BROOKLYN REMEMBERED

THE 1955 DAYS OF THE DODGERS

MAURY ALLEN

FOREWORD
BY BOB COSTAS

SportsPublishingLLC.com

ISBN-10: 1-59670-220-6
ISBN-13: 978-1-59670-220-2
ISBN: 1-58261-943-3 (hard cover)

Front cover photo: National Baseball Hall of Fame Library, Cooperstown, New York.
Back cover photos: Don Zimmer, Duke Snider, and Tommy Lasorda: © Los Angeles Dodgers, Inc.; Rachel Robinson: National Baseball Hall of Fame Library, Cooperstown, New York.

Publishers: Peter L. Bannon and Joseph J. Bannon Sr.
Senior managing editor: Susan M. Moyer
Acquisitions editor: Mike Pearson
Developmental editor: Laura Podeschi
Art director: K. Jeffrey Higgerson
Cover design, photo insert design, and imaging: Dustin J. Hubbart
Photo editor: Erin Linden-Levy

Printed in the United States

Sports Publishing L.L.C.
804 North Neil Street
Champaign, IL 61820

Phone: 1-877-424-2665
Fax: 217-363-2073
www.SportsPublishingLLC.com

CIP data available upon request.

For Janet:

My wife, my pal, my partner, in all things personal and professional, with total love and affection, devotion and dedication, joy and emotion for all the years past, present and future.

CONTENTS

FOREWORD

Over ten years ago, Ken Burns' epic documentary, *Baseball*, premiered on PBS. I was among the scores of baseball observers and participants interviewed for the film. I hope I contributed something worthwhile, but in the process I learned a lesson.

Ken asked me about dozens of baseball events and topics, among them Willie Mays' catch in the 1954 World Series, and Sandy Amoros' Game 7-saving play a year later. While my comments in each case were pertinent and valid, there was certainly no attempt to position me as someone who recalled those moments first-hand. And in fact, many who did were also included. Still, there was some irritation at Ken (and me I guess), since, it was pointed out, I was born in 1952, and thus lacked the requisite credibility to comment on these happenings. Leaving aside that this same reasoning might have disqualified Shelby Foote from commenting on the Civil War, or Burns himself from tackling any subject pre-1960. I took the point . . . sort of.

Anyway, here we go again. My friend, Maury Allen, asked me to write a foreword for his book on that memorable baseball season when "next year" finally arrived in Brooklyn. Now that would be 1955. I was, uh, three. Okay, there you have it—full disclosure. I WAS THREE. And for the record I didn't call any of the games. But as I grew older, did I have a sense of it, even as a kid? Damn right. Because growing up in New York in the 1950s and 1960s, the way you experienced baseball, the sense of the game that was transmitted to you came out of that incredible run of seasons from just after World War II up until the Dodgers and Giants moved west. The unique and rich flavor of that baseball era—the players, the personalities, the writers, the announcers, the rivalries, the debates—they were all resonating.

The Dodgers and Giants were gone, but their loyalists remained. And the Yankees—well, they were still the Yankees. Anywhere the baseball fans I knew gathered—dinner with my father's family and friends in Brooklyn, stickball games with my cousin in Bayside, the candy store where an egg cream was 20 cents, the newsstands where the tabloids cost a nickel—baseball talk raged; all of it tinged with the memories, perspectives, and attachments forged during that stretch when, as Burns points out, New York was the capital of baseball.

Mantle, Mays or Snider? Reese or Rizzuto? Ford or Newcombe? Yogi or Campy? Stengel or Durocher? And do we hear a vote for Dressen or Alston? Dick Young or Jimmy Cannon? Willard Mullen or Bill Gallo? Mel Allen or Red Barber? And what about that young Vin Scully?

This was the baseball soundtrack of my youth. And in a baseball decade that produced countless high points and milestones; Robinson's arrival, DiMaggio's departure, Thomson's homer, Mays' catch, Mantle's Triple Crown, Larsen's perfect game; the season that produced Brooklyn's first and only world championship ranks way up on the list. The year that Mullen's Bums became baseball's Kings. Many of us know the cast of characters, the band of baseball brothers Roger Kahn captured so vividly and poignantly in *The Boys of Summer* and even younger fans probably have seen film of Amoros' catch and Johnny Podres getting Elston Howard to bounce to Pee Wee Reese and end the Series and start the celebration.

But what about all the twists, turns and subplots that brought the Dodgers and Yankees to that moment? Well, Maury Allen has been around a bit longer than I. He was there in the press box, at the batting cage, in the dugouts and clubhouses going on five decades. Let's let him turn the clock back over 50 years and make us all feel as if we were there, too.

—Bob Costas
NBC and HBO Sports

ACKNOWLEDGMENTS

At the heart of this book are the interviews with the 11 surviving members of the 1955 World Champion Brooklyn Dodgers. Oh, how I love to write those words. I salute them now as heroes as I saluted them half a century ago—Duke Snider, Don Zimmer and George Shuba, Johnny Podres, Clem Labine, Roger Craig, Don Newcombe, Carl Erskine, Ed Roebuck, Billy Loes and Sandy Koufax. As Yogi Berra might say, they made this book possible and necessary. The families of lost Dodgers, Jackie Robinson, Gil Hodges, Pee Wee Reese, keep them forever alive. Then there were the kind contributions of two other spring '55ers, Joe Pignatano and Tommy Lasorda. Dodger owner Peter O'Malley and Dodger GM Buzzie Bavasi contributed and encouraged. There were so many others who gave their time and stories, from Tom Brokaw to Robert Merrill, Marty Hanfling to Phyllis Cash, Tom Villante to Alan Boroff. My thanks also to the working sportswriters of the day who filled my early years with their wit and wisdom—Dick Young, Jack Lang, Stan Isaacs, Jimmy Cannon, Milton Gross, Herb Goren, Arthur Daley, Harold Rosenthal, Joe Trimble, John Drebinger, Red Smith, Sid Friedlander, Bill Roeder, Barney Kremenko and Joe Sheehan. Much baseball lore was gained from Roger Kahn's breakthrough *The Boys of Summer* and Larry Ritter's glorious *Glory of Their Times* and other journals of the day. Jane Leavy's incisive *Sandy Koufax: A Lefty's Legacy* was a working tool.

There were the radio and television broadcasts by Red Barber, Connie Desmond, Vin Scully and by Mel Allen, Russ Hodges, Al Helfer, all spilling baseball into me through audible osmosis.

As always, my own troops were miraculous through the process, Janet, of course, Jen, Tom, Amanda and Matthew Blazkiewicz, Ted, Sheryl and Benjamin Harry Allen.

Most of all, thanks, to the other kids in Brooklyn, the stick ball soldiers, the guys down at the luncheonette arguing the game while waiting for the pink edition of the *Daily News* and to all the millions of loyalists. We have our lives, our families, our work, our hobbies. We have, together, the 1955 Brooklyn Dodgers.

1955 BROOKLYN DODGERS

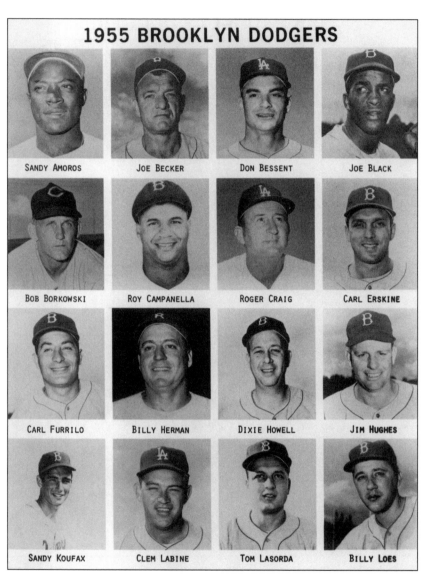

SANDY AMOROS   JOE BECKER   DON BESSENT   JOE BLACK

BOB BORKOWSKI   ROY CAMPANELLA   ROGER CRAIG   CARL ERSKINE

CARL FURRILO   BILLY HERMAN   DIXIE HOWELL   JIM HUGHES

SANDY KOUFAX   CLEM LABINE   TOM LASORDA   BILLY LOES

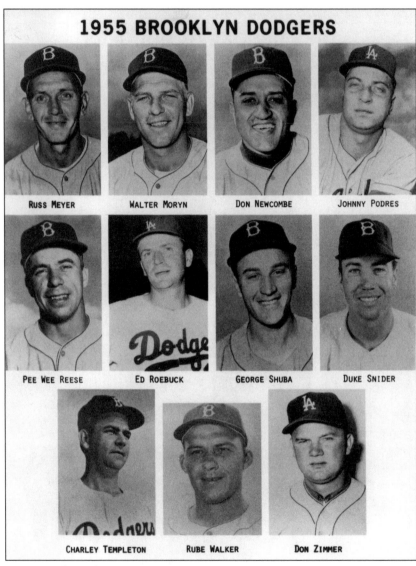

1955 BROOKLYN DODGERS

RUSS MEYER WALTER MORYN DON NEWCOMBE JOHNNY PODRES

PEE WEE REESE ED ROEBUCK GEORGE SHUBA DUKE SNIDER

CHARLEY TEMPLETON RUBE WALKER DON ZIMMER

The Count of Queensbury

Kenneth Shakir sat alone at a back table of the KFC/Pizza Hut restaurant across from the Ebbets Field Apartments at 1700 Bedford Avenue in Brooklyn, New York, sipping a cup of coffee on a cold winter morning early in 2005.

He stared across the street at the 21-story, low-income housing development and focused his eyes on the cornerstone reading 1962 inside a stitched outline of a baseball with the words etched into the brick wall reading, "This is the former site of Ebbets Field."

He was wearing a gray baseball cap with the NY logo of the New York Yankees, a heavy reversible jacket and work clothes. He shook his head a few times as he looked out the window at the wide street, the parked cars and the huge building.

A visitor approached him, asked if he could join him at the small table and inquired about his life and times.

"I ran a printing press for the Human Resources Administration at a plant not too far from here on Third Avenue and Third Street," he said. "I'm 69 years old and I retired last year. I come around here every so often to relax, see some friends and just think about those old days. I used to live nearby here when I was a kid."

His lips pursed and his eyes grew a little misty as he looked out again at the complex across the street. Some mothers with small children and a couple of elderly men stood in the courtyard.

"You know Jackie played here and that meant so much to us," he said. "The team didn't accept him right away, of course, but after a while they saw he could play. The Duke and Pee Wee, they were all for him from the beginning. Then Campy and Newk joined the team and things got easier all around."

There was a barbershop near this location in those long ago days, maybe half a century removed, and Shakir said he got his haircut there every couple of weeks.

"Well, one day I was sitting in the chair, all blacks in this place, you know, what they called us then—Negroes, and this big fellow walked in. He was alone and he seemed very tall. He didn't say much, just sat in the empty chair, and the barber got up from his seat and moved to him. He put that barber cloth around him and just started cutting his hair. I heard one of the other barbers, they had maybe four or five in there, start whispering, 'That's Jackie. That's Jackie.' They just tried to go about their business," Shakir said.

Shakir smiled at the memory of more than 50 years ago and closed his eyes.

"I leaned back in my chair as my hair was being cut but I kept peeking over at him, just to look at how he sat, how he moved, just everything about him. The barbers talked like they always did but Jackie never really got into it. You could see he wanted his hair cut and he wanted to get on. They finished up with him. He paid for the cut and when he walked out the door, there were 20, 30 little kids out there. I don't know how they found out he was in there. They just did. He signed a few pieces of paper but he kept moving, and soon I couldn't see him any more."

Shakir said he went to about a dozen games a year after Jackie Robinson joined the Brooklyn Dodgers in 1947.

"We sat way up in the top of those left-field seats or down low in the bleachers in center field. That's where the seats were 55 cents or something like that. I sold papers door to door in my neighborhood so

Kenneth Shakir has been a Brooklyn fan for 50 years.
Photo by Maury Allen

Ebbets Field Apartments at the site of the Bedford Avenue wall 2004.
Photo by Maury Allen

I always had money for the games. We just loved the Dodgers, you know. That was our life, especially after Jackie came and we could see him play. Boy, was he exciting fun."

Shakir said he still watches baseball. He roots for the Yankees but not with the same emotion he rooted for the Dodgers when he was a youngster growing up in Brooklyn.

"Ahh, it's all different now. This game is all about money and who can get rich. When we watched the Dodgers they played from the heart. Every one of them, Jackie and Duke and Campy and Pee Wee and Erskine and Furillo. See, they cared about Brooklyn and Ebbets Field. They wanted to win for us, the fans, they knew how much we cared.

"You know I still miss them, the Dodgers in Brooklyn, I mean, after all these years. I sit out here in this spot every once in a while and I think back to those days and I can see Jackie running. In my mind, I really can and all of us kids just screaming our heads off for him. You just told me it is now 50 years since they beat the Yankees that time. And then they were gone."

There are 1,300 apartments in the 21-story building that once was the site of the home of the Brooklyn Dodgers at Ebbets Field from 1913 until 1957. The rents run from $700 a month to $1200 a month for the larger three-bedroom apartments facing the front on Bedford Avenue.

In the office of the building, a bearded man wearing a yarmulke named Moshe Rosenbaum sat behind a small desk with computer printouts of the rentals in front of him.

Three colored photographs sat framed in the reception area of the offices. One showed Jackie Robinson in a rundown at third base. Another was a picture of the crowd at the 1952 World Series at Ebbets Field. There was a glowing photo of a 1954 Brooklyn game at night. The last photo, in black and white, was a 1960 scene when the field was being demolished.

"People still come around here and take pictures of the front of the building with the sign, Ebbets Field Apartments, and of the cornerstone," said Rosenbaum. "It goes on all year. But the summer is always busier. Sometimes we might get 10 or 15 people in one day, just standing out there, husbands and wives and kids, posing in front of the sign, young ones, old ones, every kind. I think this is like a historic building for some people. I don't know anything about baseball. The people who come here know a lot. They talk a lot about it when they ask permission to take pictures."

Rosenbaum said his job is to keep the building operating efficiently, making sure all residents are comfortable with their apartments and all rents are paid on time.

"Baseball, Ebbets Field," he said, "that's for others. For me it is Fieldbridge Association Apartments for rent."

Over fifty years ago. Duke. Jackie. Campy. Newk. Pee Wee. Erskine. Hodges. And Johnny Podres. John Joseph Podres, the left hander from the tiny upstate New York village of Witherbee, two wins in the 1955 World Series, the third game an 8-3 victory after the Dodgers were down two games to none and that seventh game, 2-0 win, that most emotional of all baseball triumphs for so many millions of fans. *Wait 'Till Next Year.* It WAS next year.

🏳️🏳️🏳️

The car in his garage at his handsome split-level home in Queensbury, New York, just a few miles from Glens Falls and about 60 miles south of Witherbee reads, "MVP 55."

"If I did it against the Saint Louis Browns, you wouldn't be here, would you? It's the Yankees, right?"

Johnny Podres was a cocky, witty youngster just turning 23 on October 4, 1955, and the same air, the same wit, the same infectious smile was on his face as we sat in the living room of his picture-filled home in the summer of 2004. His wife, the former Joan Taylor of Ardmore, Pennsylvania, as striking a beauty as she was when they first met in 1966 while she was in Los Angeles with the Ice Capades and Podres was finishing his Dodger days, provided a cold drink.

"I still get those calls and those emotional letters from fans," Podres said. "Nobody makes much of a fuss around here. We've been here about 20 years now and I'm just another neighbor. But I'll get a note from a guy who said he was there at the Series and he wants an autograph. Sometimes they forget to send a stamp and it costs me money."

Podres was wearing a dark sports shirt, blue jeans, white socks and sneakers as he leaned back on his favorite sofa. His hair was thinning and his face showed some fun and wear as he talked of those Dodger days. The voice was the same as I remembered from the middle 1990s when we last talked while he was finishing his almost 50 years in the game.

"My father got me into the game. He was a good pitcher around home. I started as a kid and then I was pitching at Mineville, the local high school. Up here we played maybe 10 games a year. In four years I might have thrown a total of 10 games. But I could throw hard and I had that curve ball," he said.

His father, Joe, worked as a miner for Republic Steel Company, and his mother, Anna, hearty still at 95, raised the five Podres children. One brother, Jimmy, died of leukemia at the age of 32, and Joe Podres,

John's father, died of lung cancer in 1961, at the age of 50. The family lived at 192 Lamos Street in Witherbee, a town of about 500 people.

"There used to be a lot of stores, a post office, a grocery, a bunch of bars where the miners hung out. Not any more. We moved away because there wasn't anything there anymore for our two sons," said Anna Podres.

"He's the greatest hero to come out of the area," said Jack Woods, 54, the owner and operator of Sagan's Clothing and Footwear store in nearby Moriah. "The local recreational field was dedicated to him some years back and about 4,000 people showed up. There are pictures of Johnny in a lot of the stores around here. His mother comes into the store once in a while. A wonderful lady. When you hear the Podres name around this area you know how well respected they are."

Podres' high school principal and coach, Alex Isabell, wrote a letter to several baseball teams in 1950 about the young pitcher. He received a response from the Phillies and the Brooklyn Dodgers.

"I went down to Philadelphia and worked out with them. Benny Bengough, the old Phillies scout, watched me and told me that he would get back to me. Then I went to Ebbets Field a few days later and threw for them. I was taken upstairs to the office and met Mr. [Branch] Rickey. He turned to one of the scouts and said, 'Don't let this boy get away.' Then they told me they would give me a $5,200 bonus and an $800 salary. That was $800 for the whole year," laughed Podres.

He celebrated his signing with the Dodgers by taking a five-cent subway ride to Coney Island and spending five dollars on rides, a hot dog, cotton candy, a boardwalk look and a soda pop.

"I was on a train out of Fort Henry, New York, for the first time in my life headed for Vero Beach, Florida, Dodgertown. I was with a Dodger scout, Arthur Dede, and we were having dinner together in the dining car. I never was on a train, I never was near a dining car. I ordered chicken and they brought this little bowl with water to the table. I thought it was a juice or a sauce for the chicken or something. I took a few tastes. Then Dede waved his fingers at me. He put them into the bowl. It was a finger bowl for cleaning your hands after touching the chicken. Ah, hell, I was only 18 years old."

This was 1951 and the Dodgers were to have a memorable year ended by a Bobby Thomson home run but hopes were high in March in Florida.

"The train got into Florida and just chugged along. Soon I could smell the orange groves and see them out of the train window. Everything was just so exciting. I got to the camp and they put me in the main clubhouse with all those famous Dodgers I had read about, Jackie and Pee Wee and all the rest. I got into a uniform and we sat around for a few minutes and then there was an announcement to take the field. All the clubhouse doors opened and I jogged out and looked around and I could see ball players coming out of those doors, dozens of them, hundreds of them, maybe six or seven hundred all together from the 20-25 teams in the Brooklyn organization. 'How in hell am I gonna pitch against all these guys?' I didn't think I had a chance of making it with that competition."

The Dodgers sent Podres to their A ball club in Newport News, Virginia. He was hit hard in his first two games and then was sent to the D league club of Brooklyn's at Hazard, Kentucky. He found his level. He was 21-3 at Hazard and earned an invitation to the early spring camp of the 1952 Dodgers.

"I was visiting my aunt in Staten Island, Mary Dambroski, and a note came there from the Dodgers for me to get to Florida. I thought it was too early and wasn't ready to leave. 'Go to spring training,' my aunt said. The next day I was going down for my second Brooklyn camp.

Charlie Dressen was the manager of the Dodgers then. He had lost the 1951 playoff to the Giants when he asked for Ralph Branca from the bullpen to face Thomson instead of Carl Erskine. It had no impact on Charlie's confidence as a skipper. He would often march up and down the dugout when the Dodgers were behind in a tough game and announce, "Keep it close and I'll think of something."

Dressen watched Podres work out one afternoon and walked up to him.

"You got a change?" he asked.

"No," said Podres. "Just a fast ball and a curve."

"Gotta have a change," Dressen said.

Dressen put a baseball into Podres' left hand. He closed his fingers over the ball and showed Podres how to release the baseball so that the rotation and the speed of the baseball would dramatically change as the ball neared the plate.

"I threw a couple and damn, they moved and sunk and threw the hitters off," Podres said.

Podres got into a squad game and threw his changeup pitch. Two hitters struck out in the inning. Dressen walked over to his pitcher, now 19, and said, "Go in the clubhouse and tell the clubhouse attendant to give you a beer. Wait. You struck out two guys. Tell him to give you two beers."

Podres celebrated his big Dodger day that evening with his first baseball roommate, Brooklyn pitcher Ed Roebuck.

"I was assigned to a room at Vero Beach and Roebuck was already in it. I walked in and there were 20 or 30 cartons of cigarettes spread out on the bed. Roebuck had driven to camp and stopped in North Carolina and picked up those cigarettes. They cost a lot less there than anywhere else. I started smoking a lot that spring and I still haven't stopped. I remember when Pee Wee was trying to stop smoking. He would bum cigarettes off me. One time I asked him, 'Pee Wee, when are you going to buy your own cigarettes?' Pee Wee said he was trying to stop smoking. 'Yeah, I know, but you've been trying for three years.' I think he didn't bum another for a week," Podres said.

While their white French poodle, Andre, barked at a doorbell ring, Podres continued his tale of his early Dodger days.

"That year, 1952, I had a great spring. Dressen said he would like to take me north with the club. He just couldn't because I was 1A in the draft and they didn't want to have me on the club and then lose me to the service," Podres said.

A bad back got Podres a 4F classification in the draft and a deferment. He later served a year in the Navy in 1956.

Podres remained with the Dodgers in 1953. His first two starts at the age of 20 were against the Giants and the Phillies. He pitched against Sal Maglie and lost his first big league start. "I hung a curve ball against Wes Westrum and he hit it in the upper deck of the Polo

Grounds and beat me," Podres said. He pitched against Robin Roberts and lost his second start. He didn't start for a while but had an impressive performance in the Mayor's Trophy exhibition game against the Yankees.

"I struck out eight or nine that game, Mantle and all of them and pitched in rotation the rest of the way. I even earned a start in the 1953 Series. I was tied 1-1 in the third inning of the fifth game of the Series. Then Hodges made an error, they got a couple of hits and I gave up a grand slam to Mantle. That took care of *that* Series. I'll tell you what. That was the best Dodger team I ever played on, the best. All those great players were at their peak. By 1955 a lot of the same guys were going down. It was a good thing we had enough pitching to win that year," he said.

Podres finished with an impressive 9-4 mark in his rookie season of 1953. He was 11-7 in 1954 despite being set back from late June until late July with an appendectomy. He finished strong and gave all indication that at age 22 in 1955 he was ready to add to the Brooklyn pitching depth.

"That was really one hell of a staff that year of 1955 with Newcombe, Loes, Erskine, Labine and me. We had depth and we had experience. It was going to take a hell of a team to beat us, and it turned out nobody could," he said.

Podres was in and out most of that 1955 season with a 9-10 mark. The Dodgers exploded from the gate with ten straight wins, lost one and then won ten more out of 11 before the next loss.

"We were 21-2 and I had the two losses," Podres laughed.

He made up for the slow start with seven wins in the month of June. The real pitching crisis came for Podres late in August.

"We were playing a game in Ebbets Field and I was hitting fungoes to the outfielders," Podres recalled. "I was standing in that circle near third base and knocking them out to the field. All of a sudden I felt this incredible jolt against my body and went straight down. I had been knocked over by the batting cage."

Grounds crew staffers rolled the batting cage out towards center field in Ebbets Field when batting practice was finished. The cage was pushed by three or four men to the center-field gate 389 feet away from home plate. The gate would be opened, the cage broken down and the batting practice equipment was stored in a chilly ramp under the stands.

Only this time it caught Podres on its trip to center field.

"I had a bad back anyway, and now I had sore ribs for about three weeks," Podres said. "Around the middle of September I got another start against Pittsburgh. The rosters had to be set for the Series soon, so this one really counted. I threw the hell out of the ball. The Dodgers were thinking of bringing up another left-hander, Ken Lehman, but they decided to add me to the roster after the Pittsburgh start. Things might have been different if I didn't get in there, right?"

The Dodgers lost the first two games of the 1955 Series with Don Newcombe losing the opener at the Stadium 6-5 to Whitey Ford and Billy Loes losing the second game 4-2 to Tommy Byrne.

Roy Campanella slugged three hits, including a two-run homer, Bob Turley couldn't get out of the second inning, and the Dodgers won the first Series game at Ebbets Field that year 8-3.

"I used my changeup a lot in that game," said Podres. "Except for the home run Mantle hit off me, nobody really hit a ball hard. As soon as the game was over [Walt] Alston came up to me and said, 'Kid, if this thing goes seven games, you're my starter.' That made me feel real good."

Campanella, Hodges and Snider homered in the fourth game with the Dodgers evening the Series at two all in an 8-5 victory. Clem Labine got the win with 4 ⅓ innings of splendid relief pitching. There was no such thing as short relief pitchers then. The reliever stayed in there until the manager decided he had lost his stuff.

Duke Snider hit two homers in the fifth game, Sandy Amoros hit one and rookie Roger Craig pitched six strong innings in the win. Labine saved it again with three innings of relief.

Yankee manager Casey Stengel turned to his Chairman of the Board, Whitey Ford, for the sixth game. Ford responded with a four-hitter as the Yankees won 5-1. Moose Skowron's three-run homer in the first inning locked it up.

After five straight Series wins over the Dodgers in 1941, 1947, 1949, 1952 and 1953, the Yankees only had to win the seventh game the next day to stretch the torturous streak to six. It would be Podres against Byrne at Yankee Stadium.

"I've always kidded Whitey through the years about winning that sixth game for the Yankees. If he didn't do that, there wouldn't have been a seventh game and nobody would have heard of me," said Podres.

On the morning of October 4, 1955, Johnny Podres drove his blue Oldsmobile, a car he purchased with his Brooklyn bonus money in 1951, from his aunt's Staten Island home, where he was staying during the Series, to Ebbets Field in Brooklyn. He parked his car across the street in the area reserved in a nearby garage for the Dodger players and walked to the Brooklyn clubhouse through the front rotunda.

"I was wearing the same suit, the same tie and the same shoes I had worn when I came in for the third game at Brooklyn," Podres remembered. "I wasn't real superstitious, but why take a chance?"

Several of his teammates were sitting in the clubhouse smoking cigarettes. Podres took off his jacket and lit up a cigarette from his pack of Camels. Soon the word was given to board the bus for the short 20-minute ride to Yankee Stadium.

"A lot of guys say that I got on the bus, looked at the other guys and said, 'Get me a run and we'll win it.' I can't remember if I said it or not. I always thought you saved that kind of talk until your career was over. No matter what happened that day I figured I would pitch against the Yankees again," Podres said.

Podres recalls that he was throwing bullets for the first four innings of the game. Then he eased off a bit and the Yankees got a couple of hits. Hodges knocked in a run with a single after Campanella doubled in the fourth and hit a sacrifice fly in the sixth for a 2-0 Brooklyn lead, a rather fitting response for Hodges in 1955 after his hitless (0-for-21) 1952 Series.

Walter Alston made the move that won the Series in the top of the sixth. He sent George Shuba up to pinch hit for second baseman Don Zimmer with two on and two out. Shuba grounded out. In the bottom of the sixth Alston sent left fielder Jim Gilliam to second base to replace Zimmer and moved Sandy Amoros to left field.

After Billy Martin walked and Gil McDougald was safe on a bunt single, Podres faced Yogi Berra. He hit a sinking, slicing fly ball to left field.

"It wasn't hit that hard," said Podres. "I turned around to watch it and said to myself, 'That's one out.' Then I saw Amoros still chasing the damn thing. Pee Wee turned around from short left field and looked at the runners. Martin was holding up just past second, but McDougald was only a few feet from second after running hard from first base. Pee Wee was just the smartest guy I ever saw play baseball. As soon as Amoros leaned over near the fence to grab it, he threw it to Pee Wee. Pee Wee knew where to throw it. He got it to Hodges at first and I got out of the inning with the double play."

Podres still had to retire tough Hank Bauer to end the inning. He got Bauer to hit a curve ball to shortstop. Reese had an instant of delay in getting the baseball out of his glove but recovered in time to nip the hustling right fielder of the Yankees by a half step. Podres took a deep breath as he saw umpire Frank Dascoli punch Bauer out in the air with his raised fist.

When he walked out to the mound for the ninth inning with the 2-0 lead, Podres said he had only one thought in his mind. "I can't let this one get away," he told himself.

Moose Skowron hit back to the mound and Podres had a little trouble with the hard bouncer.

"It just stuck in my glove and I thought I would throw the glove and the ball over to Gil at first. I moved towards first and finally got the ball out. I lobbed it underhand to Gil for the out. [Bob] Cerv then hit an easy fly to left for the second out. I had to get the next hitter, Elston Howard, to end it," Podres said.

The count went to 2-2 and Campanella flashed the fastball sign.

"I just decided I wanted to change up on him. I shook Campy off. It was the only time all game I shook him off. Campy came back with the curve and then with the change as I went into my motion. Howard had to stretch out to make contact with the pitch and rolled it to Pee

Wee at short. I turned around and saw this big grin on Pee Wee's face. He didn't want to make a mistake and sort of goosed the ball to first. It was low but Hodges caught it for the final out. Some of the guys kidded Pee Wee that it bounced and Gil saved him. It didn't bounce but Pee Wee didn't fire it over there, either. It was a good thing that Howard couldn't run faster," Podres said.

Podres leaped into the air with joy as the fans at Yankee Stadium, even the most devoted of Yankee fans, stood up to applaud and cheer the Dodgers.

"My father and uncle were at the game. My uncle came into the clubhouse but my father stayed in the car. He was just too emotional. A lot of guys were crying in the clubhouse. I drank some champagne and then I showered and dressed. I wanted to see my father. I was the last guy out of the clubhouse on the way to the bus back to Brooklyn. I was surrounded by a hundred cops. I walked out there like I was the president of the United States. I went to my father's car and we both just cried. Then I got up and walked to the bus for the ride back to Brooklyn. When we crossed into downtown Brooklyn, near the Dodger offices at 215 Montague Street, there were thousands of people out there, just shouting and waving banners and screaming our names and applauding. Just smiles. Everybody had smiles. We had finally won. We had gotten that monkey off our backs. We had beaten the Yankees. What a joy."

Podres got a little emotional, a little teary, as he relived those days of half a century ago. He excused himself, walked off into his bathroom for a while and then returned.

He showed the huge urn he got from *Sports Illustrated* magazine, just starting publication that year and a photo of himself in the Corvette they presented to him as Series MVP. Another photo showed Podres in his room at the Bossert Hotel the next morning after the Dodgers partied all night at the expense of owner Walter O'Malley.

Podres had offered his hotel key to the young daughter of farm director Fresco Thompson and kidded about it for years. When asked about the invitation [declined] years later, Podres would say, "If I live to be a hundred I'll never forget what's her name."

"I was in the Navy the next year. That was good for me. It helped ease some of the public attention," Podres said.

He returned to the Dodgers in 1957, pitched six shutouts, had a 2.66 ERA and ended the season with a 12-9 mark. One day he turned to Pee Wee Reese and asked, "When are you guys going to get me some runs?" Reese, quick with a quip, responded, "John, you gotta win some of them 1-0."

It happened to be a formula the weak-hitting Dodgers followed in Los Angeles in 1963 with Don Drsydale and Sandy Koufax—a lot of 1-0 wins.

The Dodgers moved west after the 1957 season. That saddened Podres, who lived in Witherbee, about a six-hour drive from Ebbets Field.

"I used to take off after the Sunday games, drive to Glens Falls, have dinner at Massey's and drive on home to Witherbee. I was there about 1 a.m., got up early, hung out with the guys and had lots of fun," he said.

Podres always had lots of fun. Part of the recreation revolved around the racetracks in New York and everywhere else the Dodgers went.

"One day in Brooklyn Zimmer took me to the track. We went up to Belmont, I won a few bucks and I fell in love with racing. That's the only game to watch. I can watch baseball for two or three innings now, but I lose interest. I never lose interest at the track," he said.

Podres said he loved every minute of playing with Brooklyn at Ebbets Field.

"This was just a great bunch of guys. I remember once when Jackie was 0-for-12 and he came up to me and said, 'I hope I can help you tomorrow.' It was all about winning. It wasn't about individual numbers. That's what made the Brooklyn club so good," he said.

Podres was 13-15 and 14-9 in the first two seasons in Los Angeles. He won another Series game with the 1959 Dodgers over the White Sox. He won 14, 18, 15 and 14 games in the next four seasons. In 1963 he beat the Yankees again in the second game of the Series after Sandy Koufax struck out 15 in a 5-2 win over the Yankees in the Series opener.

Warren Spahn hit Podres on the left elbow in 1964 after he had driven in three runs in a game against the Braves. That was the beginning of the end of his effectiveness as a big-league pitcher. Podres was 0-2 that year, won seven games the next year and was traded to Detroit. He finished his pitching days with San Diego in 1969 with a 148-116 lifetime record and a 4-1 World Series record.

"Buzzie [Bavasi] was running the San Diego club and he asked me if I wanted to become a pitching coach. I knew I was finished, so I agreed. So I took voluntary retirement and agreed to a contract as a coach for $8,000 a year. I coached in San Diego, in Boston with Zimmer and then with the Phillies for six years. I had Curt Schilling there as a kid. I saw how hard he could throw and I told him to just throw and throw and his arm would get stronger. It did. Look at him now," Podres said.

In 1996 he had to undergo a heart bypass operation. Jim Fregosi was the manager of the Phillies. He told Podres he would be better off if he just forgot about the game and went home.

"I came home, did card shows, went to the track whenever I could and enjoyed relaxing. Once in a while I would meet up with Zimmer when he was with the Yankees and they had an off day and we would go to the track. Zim got me my first winner. I made 20 bucks and said, 'Nice going, Popeye.' That's easy money," Podres said.

His hips bother him now from a half-century of pitching. He suffers from arthritis and had some circulatory problems in 2003. After surgery he received a call from Brooklyn teammate Duke Snider. It was the November day Warren Spahn had died.

"Johnny, how are you feeling?" Snider asked.

"Better than Spahn," Podres responded.

Podres was told some old Brooklyn Dodger fans were planning a reunion of the team in 2005 for the 50th anniversary, a parade in downtown Brooklyn and a reunion of many people who made October 4, 1955 so memorable in so many hearts.

"I hope I'm alive," said Podres.

Almost 50 years after that historic Brooklyn date, Podres was still quick with a line, a smile and a memory of half a century ago.

The last thing I saw as we said our goodbyes for the day was Podres getting into the driver's seat of his car, pulling out of his garage and seeing that license plate, "MVP 55," glowing in the summer sun.

This was a guy who would live forever.

Ebbets Field Frolics

Betty Smith wrote *A Tree Grows in Brooklyn* and Dick Young wrote *The Tree That Grows in Brooklyn Is an Apple Tree.*

Smith's novel about a young girl fighting her way out of the poverty of early 20th century Brooklyn, New York life was made into a classic 1945 film starring Dorothy McGuire, Joan Blondell, James Dunn, Peggy Ann Garner and Lloyd Nolan. Dunn won the Academy Award for his portrayal of the down-on-his-luck father, and the teenage Garner earned a special Academy presentation. The film can still be seen on late-night television and purchased in the classic corners of most video stores.

Young, a New York *Daily News* sports reporter and columnist, parodied Smith's title as he described a Brooklyn team he charged with choking, a baseball term for excessive collapse under pennant pressure.

Young was the voice of the Brooklyn fan in print for more than two decades as he covered the Dodgers and became identified as the conscience of the club. He campaigned for Jackie Robinson when the Negro star first joined the club in 1947 and later battled verbally with him as Robinson campaigned for his equal standing in the game. He attacked Duke Snider for sitting down against some tough left-handed pitchers with mock injuries and he was quick to point out mistakes made by a rock-headed outfielder named Carl Furillo. He sided with Pee Wee Reese, the captain of the team, and chided the Dodgers for bad trades and inability to spend enough money to lift the team.

He was a raging liberal, politically and professionally in his younger years. He typified the gritty New Yorker who had fought his way to newspaper fame despite a poor background and lack of classical education. He was from a mixed religious marriage, was raised by a single mother, grew up on the streets of Manhattan's Washington Heights and abrasively controlled the doings of the Dodgers as regards media coverage.

While Arthur Daley, Red Smith and Dave Anderson of *The New York Times* won Pulitzer Prizes for their sports coverage, Young was ignored by the effete snobs of that Columbia University annual convocation. He had more readers than all three put together in their best days and created more subway and candy store arguments with his writings than any print scribe in the 1940s and 1950s.

Young was part reporter and part family in his time around the Brooklyn Dodgers. He could excoriate members of the team in the *Daily News.* Then, for instance, he could show up in the Brooklyn clubhouse with a box of cigars. He had eight children with six of them born in little more than eight years. He offered cigars one day to all of the Dodgers and several members of the working press.

"Did your wife have another baby?" asked Pee Wee Reese.

"No," replied Young with a wry smile, "she had her period."

He was a small man with a loud, crackling laugh who dominated his press box scene as no writer had done before or has since. He aged sluggishly and dealt poorly with the new crop of sportswriters who arrived in the 1960s, known as the chipmunks for their incessant chattering involving politics, war and restaurants. He often alluded to "My America," the painful changes of mores he saw around him in his writings, certain that the new generation of sportswriters could not carry his typewriter or those of his peers.

He later helped create the joyous scene around the new New York Mets in 1962 and glorified the rowdy, banner-waving fans by calling them, "The New Breed." He peaked in 1955 when the Dodgers did and died in 1987, an angry, bitter, unappreciated 69-year-old man. He was still on his job as a columnist at the *New York Post* after jumping his *Daily News* deal.

Young's ridicule of the Dodgers with his "apple tree" remark caused the greatest furor around the team since Robinson's arrival as an historic color-barrier breaker.

Brooklyn fans did not take criticism of their team lightly. This was family. The fans could criticize them for a bonehead play, a bad trade or obnoxious conduct under stress. Just let others try, especially if those others were arrogant Yankee fans or misguided fans of the New York Giants.

A Brooklyn baseball team bounced around professional baseball from its earliest days in the late 19th century. The game may have been invented or developed from Civil War days with soldiers playing with a ball in between battles. Hoboken, New Jersey, claimed its founding as did Cooperstown, New York, with the location of the Baseball Hall of Fame there starting in 1939. Pittsfield, Massachusetts, even got into the act of creation in 2004 with a discovery of a local document warning baseball players away from nearby windows as early as the 1820s.

However the game came about, Brooklyn always seemed part of it. The team had a few other nicknames outside of Dodgers in its time, including the Superbas, after a Broadway musical; the Bridegrooms, because so many of their young players married in one season; the Robins after longtime manager Wilbert Robinson; the Trolley Dodgers, for the frequent fear of misdirected Brooklyn trolleys; and finally and faithfully, the Dodgers. They were often called "the Flock," by fans and finally, affectionately, were known by loyal fans as "Dem Bums," an intimacy allowable only by dedicated loyalists. The *Daily News* would solidify the identification with a front-page headline bellowing, "Who's a Bum!" after the 1955 World Series triumph.

With war waging in Europe and the United States only months away from being dragged into the conflict, the Brooklyn Dodgers finally won a pennant in 1916. Wilbert Robinson was the manager, Zach Wheat was the hitting star of the team, and a flaky outfielder from Kansas City, Missouri, named Casey Stengel was the comic relief. He batted .279 in the regular season and starred in the World Series as was his wont with a .364 average.

The Boston Red Sox won the World Series in five games. The Red Sox used to do that with regularity in the early part of the 20th century. No kidding. Right-hander Ernie Shore won two games, and a bulky left-handed pitcher, who showed he could also hit a little, named George Herman "Babe" Ruth, out-pitched the Dodgers in a 14-inning victory.

Years later, as he sat around hotel lobbies across America as manager of the New York Yankees or New York Mets, Stengel would discuss his teammates on that Brooklyn team or his opponents. His references to his pal Wheat or that great lefty Ruth would often begin with the reference, "He's dead at the present time."

Dead or alive, those Brooklyn names stayed vivid in the hearts and minds of all who watched them play there in Brooklyn. No matter where else their careers in and out of baseball would take them, a former Dodger remained a significant character on the American social scene.

The Dodgers won the National League pennant again in 1920 and lost that World Series to the Cleveland Indians five games to two in the old nine-game World Series set. Was some kind of a World Series jinx starting here?

Stan Coveleski won three games for Cleveland that Series and a right-hander named Jim Bagby picked up another. Bagby had a son, Jim Bagby, Jr. who also became a big-league pitcher with the Cleveland Indians.

Bagby Jr. was on the mound for the Indians in the eighth inning as a relief pitcher for left-hander Al Smith on July 17, 1941. Smith had retired Joe DiMaggio twice on that July night and walked him once as DiMaggio threatened to stretch his consecutive game-hitting streak to 57 straight games and earn a $10,000 bonus from the Heinz 57 company. Bagby Jr. got DiMaggio out on a hard ground ball to shortstop in the eighth inning that Lou Boudreau handled cleanly, ending the historic streak that most baseball observers believe will last forever.

"Bagby was gone from Cleveland by the time I joined the Indians for my final playing year," home run king Ralph Kiner once said. "He was famous around town and his name would come up often when some hitter had a 10- or 15-game hitting streak. He was the guy who stopped DiMaggio."

There was one other baseball story about young Bagby that the Cleveland veteran players told Kiner after he joined the team.

"Bagby had this terrible stutter," said Kiner. "He could hardly get a word out without repeating everything two or three times. 'My name, name, name is Jim, Jim, Jim, Bag, Bag, Bagby.' It was very difficult for him to talk clearly. One time the manager thought the players were running wild and called Bagby's room to check if he and his roommate were in. Bagby answered the phone. He stammered that he had been in the room all night and hadn't broken curfew. The manager was satisfied, but he was certain that Bagby's roommate was out on the town against club rules. 'Put him on the phone,' ordered the skipper. Bagby was trying to protect his roommate and pal, put down the phone, walked to the end of the room, came back to the night table and tried to disguise his voice. 'I'm here, here, here, skip, skip, skipper.' I don't think it worked. They were both fined, the roommate for missing curfew and Bagby for covering up for him poorly."

The Dodgers cornered the market on sixth place in the 1920s with seven finishes in that position out of the next 10 years. They finished in second in 1924, fourth in 1930 and fifth in 1921.

Still, the romance continued. Ebbets Field, which had opened in 1913 under the guidance of the club's former bookkeeper, Charles Ebbets, was an easy subway stop from the edges of Coney Island to the outer regions of the borough. Fans filled the small stadium with its original seating of 31,500, and the loyalty and the legend grew. With no radio or television coverage in the 1920s and early 1930s, kids hung around candy stores at eight o'clock on summer nights for the first edition of the *Daily News* and the *Daily Mirror*, the two local newspapers that covered the Dodgers thoroughly and took the team to its journalistic bosom with far more stories than the broad sheets, *The New York Times*, the *New York Herald-Tribune* or the *Sun* would deliver.

Youngsters would play with their red spaldeen balls under subway tracks while waiting for the details of the games that day. A fraternity grew up in those nightly waits for the papers unlike any other in New

York City or around the country for that matter. These were kids who cared about the Dodgers first, family second and school last.

The small newspaper trucks would arrive and the papers were bounced in bundles onto the streets. The storeowner would shoo the kids away until he counted the delivery, packaged them neatly on the stands and collected back payment. Then he would collect the two cents from each kid for a paper and maybe sell an egg cream, a delicious effervescent special New York chocolate drink, to a waiting parent.

The kids would see that Ebbets Field was filled that day, that the Dodgers lost another heartbreaker to the Cardinals or the Cubs or the Reds, that Dazzy Vance pitched another strong game, that Max Carey stole another base or that Babe Herman crashed another double off the friendly right-field wall only 297 feet away from home plate.

Floyd Caves Herman came to Brooklyn in 1926 after signing with Detroit and lasted there through 1931. He hit .381 and .393 in two separate seasons. His lifetime average over 13 seasons was .324, the highest for any regular player not elected to baseball's Hall of Fame. Babe Herman almost personally was the personification of the Brooklyn Dodgers in his first six seasons with the team. He did make a quick comeback in 1945 during the depth of the World War II years, singled as a pinch hitter, fell down rounding first base and still batted .265 at age 42 after a six-year playing absence from baseball.

He coached and scouted for more than 50 years and clearly understood why he was not elected to the Hall of Fame.

"My image was set by the writers because I let them go along with a gag," he once said. "A fly ball hit me on the shoulder in the shadows of the outfield. I lost it. One of the writers wrote that it hit me on the head because that sounded funnier. I thought it would be entertaining for the team so I let him go along with it."

Even though he slid into second base once with a lighted cigar in his back pocket, slid into third once despite the fact that two teammates were already there, Herman was a very smart fellow. He spoke with eloquence of his Glendale, California pal Casey Stengel and later Yankee Yogi Berra.

He made a lot of money in his orchid business in California, lived in a magnificent home in Glendale and was a fan of serious opera. His son, Robert, served as the assistant to Rudolph Bing at the New York City Metropolitan Opera and later ran the Miami Opera company.

"The thing about baseball," he said, "is that the writers can portray you any way they want. They can set a tone for you that you can never escape. You get locked into a groove because of one or two small things you might do and that will be your image, your identification until the day you die."

Herman played the outfield and first base with average skills. His hitting was as good as anybody in the game during the middle 1920s and early 1930s. Unfortunately for his Hall of Fame credentials, he had been pictured as a character, a flake in baseball jargon, a subject for funny tales. It worked well for Yogi Berra with Joe Garagiola being his front man in his early days. Babe Herman had no front man, so his image remained tarnished. He was the best player on some bad teams, and they soon became known in Brooklyn and throughout the league as the Daffiness Boys.

Babe Herman was honored with election to the Brooklyn Dodgers Hall of Fame in the early 1980s. His appearance on a flatbed truck in downtown Brooklyn brought out huge crowds as he reminisced about his Dodger days in the 1920s and 1930s.

"My son lived in New York and I always loved coming here," he said before his Brooklyn Hall of Fame induction. "I don't think there ever was a baseball town like Brooklyn. The people here just loved the game so much, loved the players and understood baseball so well. I cried when the Dodgers left Brooklyn after 1957 even though I lived near the new stadium in Los Angeles. Brooklyn without baseball? Who could believe that?"

The Dodgers finished in last place in 1905. They never finished at the bottom again. All the fifth- and sixth-place finishes did not discourage the kids waiting for the *News* and *Mirror* at night or the fans who would dress immaculately for each game they attended. The fun was just in being there, getting off that subway stop at Prospect Park, walking those few streets to Bedford Avenue and Sullivan Place, buying that grandstand seat for $1.25 or that bleacher seat for 50 cents, waiting always for improvement, dreaming that the slogan "Wait 'Till Next Year" would finally, finally mean something.

Herman was gone after the 1932 season and the Dodgers, now
being run by Ed and Steve McKeever, who had come up with needed
money for Ebbets Field as wealthy Brooklyn contractors, looked for a
man to bring the Dodgers out of the Depression years as World War II
approached.

The Dodgers had not finished higher than fifth in the 1930s until
they climbed all the way to third in 1939. A new team president named
Leland Stanford MacPhail and a new shortstop, soon-to-be manager
named Leo Durocher would bring glory to the team.

Larry MacPhail was a bombastic, large, hard-drinking man with a
thick head of red hair and an insatiable lust for competition. He loved
the idea of beating out his baseball partners for players, fans or attention.

Durocher had been a spindly shortstop with the Yankees in the
1920s who was most famous for his raunchy mouth, his flaming temper and his alleged stealing of Babe Ruth's watch. He had played for the
Reds, the famed Gashouse Gang of the St. Louis Cardinals, and a year
as Dodger shortstop before being named the team's player-manager in
1939. Leo the Lip would put fire into the Brooklyn scene.

With MacPhail on top of the team, Durocher leading the club on
the field and fans starving for improvement as well as excitement, the
Golden Era of Brooklyn baseball was about to begin.

It would all play out around Ebbets Field, that cute little baseball
park that had grown so identified across the country as the home of the
Dodgers. People made jokes about Ebbets Field and the Dodgers on
radio shows, in newspaper articles and in films. Hardly a World War II
movie could be made without a character with a Brooklyn accent talking about Ebbets Field. If Hyde Park and the White House were the
two homes of President Franklin D. Roosevelt in the 1930s and early
1940s, Ebbets Field was equally famous as the home of Dem Bums.

"I remember when I first came there in 1946 with the Pirates," said
Ralph Kiner, early in 2005 as he prepared for his 43rd season as a New
York Mets broadcaster. "I just loved playing there. The fans were so
quick to recognize players, even on the opposition. I remember how the
Brooklyn Dodgers Sym-Phony would play that bouncing music as I
walked back to the bench after striking out. We had a big game going,

me and the Sym-Phony. When I sat down they boomed their instruments. When I stood up in the dugout they were silent until I sat down. A lot of times I just tried to hang at the end of the dugout until the half inning ended."

The Brooklyn Sym-Phony was a group of amateur musicians who had other jobs but played music at Ebbets Field in their spare time with an old trumpet, an out-of-tune horn, a trombone and that base drum. They were led by a couple of little guys named Shorty Laurice and Eddie Bataan who became as famous at Ebbets Field as some of the Brooklyn players.

"Everything about Ebbets Field was special," said Kiner. "They had that sign in right field put up by the clothing guy, Abe Stark. It said, 'Hit sign, win suit.' It was so damn low on the wall nobody could hit it."

Red Schoendienst, the Hall of Fame second baseman of the Cardinals and the closest pal to Stan (The Man) Musial, said he once hit it.

"I cracked a low drive to right field," said Schoendienst. "It got past Carl Furillo in right field and hit the sign. The next day I was told I could pick up the suit. I got into a cab from the Commodore, our Manhattan hotel, and took a ride over to Brooklyn for the suit. I think the cab ride cost me 15 bucks and the suit was about 10."

Kiner never hit the sign but he hit lots of home runs in Brooklyn and everywhere else he played. In his first seven seasons in the big leagues from 1946 through 1952 with the Pirates, he tied or led the league in home runs. Not even Babe Ruth could do that. Of course, Ruth was pitching in his early years, but even after he became a Yankee outfielder he could only win six in a row of the 12 home run titles he collected.

Kiner challenged the Ruth record of 60 homers with 54 in 1949, but a bad back after the 1952 season cut his career short. After he finished up with old Pittsburgh pal Hank Greenberg, the general manager, in Cleveland in 1955, Kiner became a general manager himself for the minor-league San Diego team. He was a broadcaster with the Chicago White Sox in 1961 when he got a call from new Mets general manager George Weiss asking if he was interested in teaming up with Lindsey Nelson and Bob Murphy on the Mets broadcasts.

Kiner was very popular in New York from his visiting days in Brooklyn. He had also played against the Giants in the Polo Grounds in Manhattan, the first home of the Mets.

"I just enjoyed being in New York so much as a player with the theater, the night clubs, the movies, the great restaurants," Kiner said. "I knew I would like it in New York as a broadcaster."

Kiner was always a wonderful storyteller on the air. He would recount tales about himself and about other players. One of the classic baseball lines is about Kiner. His Pittsburgh teammate, pitcher Fritz Ostermueller, saw him drive up to the ballpark once in a fancy automobile. Ostermueller was pulling into the players' parking lot in a small sedan.

"Home run hitters," said the pitcher referring to his slugging teammate, "drive Cadillacs. Pitchers drive Fords."

Kiner was one of those drop-dead handsome guys in his youth at Pittsburgh some 60 years ago. He was a California resident and was often seen around Hollywood with the beauties of the day, actresses Elizabeth Taylor and Janet Leigh or dancer Ann Miller.

"Oh what legs she had," Kiner recalled during a rain delay while sitting in the Mets press room late in 2004, "and what a chest Elizabeth had."

One of Kiner's favorite stories revolved around his first wife, tennis great Nancy Chaffee.

"After we were divorced I took a trip to France," Kiner said. "I was visiting in the wine country and walked up to the entrance of one of those caves where the wine was stored. The guy recognized me and said he had watched me play in Pittsburgh when he was a youngster. His father worked for an international banking company with Pittsburgh offices. He told me to wait there for a moment while he got a bottle of wine for me."

When the man returned from the cave he was carrying a large, dusty bottle of wine as a gift for Kiner. He told the former home run king the bottle would sell for two thousand dollars on the open market.

"Two thousand dollars," said an astounded Kiner. "When would I ever have an occasion to open up a bottle of wine worth two thousand dollars?"

The Frenchman smiled at Kiner and said quietly, "When your former wife, Nancy, remarries."

Kiner told the story often. Late in the 1990s he told it again while sitting around with some old sportswriters in the Mets press room. He had one addition to the tale.

"I finally opened the bottle up," he told his listeners. "Nancy remarried. She married the broadcaster Jack Whitaker. Our kids were at the wedding and I wished her well."

Kiner couldn't recall any spectacular home runs at Ebbets Field but he said he loved every minute he spent in that old park.

"We used to come into New York by train then and we would arrive at Grand Central station. The team was in the last two cars of the train, the Pullman car and the diner. We carried our own bags then and marched that long trail to the waiting room. We could finally get a porter there to get a cab for us and take our bags. Sometimes the bags went to the hotel without us and we took cabs to Ebbets Field. Our baseball stuff had usually arrived ahead of us."

Kiner recalled a game in which the Pirates had beaten the Dodgers at Ebbets Field with a couple of ninth-inning runs. The Pittsburgh players were sitting around the small locker room sipping on their beers and talking over the joyous victory.

"There were a couple of windows in the locker room that led right out into the street," Kiner said. "A bunch of kids were screaming at us, all in fun, you know, saying how lucky we were to win and how Dem Bums would murder us tomorrow. A couple of us saw this huge, empty barrel filled with water. We lifted it up, told the kids to get closer to the windows because we wanted to tell them something about the game and unloaded the water on them. You could hear their screams for miles."

The Pirates almost always finished last in those days in the early 1950s. Branch Rickey, who had built the Dodgers into a powerhouse, was now the Pittsburgh general manager. He was known as El Cheapo as he worked hard to keep salaries down. When he traded Kiner to

Chicago in 1953 he told the slugger, "We finished last with you and we can finish last without you."

Kiner got back at Rickey and the cheapness of all baseball owners by helping form the first pension plan for players and a future union that has led to the enormous baseball salaries such as the 26 million-dollar-a-year Alex Rodriguez deal.

"In those days 50 bucks meant a lot to a player. We always tried to get on Happy Felton's Knothole Gang show after the game. This was a postgame radio show and the guy being interviewed was paid 50 bucks," Kiner said.

Felton, a huge, rotund man, also ran a pregame show at Ebbets Field. On that program, several kids, called Knothole gang kids, worked out before the contest with two or three Brooklyn players. They would be asked by Felton to select their favorite Dodger player. That player would be given 50 bucks and the kids would be given candy bars or tickets for another game.

"I had been on the show half a dozen times," a fringe Brooklyn Dodgers outfielder named Cal Abrams, said many years ago. "I had never been picked. It was getting embarrassing and I also could use the 50 bucks. So I gave each of three kids five dollars before the drill and told them when Happy asked for their favorite Brooklyn player they should give my name. All went well until we finished the little catch. The kid was asked the name of his favorite Dodger player. He looked up at Felton with this sweet smile and said in a loud voice, 'Carl Furillo.' I never got over that one."

Kiner said he goes to Cooperstown, New York for the Hall of Fame inductions each summer and always visits the old Stadium exhibit. He was named to the Baseball Hall of Fame in 1975.

"I take a look at the model of Ebbets Field. It brings back some wonderful memories, the great Dodger teams and the great games we had with them as well as Shorty Laurice and the Brooklyn Sym-Phony and Hilda Chester with that old cowbell in the center-field bleachers and all the fun in Brooklyn. I loved Forbes Field, you can bet. But there was only one Ebbets Field. Boy, would I have loved to play every day in that little park."

ᢒ ᢒ ᢒ

Leo Durocher's team finished third in 1939 and moved up to second behind the Cincinnati Reds in 1940. They were 12 games behind
the Reds at the end so only the most optimistic of Brooklyn fans could
believe 1941 would be their year. After all, they hadn't won a pennant
since 1920. Why now?

A couple of handsome kids, centerfielder Pete Reiser from St.
Louis, Missouri, and shortstop Pee Wee Reese from Louisville,
Kentucky, anchored Durocher's team.

Reese would take over the shortstop duties from Durocher, and
Reiser, an explosive switch hitter, would win the batting title with a
.343 mark in his first full season in the big leagues. If he didn't develop
this terrible habit of running into walls in the days before outfield walls
were padded, he would have been the switch-hitting guy Mickey
Mantle chased for records a decade later.

First baseman Dolph Camilli won the home run and RBI title in
1941, veterans Billy Herman and Cookie Lavagetto would handle second and third, Dixie Walker, later to be known as the People's Cherce
in Brooklyn, and Joe Medwick would play the outfield with Reiser and
two right-handers would handle most of the important pitching.
Whitlow Wyatt, a quiet family man and Kirby Higbe, a swinging
southerner from Columbia, South Carolina, each won 22 games.

It was Higbe who would supply baseball with one of its most legendary tales.

The handsome, heavy-browed drawling pitcher met a lovely lady
while the Dodgers were on a road trip to St. Louis. He spent all three
nights with her in those times of day baseball, moved with Brooklyn on
to Chicago and then returned home by train with the club. He had left
his pajamas back in the lady's St. Louis apartment.

She packed them up, doused them with a little perfume and mailed
them back to Higbe at Ebbets Field. The clubhouse attendant, Babe
Hamburger, collected the package on an off day and brought it to
Higbe's home where the pitcher's wife accepted the delivery. Higbe was
out fishing on his day off. His curious wife opened the package, saw the

pajamas, read the erotic love note and steamed until the pitcher walked into their home at dark.

"What is this?" she screamed, as she hurled the perfumed pajamas and love note across the floor.

Higbe quietly picked up the note, read it carefully, picked up the pajamas and announced, "This isn't for me, dear, this is for some *other* Kirby Higbe."

Catcher Mickey Owen, who was later to become a Missouri sheriff and Hugh Casey, one of the game's first great relief pitchers and later a suicide victim, were forever linked as a result of the World Series that year.

The Dodgers had defeated the Cardinals by 2 ½ games and moved into the World Series against the Yankees. The Yankees had won by 17 games and Joe DiMaggio had hit in 56 consecutive games that season.

The Yankees led two games to one in the Series as the Dodgers seemed set to tie it up. They led 4-3 in the ninth inning. Two men were out. Tommy Henrich, the Old Reliable of the Yankees, had two strikes on him. Casey threw a breaking ball. Henrich swung and missed for strike three and the Brooklyn win. But wait. The ball got away from Owen for a passed ball, the Yankees rallied for four runs, and Owen was locked into Brooklyn ignominy.

The soft-spoken Owen spent another 10 years as a player, went home to a political life in Missouri and passed away at the age of 90 in 2005.

Casey, the hard drinker who may or may not have thrown an illegal spitball to Henrich, hung around baseball another half-dozen years, pitched with Brooklyn against the Yankees again in the 1947 Series and shot himself in the head in 1951. He was 37 years old. Ironically, Casey had been befriended by writer Ernest Hemingway when the Dodgers trained in Cuba. Hemingway shot himself 10 years later.

The Dodgers had a big lead over the Cardinals in 1942. They blew the lead and the pennant again as a young St. Louis team rallied for the victory.

The Dodgers slipped to third in 1943 as they continued to lose young players to military service and fell all the way to seventh in 1944. Dixie Walker won the batting title with a .357 average. Walker would become a focal point on the team again three years later when the first Negro player, Jackie Robinson, joined the Dodgers. Walker was a leader of a petition to keep the black man off the Dodgers. He would later admit the error of his ways as he and Robinson learned to respect each other.

The Dodgers moved up to third place again in 1945 and tied the Cardinals for the pennant in 1946. St. Louis won the one-game play-off as Eddie Stanky, known as the Walking Man, and Howard Schultz, a tall first baseman who never lived up to his huge potential (though he was one of a few athletes to play professional baseball and basketball) struck out with the bases loaded in an 8-3 defeat.

Durocher was suspended from baseball in 1947 for gambling, for marrying an actress named Larraine Day over church opposition and for associating with nefarious actor George Raft. KOB, Kindly Old Burt Shotton, a favorite of Brooklyn boss Branch Rickey, led the team to another pennant.

The Yankees, of course, won the seven-game Series with lefthander Joe Page shutting down the Dodgers in relief over the last five innings.

The Dodgers would lose to the Yankees again in the 1949 Series. They would lose the pennant on the last day of the season for the next two years, an unenviable record.

The Dodgers and Phillies were tied on the last day of the 1950 season. The Dodgers failed to score in the bottom of the ninth when Cal Abrams tried to run home from second base on a single to center by Duke Snider via the Brooklyn Bridge. His wide turn at third base gave charging centerfielder Richie Ashburn time enough, despite a weak throwing arm, to throw Abrams out at the plate.

Dick Sisler, who stuttered embarrassingly, was typically kidded about his speech problems, especially by the Dodgers, who specialized in opposition needling, often led by Leo Durocher's lip. Even after Durocher left the Dodgers to join the Giants as their manager, Brooklyn players made fun of Sisler's struggles with his speech.

Sisler hit a tenth-inning home run off Don Newcombe to lead the Phillies to the victory and the pennant. Dodger players clearly recall him clapping his hands and shouting distinctly, "Take that, Dodgers," as he rounded third base.

The Dodgers brought all of Brooklyn to tears in 1951. They blew a 13 ½-game lead to the Giants, tied for the pennant and entered a three-game playoff. Ralph Branca lost the first game, Clem Labine won the second for Brooklyn, and the Dodgers led 4-1 in the ninth inning of the third game. Disaster struck. Alvin Dark and Don Mueller singled. Whitey Lockman doubled and Bobby Thomson hit a home run off Branca for the win.

"The Giants win the pennant, the Giants win the pennant, the Giants win the pennant, the Giants win the pennant," shouted radio announcer Russ Hodges. Shut up, already.

The Dodgers showed no aftereffects from the debacle of 1951 as they won the pennant in 1952. They still couldn't beat the Yankees in another seven-game Series. Lefthander Bob Kuzava shut them down as Jackie Robinson popped up with the bases loaded. Billy Martin made a lunging catch that is repeated on television screens across the world every October. His manager, Casey Stengel, could never stop talking about it.

The Dodgers won again in 1953. They lost again to the Yankees in the World Series. Seven pennants for Brooklyn. Seven World Series losses. Manager Charlie Dressen, who would often say on the bench during a close game, "Hold 'em close, I'll think of something," asked for a two-year contract for 1954 and 1955.

Dressen, who had thought of Branca instead of Carl Erskine, also in the bullpen, in 1951 against the Giants, was pushed by his wife. She was tired of dealing with baseball insecurity and one-year contracts. New boss Walter O'Malley thought of Montreal manager Walter Alston.

He let Dressen go and brought the laconic Alston to Brooklyn. The New York Giants won the pennant by five games over Brooklyn. They swept the Cleveland Indians in the World Series. That really hurt in Brooklyn. Who the hell was this guy Alston, anyway?

Things weren't too hopeful for the Brooklyn Dodgers as the 1955 season approached. This was an old team. Jackie Robinson was 36 and had no position. Pee Wee Reese was close to 37 and was on losing Brooklyn World Series teams since 1941. Duke Snider and Gil Hodges were at their peak years, but they hadn't been able to lead the Dodgers to a Series triumph. Roy Campanella was 33, coming off a broken hand and had batted all of .207 in 1954. There was no left fielder. There never was. Carl Erskine, Don Newcombe, Johnny Podres and Billy Loes were slated as the starting staff. Only Erskine had a real good year in 1954 with 18 wins.

Alston and Robinson had a tense relationship because the new manager was trying to move the old hero out of the lineup. Jackie knew it and said it publicly. Reese tried to keep Jackie from making waves.

One day he said to Jackie, "You know, a lot of guys don't like you and it isn't because of your color."

If all of these problems weren't enough to damper the hopes of the Brooklyn loyalists, a crazy baseball rule was about to make it worse.

In an attempt to hold down wild spending for young kids—dollars were always the heart of the game—a bonus rule had been established. Any player signed for more than $10,000 as a free agent had to stay with his team on the big league roster for two years before he could be farmed out.

On December 18, 1954, the Brooklyn Dodgers signed Sanford Koufax, a University of Cincinnati freshman pitcher, for a bonus of $14,000 and a $6,000 salary. That would guarantee him a spot on the Brooklyn roster in 1955 and 1956. He was 19 years old.

"Part of the Dodgers bonus to Sandy Koufax was a gift of the satin night game uniforms of a few years ago to the Parkviews, Koufax's team in the Coney Island League," wrote future Pulitzer Prize winner Dave Anderson in the *New York Journal American*. "They're a little big," reports Parkviews outfielder Dick Auletta, "but they're sure nice."

Anderson had been working for the *Brooklyn Eagle* in December of 1954 when the signing of Koufax was announced. Anderson reported that the left-hander from Brooklyn's Lafayette High School, a first baseman in high school most of the time there, lived at 1104 83rd Street in the Bensonhurst section of Brooklyn.

Dodger farm director Fresco Thompson was very high on Koufax after an August workout at Ebbets Field. Koufax had pitched the Parkviews to the Coney Island senior championship in that sandlot league and had pitched the Tomahawks to the junior title in the Ice Cream League.

Thompson told Anderson the three reasons the Dodgers went against the tradition of signing bonus kids in the Koufax case were that he was a local boy from Brooklyn, he was one of the scarce left-handers around as good prospects and he was a Jewish star who owner Walter O'Malley saw as a potential for boosting Ebbets Field attendance among Jewish fans.

"At the moment," Anderson wrote in the *Eagle* in December of 1954, "he's the only Jewish player on the Dodgers, but the organization has four new Jewish players in the farm system. Two are from Brooklyn, outfielder Shelly Brodsky from New Utretcht High and shortstop Howard Gershberg from Boys High."

Only the Brodsky and Gershberg families ever heard of them again.

Many of the Dodgers privately resented the idea of a Jew on their team. Others resented the idea that an untried kid would get that kind of money. All resented the reality that this 19-year-old without a minute of big-league experience would be taking up a place on their roster as they tried, hopefully, to win a pennant again, and maybe, just maybe, finally, win a World Series in 1955.

Fat chance.

Captain Pee Wee

Harold Henry Reese was born July 23, 1918, in Ekron, Kentucky. His father was a railroad engineer and away a good part of the youngster's growing-up years.

He was wild about athletics almost from the start and soon earned a nickname because of his skill with marbles. He used the most colorful marble, known as a pee wee, as his shooting marble in street games. He would soon be called Pee Wee as much for that as for his slight size, a stretched 5-foot-9 and maybe 160 pounds at his playing peak.

Reese was supposed to go to the Boston Red Sox after a fine 1939 season with his hometown Louisville Colonels team, but the player-manager of that team, Joe Cronin, thought he had a few more years of playing time left and so allowed the Red Sox to offer the services of Reese to the Brooklyn Dodgers. He came to the team in 1940, succeeded another player-manager, Leo Durocher, as the regular shortstop and batted .272 as a 1940 rookie with the Dodgers. He slipped to .229 in 152 games in 1941 as the Dodgers won the pennant but climbed back to .255 in his third season.

Reese was in the Navy during 1943, 1944 and 1945 and returned to the Dodgers with a .284 average in 1946. He hit .269 over 16 seasons. He was named to Baseball's Hall of Fame in 1984 as captain and leader of the successful Brooklyn teams from 1940 through 1957 and for that one year in Los Angeles in 1958 before being replaced at shortstop by Maury Wills.

Reese worked as a broadcaster with legendary Gashouse Gang Cardinal Dizzy Dean who mangled the English language as he had handled National League hitters. He often spoke weirdly with double negatives and malapropos filling his vocabulary. He captured the situation clearly after a snobby, journalistic attack when he replied, "A lot of people who ain't saying ain't, ain't eating."

After his broadcasting career ended, Reese was hired by his hometown Hillerich & Bradsby Bat Co., makers of the famed big-league Louisville Slugger bats.

He worked with a company executive, Rex Bradley, who traveled regularly around big-league cities and to Hall of Fame induction ceremonies every summer with Reese.

"People would just light up when they saw Pee Wee," said Bradley. "I never was around another man who got that kind of warm reception wherever he went."

Reese had a public birthday party at Ebbets Field in the team's final days in Brooklyn. More than 30,000 fans lit candles in the darkened park and sang "Happy Birthday" to the Brooklyn captain and the favorite Dodger of most fans.

฿ ฿ ฿

"I remember the story Dad used to tell," said his son, Mark Reese, a Los Angeles writer and filmmaker. "He reported to the Brooklyn training camp in Daytona in 1940. He had taken a train from Louisville to Florida, and with all the changes and delays he was late getting to the park."

Pee Wee carried a small bag to the Brooklyn clubhouse, knocked on the door and was met by the burly, gruff clubhouse attendant, John Griffen.

"Get in here, kid, and get this uniform on in a hurry if you want to work here," Griffen barked.

Griffen had mistaken the small rookie shortstop for the team's new batboy and wanted him to hustle onto the field as batting practice was about to begin.

"Pee Wee did what he was told but he also took his glove on the field and wore that little bat boy uniform," said Mark Reese. "He was just too shy and soft-spoken to suggest to Griffen that he was a player and deserved a larger uniform with a number."

Rookie Reese took the field and began having a catch with another rookie named Pete Reiser. They would establish a friendship, rare in baseball, that would last a lifetime. They played together, were married at the same time, shared a spring training honeymoon party together, confided in each other and helped and motivated each other for all their years with the Dodgers and beyond.

When manager Durocher spotted the small shortstop playing catch with the heralded Reiser he walked over to him.

"What the hell are you doing in that bat boy shirt?" he asked the baby-faced youngster.

"Uhh, that's what the clubhouse man handed me when I reported a little while ago," explained Reese.

"Get the hell in there and tell him to give you a real uniform. You're going to be the shortstop on this team," Durocher said.

Durocher had joined the haughty Yankees of Babe Ruth out of his home fields of West Springfield, Massachusetts, for a couple of games early in the 1925 season. He was a loud-mouthed 19-year-old who could field but couldn't hit much. Ruth immediately needled the youngster for his jabbering and for his attempts at squeezing into the batting cage for practice out of his regular turn with the scrubs. It would develop into an antagonistic relationship that would remain so through Durocher's Yankee years and well after Leo the Lip moved on to Cincinnati, St. Louis and then Brooklyn.

Durocher had his chance for revenge at the end of Ruth's career. He quickly got rid of Ruth when he became the player-manager of the Dodgers in 1939. Ruth finished his term serving as a Dodger prop for attendance purposes only in 1938. Although Ruth was supposed to be a coach for the Dodgers, nobody around the team during those days could ever recall any real coaching he did.

As a result of his own experiences as an unaccepted kid around the Yankees, Durocher always had a soft spot in that hard heart of his for youngsters with talent. He encouraged and aided the careers of Reese and Reiser in that first 1940 season. He would later encourage the career of an elderly 28-year-old rookie in the spring of 1947 named Jackie Robinson.

Durocher pushed a youngster named Willie Mays when he managed the kid outfielder of the New York Giants in 1951 and he would bring along several young players when he led the Chicago Cubs to an almost-pennant in 1969.

In a few days Reese had shown enough ability to be pronounced the opening-day shortstop for the Dodgers at the age of 20. Two kids, Reese and Reiser, would be the anchors of the first pennant-winning team in Brooklyn in 21 years when the 1941 Brooklyn club won the National League title.

Like hundreds of other baseball players, Reese lost important years of his career during his service time in World War II. He was in the Navy as a ball player for most of the war and later was transferred to a combat ship in the South Pacific in late 1944 as the war deepened.

The war ended in Europe on May 8, 1945, and peace was declared after the Japanese surrendered on the battleship *Missouri* on September 2, 1945.

Shortly before the signing of the peace treaty in late August of 1945, Reese was on the high seas. His ship was returning to San Francisco and he would soon be discharged from service and could resume his baseball career in 1946.

"I was sitting on the deck reading a paper and enjoying the sun," Reese once said, "when a radio man I knew came up to me. 'Hey, Pee Wee, I just heard something on the radio I think you will be interested in.' He proceeded to tell me that the Brooklyn Dodgers, my team, had just signed a new player. 'The Dodgers signed a nigger,' he said."

The name of the player was Jack Roosevelt Robinson. He was from California, had been a big athlete at UCLA and had played for the Negro League team, the Kansas City Monarchs, in 1945.

Reese said he didn't react much to what the other sailor had said. He knew that his father had the attitude common to most Kentuckians in 1945 that blacks and whites just didn't live or work together. He could only think that his father might not be too happy about the news that a black player was to have a chance in organized baseball after being kept out of the game throughout the 20th century.

"Then the sailor came back a few minutes later. He had run up the stairs to the deck. He had some other news. 'Hey, Pee Wee,' he shouted, 'that nigger I told you about. He's a shortstop.' *That* upset me."

Reese now envisioned that his return to baseball after three years in service might not be very easy. He hadn't played organized baseball for a couple of years, certainly wasn't in shape for a grinding National League season and now faced competition from all avenues, including this latest one from the newly signed Brooklyn player.

Robinson would, of course, be sent to the Dodgers farm club in Montreal for the 1946 season. He played second base there and joined the Dodgers as a first baseman in 1947. After Eddie Stanky was traded from Brooklyn the following season, Robinson moved to second base. Robinson would play only one game at shortstop in his 10-year career in Brooklyn. He and Reese played as teammates and friends from 1947 through 1956.

In 1947, Reese performed a noble public act. Robinson had been challenged and harassed by many opposition players after a Brooklyn rebellion by southern players against Robinson had been quelled by Durocher.

The manager threatened to get rid of any player who didn't want to play with Robinson. A petition begun by Dixie Walker, Bobby Bragan and Hugh Casey and signed by a few other southern players and one northerner, Carl Furillo, lost steam after stars like Reese, Ralph Branca and future Hall of Famer Duke Snider refused to go along with it.

Robinson's life had been threatened by nasty, hateful letters, several of them coming from the southern city of Cincinnati, a border town to Kentucky. One day Reese casually walked over to Robinson on the field. He put his arm over his teammate's shoulder. It was the kind of universal gesture accepted in sports by teammates for rookie players in helping them make the grade.

At the 1999 memorial service for Pee Wee Reese in New York, *Newsday* columnist Stan Isaacs suggested in his remarks that this simple comradely gesture should be immortalized in a statue of Robinson and Reese.

The statue was unveiled outside Key Span Stadium in the Coney Island section of Brooklyn in touching ceremonies with the families of Robinson and Reese in attendance in the summer of 2005. It is a fitting memorial commemorating the friendship of the two players and their contributions to Brooklyn's only World Series triumph over the Yankees in 1955.

The event had the support of the Brooklyn Historical Society at 128 Pierrepoint Street, which has stood in the same site since 1881.

Jessie Kelly, president of the Brooklyn Historical Society, said the statue unveiling would be part of an extensive exhibit in 2005 connected to the Society and showing the history and growth of Brooklyn.

"We will have an exhibit room with Brooklyn Dodger displays for the entire year," she said late in 2004. "The Brooklyn Dodgers World Championship flag of 1955 will be part of the exhibit. One of our exhibit rooms will show the history of Brooklyn through a collection called *Brooklyn Works: 400 Years of Brooklyn Working*. We have so many wonderful exhibits about Brooklyn," she said.

"Brooklyn is one of the oldest settlements in the country. We have exhibits that go far back in Brooklyn history," Kelly said.

As the Dodgers won pennants in 1947, 1949, 1952 and 1953, Reese emerged as the on-field and off-field leader and captain of these great Brooklyn teams.

He was captured brilliantly in a film biography by his son, Mark Reese, as the heart and soul of the best National League baseball team of all time. If it wasn't for those Damn Yankees, Brooklyn in Reese's time from 1940-1957 may well have been regarded as baseball's best team ever. They were certainly in that category with the 1955 Series win over the Yankees.

"Pee Wee always thought of that World Series championship season as the culmination of his career," said Mark, who often refers to his father by his baseball nickname. "That was the crowning moment of his life."

Mark Reese recalled how Pee Wee made one special request in his final days as cancer destroyed his body and took his life.

"He always had that 1955 World Series ring on his hand after 1955. It never left him. He slept with it, traveled with it, showed it off to everybody, bragged about it," said Mark Reese. "In his final days he wanted me to make him a promise. He wanted to be sure that the ring wasn't buried with him. He wanted it to go on. It was too much a part of him, a part of that Brooklyn legacy, a big part of those wonderful years, the essence of his life. I have the ring now in a safe deposit vault. I am always confused about what I should do with it."

Mark Reese has a teenage daughter by a previous relationship. He is not certain he will ever give it to her or even leave it to any future children he might have with his new wife, Patti, whom he married in late September of 2004.

He was in New York, at a reception with mayor Michael Bloomberg, a day after his marriage for the official announcement of the final fund raising effort for the statue before its creation and placement in Brooklyn's Key Span Park in 2005.

"The last time I was here in New York was when the committee was formed to decide on the statue. It was in the morning of September 11, 2001. We were in City Hall with Mayor Giuliani, two blocks from the World Trade center," Reese said. "We heard about the attacks. We just ran. My mom was 79 at the time. I said, 'Mom, run.' She just said, 'I don't run.' Joe Black was with us. He was a big man. He said, 'I don't run, either.' The women were supposed to be on their way to lunch at the Windows of the World in the Trade Center later. I believe to this day I heard Pee Wee's voice saying, 'What in hell are we doing here?' Somehow we all got out safe."

"In the meantime the 1955 ring just stays in the vault," Mark Reese said. "It is really too painful to even think about it."

Reese's Dodger uniform, number 1, the one it took him a while to prove he deserved as a youngster, was eventually retired by the Los Angeles Dodgers. Reese was elected to Baseball's Hall of Fame by the Veterans Committee in 1984 after a 20-year wait.

"That was such a sad year when he was ill," said Mark Reese. "He couldn't make it to the Hall of Fame inductions in Cooperstown and he missed that terribly. He was so connected to all those people. He loved seeing them all at the Otesaga Hotel in Cooperstown and at the ceremonies."

Reese was connected to all his Brooklyn teammates who also made it to the Hall of Fame. He would spend wonderful hours with many of them in later years, players such as Sandy Koufax, Roy Campanella and Duke Snider. Jackie Robinson was gone by the time Pee Wee made it to the Hall of Fame in 1984. Robinson had died in 1972.

The last time the two men saw each other was at the funeral of Gil Hodges after his death on April 2, 1972. He had been their Dodger teammate and first baseman. Hodges died of a massive heart attack while walking off a golf course at West Palm Beach, Florida. Hodges was with his coaches on the New York Mets, former Brooklyn teammate Rube Walker, former Dodger Joe Pignatano and former Washington coach Eddie Yost.

Pignatano turned to Hodges and asked, "What time are we meeting for dinner?"

Before Hodges could answer he collapsed on the concrete walk outside the team's hotel headquarters.

"He was dead before his head hit the ground," a doctor told Mets officials.

Pee Wee Reese sat in a front row of the Brooklyn church a couple of days later for the farewell to their teammate and pal.

Robinson walked into the church and slowly walked down the aisle to a front seat. He sat just behind Pee Wee who said, "Jack, it's me, Pee Wee."

Robinson, who suffered near blindness from diabetes, stammered an apology.

"Oh, I'm sorry, Pee Wee, I just can't see," he said.

Robinson died a few months later, October 24, 1972, at his Stamford, Connecticut home.

In their youth and vigor they were all heroes and wonderful baseball players, performing their exploits at Ebbets Field and around the other seven cities in the National League.

"I always remember those great rivalries we had with the Dodgers. Pee Wee and I would talk over a lot of those games," said Stan Musial, the greatest hitter of his time, as he sat in the lobby of the Hall of Fame hotel in Cooperstown, New York.

"It was always such a great show," said the Hall of Famer of the St. Louis Cardinals. "Brooklyn had those great baseball fans and they appreciated good ball games. They wanted their Dodgers to win, of course, but when we made a good play or got a big hit, they applauded us. They knew they would see great baseball when Pee Wee Reese's Dodgers played against us in Ebbets Field."

Musial batted .331 over 22 seasons with the Cardinals from 1941 through 1963. He did it with that famous corkscrew stance he still reveals on stage every summer when he is introduced at the Baseball Hall of Fame inductions, his harmonica in his pocket always at the ready and with his constant smile.

Musial was once asked why he always had a smile on his face.

"If you hit .331 all your life you'd have a smile on your face, too," he replied.

He would greet fans and friends with his ever-present chattering, "Whatdoyousay, whatdoyousay" welcome, put out his hand and immediately bring his hands together in that famous left-handed stance.

"The field was so close to the stands," Musial recalled about his days against the Dodgers in Ebbets Field. "I just loved hitting there. I hit about .350 against the Dodgers in my career and maybe .522 or something like that in Ebbets Field."

One year he had a five-for-five day against the Dodgers in Brooklyn and when he walked on the field the next afternoon he heard a few of the Brooklyn fans shouting, "Here comes That Man again."

"Bob Broeg [*St. Louis Post-Dispatch* columnist] heard it and he began referring to me in his columns as That Man. Pretty soon everybody picked it up and I became Stan the Man. My business is called Stan the Man Enterprises. Isn't that funny? I always loved that name," he said.

Some years back Musial was elected to the Brooklyn Dodgers Hall of Fame, an organization that honors former Brooklyn Dodgers and former star opposition players of those Dodger days.

"My wife Lil and I were invited to this big Hall of Fame dinner at some fancy restaurant in Brooklyn, Gage and Tollner, in downtown

Brooklyn before the ceremonies. We took a cab from the hotel in
Manhattan and were left off in front of this fancy place. Only it wasn't
the right place. We started walking towards the corner in hopes of find-
ing another cab that could take us to the right place," Musial said.

Just then a car pulled up alongside the restaurant and the middle-
aged driver started yelling out of the window.

"It's the Man, Stan the Man," he bellowed.

"Whatdoyou say, whatdoyousay," Musial answered.

"Hey, what are you doing here?"

"We're lost," Musial said. "We were supposed to be at Gage and
Tollner's restaurant but they left us off here by mistake," said Musial.

"Get in," the guy said. "I'll take you."

All the other guests at the dinner arrived by a bus chartered by the
group from the hotel. Those who didn't make the bus arrived by cab.
Musial arrived in a private car driven by an old Brooklyn Dodgers fan.

"That was maybe 30 years after I stopped playing," Musial said.

President George W. Bush, former owner of the Texas Rangers
baseball team, invited some 30 Hall of Famers to the White House for
dinner early in 2004.

The war in Iraq was going full blast and the president wanted to
change the subject in the press and enjoy a nostalgic evening.

"We talked about baseball, talked over those old days, especially
my games with the Cardinals against the Dodgers. We really had a wonderful evening," said Musial. "Just before we were to leave, the president asked me to play *Take Me Out to the Ball Game* on my harmonica. I pulled it out and everybody sang it. It was great fun."

At the age of 86, Musial still has the same enthusiasm, the same joy
in his face, the same warmth he showed as a St. Louis great, especially
to those Brooklyn fans as Stan the Man.

Musial's Hall of Fame teammate, Red Schoendienst, also recalled
his days in Brooklyn with much joy. As the Cardinals played the New
York Mets in May of 2004, Schoendienst remembered what it was like
being an opposition player in Ebbets Field.

"Those Dodger fans were just the best in the game," said
Schoendienst, finally out of uniform at the age of 81 after more than
60 years as a uniformed player, coach and manager. "You always knew

if you made a good play in the field you would get a great hand from the fans."

Schoendienst joined the Cardinals in 1945 and played on their 1946 World Series winner. He also played in the World Series for the Milwaukee Braves against the Yankees in 1957 and 1958.

"Ebbets Field was a special place and the Dodgers were a special team. You could see why they were so loved by their fans," the red-headed switch hitter said. "They were also a great bunch of guys, especially Pee Wee Reese. He really was my favorite."

ℬ ℬ ℬ

In those days of the 1940s and 1950s, players threw their gloves on the field after the last out of an inning and retrieved their gloves to start the next inning. A sportswriter from the New York *Daily News* named Joe Trimble immortalized the event in a story about World War II Yankee first baseman Nick Etten. Etten was a strong hitter but a weak fielder.

During one game Etten threw his glove on the field near first base at the end of the inning. A batter rolled a ball in the direction of Etten's glove. The ball hit the dirt and stuck in Etten's glove near first base.

Trimble wrote, "Nick Etten's glove fields better without Nick Etten in it."

Etten happened to be reading Trimble's line in the *Daily News* the next afternoon as the team took off on a train trip for Chicago. Etten spotted Trimble and chased after him through six cars of the train. When last seen that day, Trimble was hanging off the back railing of the train with Etten's hands around his throat.

"I threw my glove on the field once in Brooklyn and when I went out to get it the next inning I couldn't separate the fingers of the glove," Schoendienst said. "Pee Wee Reese had stuck a wad of gum in the glove gluing the fingers together. I got him back. I took his glove off the field instead of my own at the end of a game."

Schoendienst said the Dodgers were not only a great baseball team, they were a terrific bunch of needlers.

"One guy they used to beat up on was our first baseman, Dick Sisler, because he had a speech problem and stammered terribly. Leo Durocher used to drive him nuts. One time Sisler was playing first base and the last out of the inning was a ground ball to me. I threw it to Dick. He took the ball out of the glove and threw it into right field and threw his glove out to the mound for the start of the next inning."

The Dodgers had won six pennants and not one World Series from 1941 through 1953. The Giants had won in 1954. As the Dodgers prepared for the 1955 season there wasn't a great deal of optimism around the Brooklyn offices at 215 Montague Street that this would be that very special year. The Brooklyn cry, "Wait 'Till Next Year" was getting a little old and weary. The fans were getting restless. Ebbets Field was showing its age and stories began appearing regularly in the press about the possibility of a new stadium for the Dodgers in downtown Brooklyn. Owner Walter O'Malley and parks commissioner Robert Moses, the most powerful figure in the city because he controlled most of the city's lands, met several times to explore the possibilities. They didn't like each other immediately. Egos and self-interest were at stake. It was going to be a tough fight.

The Dodgers had traded a veteran left hander, Preacher Roe, and the great-fielding third baseman, Billy Cox, late in December of 1954. The reconstituted team, with the addition of the kid left-hander from Brooklyn, Sanford Koufax, was scheduled to begin workouts March 1, 1955, under a new restrictive baseball spring training rule.

On February 28, 1955, the privately owned Dodger plane, named the Kay-O, in honor of owner Walter O'Malley's wife, Kay O'Malley, taxied down the runway at La Guardia Field headed for the team's spring training headquarters at the old Navy base at Vero Beach, Florida. Several players were on board, including Johnny Podres, George Shuba, Billy Loes, Don Hoak and Karl Spooner, several team executives, including Buzzie Bavasi, the general manager, and Fresco Thompson, the farm director, and several other club officials.

The Yankees were headed for their training headquarters at St. Petersburg, Florida. The New York Giants were on their way to their camp in Phoenix, Arizona. Thirteen other teams in the National and

American Leagues were moving to their training sites with high hopes. That's what spring training in baseball was all about: high hopes.

At the first batting practice of the Dodgers full team at Vero Beach a few days later, outfielder Duke Snider looked over at his teammates waiting around the cage to hit.

"Duke just smiled and stared at me," Pee Wee Reese once told his son, Mark, "and then he looked at Jackie and Campy and Furillo and Hodges and a couple of the other guys. He began singing, 'Father Time's catching up with that old gang of mine.' When I asked him why he was singing that, Duke just smiled and said, 'It's true, isn't it?' It sure was."

Newk, Piggy and Loes

If ever a contending team had a muddled spring, it was the 1955 Brooklyn Dodgers under the direction of laconic second-year manager, Walter Alston.

Shortstop and captain Pee Wee Reese was pushing 36 years of age, had been around the team for 14 years with three seasons out for World War II service and was slowing down in the field. He had a big year at bat in 1954 with his career-high .309 average, but he was losing ground in the infield and his throws had a little float on them by the end of the season.

"Reese is our shortstop," Alston announced at the first Vero Beach meeting with the New York press, "unless somebody beats him out."

Chico Fernandez, a Cuban comet, and Don Zimmer, the feisty kid from Cincinnati, were looked on as competitors for Reese's job.

"Both might be at shortstop in early games because they are in shape now and Reese will be getting in shape," said Alston.

He also suggested that Reese might play a little at second base or third base, the surest sign that a veteran shortstop is on his way out of the team picture. Jackie Robinson, asserting his confidence that he would be in the lineup come opening day, worked out at second base, third base and left field. Alston indicated that Jim Gilliam would probably be the second baseman, Don Hoak was the leading candidate for the third base job and Sandy Amoros, the flashy Cuban, might be ready for the left-field job.

Roy Campanella was coming off that broken hand he suffered in 1954. Billy Loes had never lived up to his enormous potential. Don Newcombe had struggled in 1954 after coming back from missing two seasons with Army service in 1952 and 1953. On and on it went. The Brooklyn picture in the spring of 1955 was a mess.

One of the youngsters fighting for a job with the Dodgers in 1955 during that spring was a kid catcher from Brooklyn named Joe Pignatano.

Pignatano, 76 years old, was born, raised and still lives in Brooklyn, New York, in the Bay Ridge section of the borough near where many of the Dodgers lived during the season of 1955. He and his wife, Nancy, have two sons, one of whom is a rocket scientist with a California Silicon Valley company.

"I was always a Dodger fan," said Pignatano, as he lounged on the porch of his Brooklyn home. "I grew up on West 15th street and Stillwell Avenue in the Coney Island section of Brooklyn. I attended Public School 212, Mark Twain Junior High School and Westinghouse Vocational School. I wanted to be a television technician."

His Westinghouse coach, Lou Green, wrote letters to several teams suggesting they take a look at the young catcher. The Dodgers signed the 18-year-old to a contract in 1948, sent him to Cambridge, Maryland, and released him in a week.

"I didn't even get carfare home," he said. "When I arrived back in Brooklyn, my mother was shocked. She called Fresco Thompson, the Brooklyn farm director, and asked why I was released. He had no idea. He didn't even know about it. Sometimes things worked that way in those days."

Lucy Pignatano arranged for her son to get another look at an Ebbets Field workout. George Sisler, the former .400 hitter, was the head of Dodger scouts. When he saw the smooth catching style of the youngster and a good-enough bat, he asked his boss, Fresco Thompson, "Why was this kid released?"

Joe Pignatano as a young Brooklyn catcher at Ebbets Field.
Pignatano Family Photo

He was re-signed for no money again, sent to Sheboygan, Wisconsin, and then on to Cairo, Illinois. He played at Valdosta, Georgia, in 1950, served in the Army in 1951 and 1952 (almost everybody was drafted in those days) and returned to catch at Asheville, North Carolina, and Elmira, New York, in the next two seasons.

In the spring of 1955 he was at the Brooklyn camp at Vero Beach with no chance of making the 25-man roster. Alston had decided early on to go with only two catchers, Campanella and the left-handed hitting Rube Walker.

"I remember catching Koufax in those first few days of spring training," said Pignatano. "I don't know if I was the only guy who caught him, but I spent a lot of time with him. He threw very hard and he had a great curve ball. All this talk about how wild he was in those days was ridiculous. He couldn't hit a spot, but what left-hander can? He could throw it over the plate. His fastball jumped and his curve was so big. I knew he was going to be a big league pitcher as soon as I put my glove on with him."

Pignatano lost his early nervousness within a few days. He lockered next to Don Newcombe and he was befriended by coach Billy Herman and the big first baseman of the Dodgers who also lived in Brooklyn, Gil Hodges.

"Just relax and you'll be all right," Hodges told him.

One of the reasons Alston was certain he could make it through the 1955 season with only two catchers was the presence of Hodges. Gil had broken into baseball as a catcher, and Alston felt that if an emergency developed he could move Hodges behind the plate again. Jackie Robinson was still around to play first base if needed as he had in 1947.

"I stayed with the team that spring until the second cut and then I went to Saint Paul before I stayed with the Dodgers in the 1957 season," he said. "Probably the best thing about '55 besides being with the only Brooklyn World Series winner was getting close to Gil."

Pignatano was one of Hodges' coaches when he managed the Mets and won a surprise World Series title in 1969. He was with Hodges when the manager suffered a fatal heart attack in West Palm Beach in 1972.

"All these years later, it is still a painful memory. Gil was the biggest, strongest, healthiest guy I knew. He had those huge hands and that large body. Who could ever imagine something like that?"

Pignatano stayed in the Mets organization under Yogi Berra after Hodges died, scouted and coached for many years and maintains his connections with the Dodger organization. He attends their Fantasy Camps in Florida, dons the catching gear occasionally to work with campers, plays a lot of golf, is active in many charities and serves on the board of the 50th anniversary 1955 Brooklyn Dodgers Reunion Committee.

"I didn't play a game with them that year of 1955, but I did go to spring training. That is a good enough connection for me," he said.

Pignatano made it to the World Series with the 1959 Los Angeles Dodgers and to the World Series again as a coach for the 1969 New York Mets, an enviable baseball record going back more than half a century.

"The '55 Dodgers—what a team, what a terrific bunch of players and great pals," he said. "Pee Wee and Duke and Erskine and the rest liked to flash their '55 World Series rings. I flash my '59 and '69 rings and we have lots of laughs."

Pignatano looks back on his career with much joy and sweet remembrance.

"I played on winners, I caught some great pitchers, I had a lot of fun," he said. "It was much better than being a television repair man. I don't think I would ever have caught Koufax if I had stayed a television repair man."

ß ß ß

The Dodgers spring training complex at Vero Beach, Florida, was the finest facility of its time and remains so to this day. The land and old Navy barracks acquired by the Dodgers for a $1 payment became spring home to many great players, Baseball Hall of Famers and famous sportswriters.

"We were all like family there," said Jack Lang, 85, the Hall of Fame baseball writer and last surviving regular baseball beat writer of the 1955 Brooklyn Dodgers. "Our wives and the wives of the players used to sit around the pool and spend the afternoons together. There never was a baseball relationship quite like the one we enjoyed at Vero."

Lang said his late wife, Winnie, would spend endless hours with Pee Wee's wife, Dottie, while their men were at work.

"When the season started, the wives of the players all sat together in one section of Ebbets Field behind the dugout with their kids and friends. In spring training the writers and the players were just together more. We used to take turns with the Campanellas babysitting their kids and they babysat ours when we went up to the dining room for dinner. The players ate from five to seven o'clock each night—there were no night spring games then—and we had cocktails in the pressroom. Then we ate from seven o'clock on, shared the bar with clubhouse guy Babe Hamburger serving and had a grand old time."

After games at Ebbets Field, Lang would often drive Campanella and Jackie Robinson to their homes in St. Alban's in the Queens section of New York City. Lang lived in nearby Elmont.

"We had pleasant conversations in the car. Campy would invite me over to his house once in a while with the kids to play with his model trains. Jackie wouldn't do that. He was bright and he was pleasant at times, but he could be angry and argumentative at other times," Lang said.

Lang sat in the living room of his new Long Island condominium in the summer of 2004 as he talked of those Dodger days. His wife is gone now and his four children are grown and on their own.

"There are a lot of rich widows in this gated community I just moved into," he said. "I'm sure some of them will be interested in hearing about the Brooklyn Dodgers."

Lang, who began covering baseball for the *Long Island Press* in 1946, said he retains one gift from the Brooklyn Dodgers he never will let go of, though he has disposed of much from his previous home.

"The Dodgers won their first ten games of the 1955 season. That was a baseball record then. Each one of the players and all of us covering the club—me, Dick Young, Harold Rosenthal, Bill Roeder, all of the guys, got this beautiful silver mug from Walter O'Malley. It marks the event, the date and the historic impact of that start."

Lang said he could recall the victory party after the Dodgers won their first World Series.

"It was at the Bossert Hotel in Brooklyn, just a few blocks down from the Brooklyn club offices and the party went on forever. The sun was coming up when we finally left that ball room," Lang said. "Now the victory parties for baseball teams are in a room filled with baseball agents, managers and advertising executives."

☞ ☞ ☞

Spring training is fantasy time for baseball teams with brimming confidence, no pressures on established players and endless hours of recreation, golf and gossip.

Players sometimes say silly things to the sportswriters for the purposes of stirring up a little emotion and making a few headlines in the hometown newspapers.

When asked to compare himself with the other New York center fielder, Willie Mays, who had returned to the Giants in 1954 from military service after his 1951 rookie season, Duke Snider proclaimed, "I'm better than Mays. I make more money, don't I?"

Snider was making $36,000 a year, about the same as Robinson, Reese, Campanella, Furillo and the other veteran Dodgers. Mays, in his second season, was still at $10,000.

"We're going to run away with this thing," said Campanella, optimistic after recovering from a broken bone in his hand. "I'm OK, and I can't see how we can fail to run away with this thing."

Much talk that spring of 1955 in the press and around Babe Hamburger's bar each night was about the team's pitching.

Carl Erskine had won 18 games in 1954, and Billy Loes won 13. Russ Meyer and 22-year-old Johnny Podres had won 11 games each. Would the 19-year-old kid Koufax provide any help? Joe Black hadn't been the same pitcher since his sensational 1952 rookie season, Jim Hughes had led the league with 60 appearances in 1954, and that left-hander from the Montreal Royals minor league club, Tommy Lasorda, always seemed to win in the International League. Could he win in Brooklyn?

Don Newcombe had won 17, 19 and 20 games in his first three seasons. He had fallen to 9-8 in 1954 with arm trouble and some sour

Don Newcombe was a lifelong executive with the Dodgers.
© Los Angeles Dodgers, Inc.

exchanges with manager Walton Alston. A big year by the big guy from Madison, New Jersey, could ease the Brooklyn situation incredibly.

Shortly after Jackie Robinson was signed by the Brooklyn organization, the Dodgers quietly added two more Negro players to the organization, catcher Roy Campanella and pitcher Don Newcombe. They sent them off to their farm club in rural Nashua, New Hampshire.

The hulking 6-foot-4, 220-pound Newcombe could throw as hard as a hundred miles an hour. He could hit as far as any batter in the Dodger organization. This was an exceptional talent and he proved it quickly with his Rookie of the Year debut in 1949.

He lost a crusher game in the opener of the 1949 World Series when Tommy Henrich hit a ninth-inning homer to beat Newcombe and the Dodgers 1-0. The only serious blot on his marvelous career (149-90 in ten seasons) was the winless 0-4 World Series record.

Don Newcombe, who works for the Los Angeles Dodgers in community relations and also runs his own sports consulting business, Don Newcombe Enterprises in L.A., sat at his desk in the summer of 2004.

"I'll be with the Dodgers 48 years. I'm pretty proud of that," said Newcombe, as he approached his 80th birthday. "This team has had such a marvelous history. I guess that '55 season was something special. There aren't that many of us around now to celebrate the 50th anniversary."

As the Dodgers blasted out of the gate with a ten-game winning streak and a 21-2 start, Newcombe won his first ten starts in a row, was 17-1 at one time in 1955 before arm trouble slowed him down and he finished with a 20-5 mark. He won 27 games the next year and captured the Cy Young award and the National League Most Valuable Player award to go with his rookie honors, the only pitcher to ever achieve those three honors.

"We thought we had a pretty good ball club in 1954, but we didn't win it," Newcombe said. "The start convinced us all that we would win in 1955 and this was going to be the year we would finally beat those Yankees. If you look at those old photos after Podres won the last game, I'm the first guy out on the field to congratulate him. It had been a long wait. I was just about the happiest guy there was."

Newcombe was the pitcher in many significant games during his Brooklyn career. He was the starter in the final game of the 1949 season when the Dodgers edged out the Cardinals by one game for the pennant. He was the starter and loser in the final game of 1950 when Dick Sisler hit a tenth-inning homer to beat Brooklyn out of a pennant. He was the starter and pitched brilliantly in the final game of the 1951 playoff when he held the Giants to one run through eight innings. Bobby Thomson's ninth-inning homer off Ralph Branca ended that dream.

One of the most touching baseball scenes is that of Newcombe walking past Branca near second base as the Dodgers exchanged pitchers and the two large Brooklyn right-handers exchanged pats on the back on that October 3, 1951 date. Newcombe had barely walked up the steps to the Dodger clubhouse in the Polo Grounds before he was to hear The Shot Heard 'Round the World.

Newcombe was in service in 1952 and 1953 and struggled to regain his form in 1954.

"I knew I was going to have a great season when I started pitching in 1955," said Newcombe. "My arm felt good and everybody on the club suggested this would finally be our year. Pee Wee had been around the Dodgers since 1940 and he knew this might be the last time we had a chance to win for him. I remember him saying to me in spring training that he wanted it so badly it hurt."

Newcombe had been caught up in so many dramatic games, winning many and losing some, that his psyche always seemed up for examination in those Brooklyn years.

Jackie Robinson had gone through hell as the first Negro in modern baseball. By 1955 he was filled with self-confidence. No longer was he anything more than another great Dodger. He had started as such an historic figure, but now it was clear that Robinson's playing time was almost over.

The third Dodger Negro player, Roy Campanella, had joined the club in 1948 and fit in perfectly. He had a high-pitched, squeakily friendly voice. Robinson had an articulate, modulated sound. Newcombe's voice could shatter glass. People were physically afraid of Newcombe, whose scowl on the mound was similar to the later looks of Bob Gibson. Only Sal Maglie, the wonderful New York Giants pitcher, who would later join the Dodgers, could scare batters as easily with his countenance.

Newcombe was traded to Cincinnati in 1958, won 13 games for the Reds in 1959 and finished up his big-league career with the Indians. He then went on to play first base for the Chunichi Dragons in Japan and hit some of the longest home runs ever seen there.

Newcombe had batted .359 with seven home runs for the 1955 Dodgers and with his 17-1 start and 20-5 record was as responsible as anyone for the lasting glory of that team.

Some personal problems, including difficult bouts with alcohol, cost Newcombe some of his skills and probably denied him a Hall of Fame ending to his career. Still, he remains one of the most significant figures in Brooklyn Dodgers history.

"I remember just how happy our guys were after we beat the Yankees," Newcombe said. "That's the kind of memory that stays with you for a lifetime."

His company provides funds for charity events around Los Angeles, works with youngsters and creates business opportunities.

"I remember dining with Martin Luther King when he came out here to Los Angeles in the late 1960s. We talked of his movement and how much Jackie meant to America. I mentioned something to him about a national holiday for Jack. He agreed. Now there is a holiday for Martin, but there is not one for Jack. I hope this 50th anniversary can create excitement for the Brooklyn Dodgers and remind people what Jackie did for the country. Wouldn't it be fitting to mark 2005 as the 50th anniversary of the Brooklyn Dodgers victory over the Yankees and the year the country paused to honor Jackie Robinson?" he said.

⚾ ⚾ ⚾

The other pitcher manager Walter Alston hoped would come through for the Dodgers in 1955 as a big winner was Billy Loes. He was 10-4 in 19 starts for the champions. He had won 13, 14 and 13 games the previous three seasons. Dick Young suggested in print that he had the stuff to win 20 games.

"Nah, I'll never do that," said Loes. "You win 20 games and they want you to win 20 every year."

After arriving in Florida for the 1955 spring training, Loes was asked by the press what his feelings were about the team.

"All I care is if we win the pennant," he said. "That's all that counts with me."

He had started 21 games in 1954 and relieved in seven others.

"A fellow can't pitch in relief so much and still start in a regular rotation," complained Loes. Then he quickly added, "But I'm not complaining."

William Loes was born in Long Island City, New York, grew up in Astoria, Queens, and was signed by the Dodgers out of high school. He was a skinny right-hander, standing 6-foot-1 and weighing no more than 165 pounds at his peak. But he could throw hard and had a vicious curve ball.

Loes was 80-63 in his 11 big-league seasons, pitched in three World Series for the Dodgers and retired from baseball after signing a contract with the expansion 1962 New York Mets. He appeared in the 1961 Thanksgiving Day parade down Fifth Avenue in Manhattan with the Mets float that carried first baseman Gil Hodges and manager Casey Stengel. Loes quit baseball before the team went to spring training. He must have known something. The Mets lost 120 games without him.

Loes drove a cab in New York, stayed away from most baseball events, married and divorced, had some health problems and now, at 77, lives in a small apartment in Tucson, Arizona.

Tom Villante, a former New York Yankee batboy who grew up to become the executive producer for the Brooklyn Dodger broadcasts in the 1950s and later an advertising executive, still hears from Loes occasionally.

Villante said he was always amused by Loes and loved being around him.

"His mother was ailing once and when I asked him how she was doing Billy replied, 'She's all washed up.' He was one of those guys who could never sit still. We would play cards together with Pee Wee and Duke and Zimmer. Loes would make some crazy noises with his mouth. I asked him what he was doing and he would say, 'I'm idling.' If I asked him to sit down and deal his hand he would often say, 'As the city sleeps, Billy Loes creeps.' He just said funny things in a funny way. I remember working with Yogi Berra on a show he had later on television called *Yogi at the Movies*. He reviewed films and did one with actress Glenn Close starring in it. We went over the script half a dozen times before going on live. Then Yogi called the actress Glen Cove, like the town in Long Island. Billy would do things like that all the time."

Loes was once asked who would win the World Series between Brooklyn and the Yankees in 1952. "The Yankees in five," he said. When many of his teammates jumped all over him for saying that in the next day's newspapers he took it all back. "Ok," Loes said, "the Yankees in six."

Columnist Arthur Daley of *The New York Times* made fun of Loes in print because Billy had said he had lost a ground ball hit back to the mound in the sun. Any driver who bumped into the car in front of him because of sun glare understood that was not very funny.

Villante recalled how he just loved being part of that 1955 Brooklyn team and organizing the broadcasts with Red Barber, Connie Desmond and Vin Scully.

"Walter O'Malley wanted me to go along with the team to Los Angeles when they moved, but I decided to stay in the New York area," Villante said. "I missed all the guys, of course, after they moved west, but I didn't want to uproot my family. My wife had a big job with Merrill Lynch and she couldn't transfer to Los Angeles."

Villante said he was very close to all the Dodgers, especially Loes, Pee Wee, Zimmer, Snider and Clem Labine.

"It's hard to think that 50 years have gone by," he said. "These were all such great ball players and such wonderful guys. So many of them are gone now and so many others are ailing. I guess it's like that old movie news program *The March of Time*. That's what happens. They all seem to have made out OK as the years went on. Loes probably had the toughest time of all, but he did things his own way."

Villante, spending his winters now in the Dodgers training camp-site of Vero Beach, Florida, said there was one more memory of Loes he wanted to share.

"The Dodgers got this call from a young woman who claimed Loes had fathered her baby. She was threatening a paternity suit and she wanted millions of dollars. The Dodgers called Loes in to confirm or deny the story.

When he was confronted by Brooklyn executives wanting the truth before they acted, Loes simply said, "Ahh, she wants attention. It's a publicity stunt."

Villante, who has two children and four grandchildren, said Loes is just one of the most unique characters he ever met in his more than 50 years around baseball players.

"There may be only one Yogi," said Villante, who worked closely with Yogi on many commercial projects, "but there is only one Billy Loes. Thank God."

Zimmer and Torre
of Brooklyn

The aging Jackie Robinson proved to manager Walter Alston that he had a lot left in the spring of 1955. Alston's starting lineup for the opener against Pittsburgh included Robinson at third base.

Jim Gilliam, a speedy switch hitter, had stolen Robinson's job by now at second with two strong seasons in 1953 (.278) and 1954 (.282), and Robinson had bested Don Hoak for the starting position at third.

Alston's first 1955 lineup would list Gilliam leading off, Reese batting second, Snider in the third spot, Hodges at first batting fourth, another speedster, Sandy Amoros, in left field, Robinson at third, right fielder Carl Furillo, the Reading Rifle hitting seventh, Campanella, seemingly recovered from the 1954 hand injury behind the plate and 18-game winner Carl Erskine as the opening-day hurler.

One grouchy guy was on the bench. That was Don Zimmer.

"We were staying in the St. George Hotel in downtown Brooklyn the night before the opening game," recalled Zimmer in the summer of 2004 as he marked his 56th year in baseball as the special advisor for the Tampa Bay Devil Rays. "I was real close to Pee Wee. He had helped me a lot and knew I would succeed him as the Dodger shortstop. Alston had asked if I could play second during that spring. What would I do, say no? I really thought I would start somewhere."

Zimmer went to his room that evening and soon received a call from Reese. Pee Wee wasn't feeling well and wanted to go over some defensive assignments against the Pirates (in those long, lost baseball days before computers) so that Zimmer would be ready against Pittsburgh.

"You'll be in there so I want to talk about how we play these guys," said the Brooklyn captain.

Zimmer spent a good part of the evening with his captain as Reese complained of a bad stomach. He could hardly keep down the ordered room service meal and moaned about his aches.

"I was so certain I was going to start that I tossed and turned all night long," said Zimmer.

Reese was fine by morning. He never mentioned his problem to manager Alston and Zimmer sat suffering on the Brooklyn bench.

Erskine pitched a strong game, Robinson got a couple of hits and the Dodgers beat the Pirates 6-1.

Furillo hit five home runs in the first eight games as the Dodgers jumped to an 8-0 start, Snider had three home runs, the pitching was impressive with Erskine, Russ Meyer, Billy Loes, Don Newcombe and Johnny Podres all pitching well.

Robinson had been moved up to the second spot in Alston's line-up, was hitting and running like a young infielder and was leading the Dodgers to the National League's best start in baseball history, a 10-0 mark.

"Meyer was really the surprise in the rotation," said Jack Lang of the *Long Island Press*. "Everybody else was hitting and pitching well in that streak and the Dodgers looked better on the field in those early games than they had on paper or in spring training."

The Dodgers pushed the winning streak to ten games with a 14-2 victory over the Philadelphia Phillies. The Brooklyn batters unloaded on future Hall of Famer Robin Roberts with 10 hits and 10 runs— small payback for the torture Roberts had inflicted on Brooklyn fans in his winning 1950 tenth-inning Whiz Kid finale.

Casey Stengel, the manager of the New York Mets in their inglorious 1962 120-game losing season, once asked, "Can't anybody play this here game?"

Around the rest of the National League cities in early 1955 they were beginning to ask, "Can't anybody beat this here team?"

It all came to an end as the Braves beat Brooklyn 5-4 with Warren Spahn besting Johnny Podres. The Dodgers failed to tie the game in the bottom of the eighth when Zimmer was thrown out at home on a squeeze play attempted by Robinson.

"They just got me," Zimmer recalled. "It took a perfect play by the Braves to beat us."

"Zimmer could run like a deer," said former Dodger coach Clyde Sukeforth, in an interview many years ago. "He did everything in baseball pretty good."

It was not unusual for Alston to call on Zimmer for a steal or a squeeze play attempt at home. It had worked several times. It was just a miracle that the short, stocky infielder from Cincinnati, Ohio, could even be playing big league baseball.

B̄ B̄ B̄

Donald William Zimmer was born in Cincinnati on January 17, 1931. He and lifelong neighborhood pal and fellow big league manager Jim Frey starred in high school baseball and the local American Legion team together. Their reward was a trip to Yankee Stadium for the 1947 World Series games between the Dodgers and the Yankees.

"We sat way up in the top of the bleachers, watched the game and ate about a dozen hot dogs," said Zimmer. "It was just the greatest day of my life until then."

Zimmer was soon signed by the Dodgers and was playing at Saint Paul in 1953, a step away from the Dodgers, when he almost lost his life. He was hitting .320, had 23 home runs and led the league with 63 runs batted in when he was hit in the head before baseball helmets were in vogue by a fast ball thrown by pitcher Jim Kirk.

He was unconscious for two weeks, lost his speech for almost six weeks and lost 44 pounds. He had been a stocky 5-foot-9 and 170 pounds when he was injured.

"They put four pieces of metal in my head, like buttons," Zimmer once explained. "These were like tapered corkscrews in a bottle."

Years later he would set off the metal scanners at airports as he traveled around baseball cities.

"That's nothing, only the screws in my head," he reassured startled security guards when passing through airport metal detectors. He was constantly setting off alarms as a coach on the Yankees under Joe Torre.

Zimmer made it through 1955 without a major injury but was victimized again in 1956 when outfielder-turned-pitcher Hal Jeffcoat fractured his cheekbone with an errant fastball.

Zimmer batted .235 in his 12-year career with the Dodgers, Cubs, Mets, Reds and Washington Senators before becoming a minor-league manager, a coach for the Expos and Padres and later a big-league manager with San Diego, Boston, the Texas Rangers and the Chicago Cubs under old pal Jim Frey, then the general manager.

Zimmer was one of the 26 original drafted New York Mets when the team began play under Casey Stengel in 1962. He was given the third-base job at age 31 and seemed certain, finally, to have a permanent position with a New York ball club after all those frustrating years behind Reese with the Dodgers.

He started the season by going 0-for-32. Then he got a single, and the next day the Mets traded him to Cincinnati.

"I had to trade him while he was hot," explained Stengel.

After managing in San Diego he was named a coach of the Boston Red Sox and took over the team in 1976. In 1978 he was the Boston manager when Bucky Dent hit a three-run home run off Mike Torrez in the famous playoff game between the Red Sox and Yankees, locking the Curse of the Bambino into historic lore.

He joined the Yankees in 1996 under new manager Joe Torre, with whom he had never played in his long career, and became baseball's first successful bench coach, the up-close advisor to the skipper. It worked well enough for the Yankees to claim four World Series titles in the eight years Zimmer worked under Torre's hand.

Zimmer was a team favorite with most of the Yankees. Shortstop Derek Jeter would rarely go to bat without first lifting Zimmer's cap, freeing his bald head to the elements, rubbing it for luck and placing the hat back on his head in an awkward position.

When Zimmer was hit by a foul ball at his dugout seat during one postseason he showed up the next day wearing a battered old Army helmet.

His serious combative side also showed when he took over as manager for Torre when the Yankee skipper was being treated for prostate cancer.

Zimmer's Yankee years ended in a blaze of glory. After Boston pitcher Pedro Martinez had thrown tight to many Yankee hitters and threatened others in the 2003 playoff, Zimmer, at age 72, raced on to the field and attacked the pitcher. Martinez threw Zimmer to the ground. His hat came flying off again and that old, bald, battered head was seen on millions of television screens.

For that reason and for so many others, like Yankee owner George Steinbrenner's intrusive personality and blame game with Zimmer when the team slumped, Zimmer decided he was finished with baseball.

He returned to his St. Petersburg, Florida, home to be with his wife, the former Jean Carol Bauerle, a Cincinnati girl he had married at home plate in his Elmira, New York, ballpark on August 16, 1951. His wife is known by the nickname of Soot.

"In German," explained Zimmer, "it is a word that means 'My little sweetheart.' Whenever I introduce her at a banquet and say her name 'Soot' I always add, 'Like the soot that comes down your chimney.' It makes people laugh and it gets them to understand the name."

Zimmer was named as the special advisor of the Tampa Bay Devil Rays in time for spring training in 2004. It was the 55th time he would spend the month of March on a baseball field.

"I've never cashed any check but a baseball check," he points out.

He spends the pregames in his Tampa Bay uniform, showers and dresses after the workouts, sits upstairs with customers and club executives and adds more memories to his huge storage bank. None can be as memorable as those from the 1955 Brooklyn Dodgers.

"Ah, you have to remember how much it meant to those guys that had been around Brooklyn so long," said Zimmer. "All those years, all that frustration of losing to the Yankees for Pee Wee, Jackie, Furillo, Snider, Erskine. I was glad I could contribute by getting off the field."

Zimmer laughed when he said that. He had been removed by manager Alston for pinch hitter George Shuba in the seventh game of the Series. Jim Gilliam moved to second base and speedy Sandy Amoros was put in left field. Amoros would catch Yogi Berra's line drive, double up Gil McDougald at first base with a throw to Reese and a long relay to first base that ended the last Yankee threat in 1955.

"We lived off Fort Hamilton Parkway in the Bay Ridge section of Brooklyn in those days with the Dodgers," said Zimmer. "I shared the ride in to Ebbets Field, maybe 15 minutes away, with Ed Roebuck, Pee Wee, Erskine, Rube Walker. It was just so much fun."

The driver parked the car across the street from Ebbets Field in a garage behind the right-field stands and the fence facing Bedford Avenue.

"Somebody would always say, 'I hope Snider doesn't break a window in our car,'" Snider said.

Some of Duke Snider's long drives over the right-field wall at Ebbets Field crashed against the cement walk of the garage.

"If Erskine was pitching that day and he wasn't driving he would say he hoped Duke hit a bunch of them out there," said Zimmer.

When Zimmer was married at home plate in Elmira in 1951 and walked with Soot under the crossed bats, they were supposed to be part of a double wedding. Teammate Ed Roebuck was also scheduled to marry his fiancée, Janice, in a home-plate ceremony. At the last minute Roebuck informed Zimmer that he wasn't going to do it. Roebuck and Janice were wed earlier that day in an Elmira church.

"There's this restaurant in New York called Nino's on First Avenue and 72nd Street. We went there a lot. In 2001, as we both celebrated our 50th wedding anniversaries, I invited Roebuck and Janice to fly in from California. This time we shared our wedding anniversaries together in that restaurant with a great party. How many former teammates have celebrated their 50th anniversaries together? What a night of memories, mostly about the Dodgers, that was," Zimmer said.

Zimmer and Soot have a son, Tom, a scout with the San Francisco Giants and a daughter, Donna, a homemaker in Windham, New Hampshire. They have four grandchildren.

"My granddaughter, Whitney Mollica, she's the best athlete in our family. She's only 17 and she has already captained her team to two straight field hockey championships. We were able to go up there and see the last one," Zimmer said.

Zimmer won four World Series rings with the Yankees but still keeps that 1955 Brooklyn championship ring on his finger.

"That was the first one, the big one. The Dodgers finally beat the Yankees," he said. "Maybe people today don't know how big that was. The only way I could explain it is by saying it would be like the Red Sox winning the World Series now or the Cubs after all these years. Hey, what am I saying? I work for the Tampa Bay Devil Rays. It would be like the Tampa Bay Devil Rays winning their first one."

ß ß ß

The Dodgers ran their 1955 record to 21-2 in early May. Don Newcombe faced only 27 batters against the Cubs in a May 10 game in Chicago's Wrigley Field. There never was much drama about a perfect game because second baseman Gene Baker slapped a ground single in the fourth inning. He was out on an attempted steal and the Dodgers and Newcombe went on to a 3-0 victory. The big right-hander slugged three hits himself in the triumph and was being looked on by his mates as one of the club's best hitters as well as the team's ace pitcher.

After the Dodgers returned from the road trip for an off day, a high school All-Star game was held at Ebbets Field. Pee Wee Reese was the manager of the kids' team and the catcher on one of the squads was a chubby youngster from Avenue T in Brooklyn and St. Francis Prep named Joseph Paul Torre.

He was 15 years old, weighed over 200 pounds, was dark haired and dark eyed and could hit a baseball hard. His brother, Frank, was a first baseman in the Milwaukee Braves organization after an outstanding high school career as a pitcher and first baseman at Brooklyn's James Madison High School.

Joe Torre sat in his managerial office at Yankee Stadium surrounded by family pictures and baseball photos. This was early in 2004 and the Yankees were moving again toward another title. Torre had won seven pennants and four World Series titles in his first eight seasons with the team. He had survived a bout with prostate cancer in 1999 and had been emotionally drained as his older brother, Frank, waited for and finally received a heart transplant during Torre's first World Series run in 1996.

He laughed when asked why a kid from Brooklyn, not that far from Ebbets Field, would be a New York Giants fan as a youngster and grow up to manage the New York Yankees.

"I was the youngest of five in my family," he said. "They were all Giant fans ahead of me, so it was only natural. I think it probably was because all the other kids in the neighborhood were Brooklyn Dodger fans. We just wanted to be different."

Torre's oldest brother, Rocco, was a New York City police officer after playing some sandlot baseball. Frank Torre was signed by the Braves after graduating from high school and had a seven-year big-league career with Milwaukee and Philadelphia.

Joe Torre had an 18-year big-league career before becoming a manager with the Mets, Braves and St. Louis Cardinals. He was named the player-manager of the Mets in 1977 and was soon explaining to the press in a steamy Atlanta clubhouse why the team's favorite player, Tom Seaver, known as Tom Terrific and the Franchise, was traded to Cincinnati over a financial dispute. As he evidenced in standing up to that press pressure, Torre would handle the press adroitly later as Yankee skipper under bombastic owner George Steinbrenner.

"I remember that one game at Ebbets Field," he said, as he relaxed before a game at Yankee Stadium. "The park looked big to me. After all, until then, I had only played on sandlot fields and high school fields. We came to the game dressed and then started throwing the ball around in front of the dugouts. Pee Wee Reese was the manager. He posted the lineup and I was catching and batting fourth. I got up and hit a ball off the wall in right field. That was pretty exciting to me. Everybody knew about the wall in Ebbets Field. It had that Abe Stark sign 'Hit sign, win suit.' We always kidded about that in our sandlot games when one of us would hit a ball towards right field."

Torre was outstanding in the game, went back to school with Ebbets Field memories and was signed by the Braves a few years later. He joined his brother in Milwaukee in 1960.

"I remember in 1957 my brother was playing for the Braves against the Dodgers at Ebbets Field and I worked out with him before the game. Pee Wee Reese came over to say hello. He remembered me from that sandlot game. He turned to Frank, sort of winked and said, 'Your little brother, he likes the groceries, doesn't he?' I don't know if Frank put him up to that or what. They were always trying to get me to lose weight in those days. It took a while but I finally did it."

ᔭ ᔭ ᔭ

On June 8, 1955, Don Newcombe beat the Cincinnati Reds 3-1. It gave him a record of 10-0. He also had two hits. It gave him a batting mark of .400. It is unlikely any pitcher in baseball history ever had a start to a season like that.

The Dodgers were off to one of the greatest starts in baseball history. All thoughts of the disappointing 1954 season and the blown pennants of 1950 and especially 1951 seemed lost to the ages. This was an incredible team with everyone on the club seemingly having a career year.

The Dodgers were blowing the league away by early July with a 56-24 mark and a 12 ½-game lead over the trailing Chicago Cubs. Since the Dodgers had led the Giants by 13 ½ games in August of 1951, none of the players on that club, including Reese, Robinson, Snider, Erskine, Furillo, Hodges, Campanella or Newcombe, now trying again for a title in 1955, would make any predictions.

The conservative skipper, Walter Alston, would only say in early July, "If we keep playing the way we are now, we should be in good shape."

There was one other small note of interest about the Brooklyn Dodgers that appeared in newspapers in the first week of June in 1955. It would be laughed about and debated for more than half a century.

The New York Times reported in sportswriter Joseph Sheehan's summary notes of the game that, "The Dodgers released Tom Lasorda outright to their Montreal International League affiliate in order to create room on their roster for Sandy Koufax, who has been on the disabled list with a broken ankle. Both are southpaw pitchers."

For the 52 years since, Lasorda would always respond to a question about that historic date the same way.

"If it wasn't for me," the man who claims he bleeds Dodger blue always says, "Nobody would have heard of Koufax."

Jack and Rachel, Gil and Joan

When Don Newcombe won his 10th game of the season against no losses on June 8, 1955, there was one small addition to the story of the game that got little attention.

Concentrating as always on the big picture, the daily sportswriters raved about Newcombe's start, how much he was contributing to the Dodgers' early runaway lead and how his hitting added so much to the Brooklyn offense. All true.

One other thing was also true. Jackie Robinson remained a significant contributor to Brooklyn success. He was 36 years old that season, hardly the player he was when he broke in with Brooklyn in 1947 but still an important part of the team and the most dramatic player in baseball.

Robinson hit a line single in that Newcombe win in the fourth inning of a bitterly cold, raw, wet June Brooklyn night. The score was 1-1 against the Reds. Gerry Staley was pitching for Cincinnati. Robinson bounced back and forth around first base, unnerving the pitcher and energizing the frozen fans.

Frank Kellert, playing first base in place of an injured Gil Hodges, hit a pop fly to short center field. Kellert played 39 games that year, batted .325, got into three World Series games as a pinch hitter, moved on to the Cubs the next season and ended his four-year big-league career with a .231 lifetime mark and no baseball pension. Early pension rules demanded five full seasons of service. Players now qualify for some pension money after one day in the big leagues.

That raw night, Kellert's pop fly danced in the sky as shortstop Roy McMillan, center fielder Gus Bell and left fielder Wally Post all chased after the baseball. McMillan and Bell later played for the New York Mets. The incompetence on this play would be good training for the horror show of the early years with the Mets.

Robinson immediately saw the situation. He raced past second as the ball floated in the sky. He moved to third without a glance and just rushed home as the ball bounced on the wet grass. Newcombe's double off the wall scored Kellert from first base in the 3-1 Brooklyn win. The story of the game was all about Newcombe. The aficionados knew better. Without Robinson's hustle, the Dodgers probably don't score that inning. Could anyone play the game smarter than Jackie Robinson?

🐦🐦🐦

By 1955, Robinson was an old story. He had been news, of course, when he first joined the team on April 15, 1947 as the first black in 20th century baseball to take the field at Brooklyn.

Jack Roosevelt Robinson was born January 31, 1919 in Cairo, Georgia. His father was a sharecropper, and his mother, Mallie, took the family of five children west to Pasadena, California, after her husband ran off with another woman.

They integrated a small street called Pepper Street and went to the local school. Young Jackie, the baby of the family of four boys and one girl, loved playing sports in the street almost as soon as he could walk. He was the star in every game he tried—football, basketball, baseball, track and field and later, as an adult, tennis and golf. He was a wonderful ping-pong player, pool shooter and gin rummy player. He was a good enough student to enter Pasadena Junior College and be admitted to the University of California at Los Angeles where he starred in football, basketball, baseball and track.

He served in the Army as an officer in World War II during which he survived the racial harassment manifested by a bus incident when he refused to move to the back a dozen years before Rosa Parks made it an historic event. He was honorably discharged by the government, happy to get this troublesome guy out of their way. Playing baseball for a year in the old Negro League with the Kansas City Monarchs came next.

After he was noticed by several Brooklyn scouts, Dodger scout Clyde Sukeforth was sent to see him in Chicago where the Monarchs were scheduled to play three games over the weekend. Robinson had fallen earlier in the week and missed all three games with a bad shoulder while Sukeforth was in town. Sukeforth had never actually seen Robinson play when he escorted Robinson by train to Brooklyn where he was meeting with Dodger boss Branch Rickey. All previous reports emphasized Robinson's talent and speed. Sukeforth was out there, really, to get to know the man. Was Robinson up to the job as Rickey proposed it?

After a three-hour meeting Robinson agreed to the difficult racial conditions imposed upon him by Rickey as a non-combatant no matter what happened, sort of the Mahatma Ghandi of the game. Robinson accepted the terms. It was announced on October 23, 1945, in Montreal that Jack Roosevelt Robinson would join the organization of the Brooklyn Dodgers as a member of the 1946 International League Triple A club of the Dodgers.

Robinson won the batting title with a .349 mark in 1946, led the league in runs scored with 113, terrified pitchers and catchers with his antics on the bases, helped Montreal to a pennant by 19 ½ games and was the leader of the team as it won the Shaugnessay Playoff for minor league baseball superiority with a victory over the Louisville Colonels. More importantly, the 1946 Montreal Royals of Jackie Robinson proved without a doubt that a black man could play on a white professional baseball team without the world coming to an end.

"During that 1946 season," recalled Brooklyn GM Buzzie Bavasi from his home in La Jolla, California, "Mr. Rickey asked me to go to California and talk to people who knew Jackie from home and school around there. Mr. Rickey wanted to know everything he could about Jackie before considering bringing him to Brooklyn. I figured why should I spend a week going back and forth to California when I could drive up to Montreal where he was playing in a few hours."

Jackie Robinson (center) is inducted into Baseball's Hall of Fame in 1962 ceremonies with Branch Rickey (left) and Rachel Robinson.
National Baseball Hall of Fame Library, Cooperstown, New York

Bavasi got to Montreal and sat in the Royals ballpark for a few innings.

"I looked over where the wives of the Royals were sitting. I saw Rachel Robinson, his new bride. She was a beautiful lady. She was dressed immaculately. I just watched Rachel with the other wives for a few innings. They chatted and enjoyed the game. I got up to leave. I told Mr. Rickey that a guy who had a beautiful wife like that and conducted herself like such a lady wouldn't have any personal problems in Brooklyn," Bavasi said.

On April 10, 1947, Jackie Robinson had bunted into a double play in an exhibition game for the Montreal Royals against the Brooklyn Dodgers at Ebbets Field, yet his teammates applauded him as he jogged back to the dugout with his head down. They had just been informed by a press release that Robinson would be moving on. In the press box the announcement read, "The Brooklyn Dodgers today purchased the contract of Jack Roosevelt Robinson from the Montreal Royals. He will report immediately."

Clubhouse man Babe Hamburger assigned Robinson uniform number 42 when he reported the next morning, gave him a locker in the middle of the right side of the clubhouse between Ralph Branca and Gene Hermanski, and showed him where to lock up his valuables. He made his big-league debut against the Boston Braves on April 15, 1947.

Robinson's Hall of Fame career ended after the 1956 season. He was traded to the New York Giants and decided to retire rather than report to Brooklyn's enemy. He batted .311 in 10 seasons, won the batting title in 1949 with a .342 mark, was named Rookie of the Year in 1947 (the annual award is now named after him) and was National League MVP in 1949. He played on six pennant winners for Brooklyn and the World Championship team of 1955.

On that April day in 1947, history recorded that, for the first time in the 20th century, a Negro, Jackie Robinson, became a member of the Brooklyn Dodgers.

ßßß

Tom Brokaw was ending his career as the anchor and managing editor of the *NBC Nightly News* early in 2004. He was asked about his connection with Jackie Robinson.

"I was a kid growing up in Pickstown, South Dakota," said Brokaw, in that voice so familiar to millions. "The Army engineers had built the town by dams and bridges over the Missouri River. We were all St. Louis Cardinal fans in our family in 1947. The Cardinals represented the westernmost city in the big leagues then. We heard on the radio that the Dodgers had signed a Negro player. I was seven years old."

Brokaw's father, Anthony (Red) Brokaw and his maternal grandfather, Jim Conley, were construction workers and helped build those projects over the Missouri.

"They were both enlightened people and had a great sense of the discrimination some people had to deal with, not only racially, but because of their educational standing, their economic position and their social positions. They had liked Joe Louis as a great fighter and were big baseball fans and decided they would root for this new guy, the Negro player from Brooklyn. I heard that and I announced that I was a Brooklyn Dodger fan," Brokaw said.

Brokaw said that his family could identify with the Dodgers, the Jackie Robinson Dodgers, without stretching the point.

"We were working-class people and the Dodgers seemed like a working-class team, in that small park in Brooklyn, with all those players who seemed like working-class guys. This wasn't a team like the Yankees with the sainted Joe DiMaggio and later the great Mickey Mantle. You know the Yankee success and their stars. It just never ends. Brooklyn was different. Brooklyn was always an underdog team, and there was so much pressure on this new Negro player. We were all for him."

Brokaw said he got to New York for the first time 10 years later in 1957. Robinson was gone by then.

"I took a subway out to Ebbets Field, just to see it, just to see where Jackie played. The Giants were playing the Dodgers and Willie Mays was in the New York lineup. He was so exciting. But I talked about Robinson with my friends. We even remembered that Jackie had grown up in California on Pepper Street and that was funny to us. We bought a pizza and walked back to the subway after the game," Brokaw said. "I think I talked about seeing where Jackie had played all the way back to Manhattan."

In 1968 Brokaw was a Los Angeles newscaster and arranged for an interview with presidential candidate Nelson Rockefeller, New York's governor, in the Los Angeles NBC studios.

"Rockefeller opened the door to the studio with that friendly smile of his and the 'Hi ya, fella' greeting and I looked up to see that Jackie Robinson was coming into the studio just behind Rockefeller. I walked right past Rockefeller and stuck out my hand and Jackie took it. I was embarrassed that I had passed by Rockefeller, but it was the one and only time I met Jackie Robinson."

Robinson was working for Rockefeller's nomination then, which eventually went to Richard Nixon.

"When Jackie died in 1972 I did an essay about him on the air and said how much I admired the man and his baseball," Brokaw said. "I pointed out that certain rights were denied to him just because of the pigmentation of his skin. That was horrible. He was truly one of the great figures of the 20th century."

Brokaw said he was always proud of those early days as a Brooklyn Dodger fan because of Jackie Robinson.

"I know what he meant to his people, black people, in America and when you think about it, to all people," said Brokaw. "He lifted the country in so many ways. I was good friends later on with Rafer Johnson, and he always talked about Jackie. He said that most black people in America just looked at Jackie as the most inspirational figure of his time."

Rachel Robinson sat in her offices of the Jackie Robinson Foundation on Manhattan's West Side one afternoon in the summer of 2004. She is in her 80s now, still as attractive, it seemed, as the first time Buzzie Bavasi saw her in Montreal or Brooklyn residents ran into her along Utica Avenue. She would have her groceries in one hand and Jackie Robinson Jr. clinging to her with the other hand. Jackie Jr. is gone now, a victim of an automobile accident, but daughter Sharon, working for Major League Baseball and son David, an entrepreneur in Tanzania in Africa, bring her endless joy. There are 10 grandchildren and a great-grandchild, Sherita, whom she visits on her African journeys.

"I think everything we did in Brooklyn—everything—built up to that 1955 season," Rachel Robinson said. "There were so many disappointments along the way. Things like winning in Jack's first year, 1947 and then losing to the Yankees. And 1949 losing again. Then the disappointments in 1950 and 1951, that horror. We lost again in 1952 and 1953, and maybe we started thinking the Yankees were invincible. Just unbeatable no matter how many times we played them. Like Boston feels now," Rachel laughed.

"Finally, *finally*, we won it all in 1955. It was like Martin Luther King said, we all felt 'free at last, free at last, thank God Almighty we are free at last.' On a personal level we felt vindicated. After all the disappointments, all the struggles, all the hard work, the Brooklyn Dodgers were the champions."

Rachel Robinson said the triumph on that afternoon of October 4, 1955, was memorable even now, half a century later.

"It was such a sweet moment, such utter joy. It was the realization of a wonderful dream," she said.

Jackie Robinson was growing old as a ball player in 1955. After the victory he began talking about life after baseball. He recognized his playing days were coming to an end.

"It was just prudent to consider the future. He knew baseball wouldn't go on forever. He played hurt a good part of 1956 and decided he could play one more year in 1957 if the injuries healed. He would play less, of course, but he still enjoyed the game and the competition and he was still good at it. Then came the trade. We never anticipated that. It was a shock. Jack just decided he wouldn't play for the Giants. That trade made up his mind. He would just retire," she said.

There were the years with Chock Full O'Nuts and the political years with Rockefeller and all the speaking and civil rights involvement in the 1960s. Jack became ill and weak in the early days of 1970 and 1971. He passed away on October 24, 1972. He was only 53, but he had looked many years older.

Baseball waited 40 years before the rookie award was named in his honor. Another 10 years went by before his uniform number 42 was retired by all teams in his honor. Only Yankee reliever Mariano Rivera, still an active player, wears number 42.

In 2004, Rachel Robinson accepted a presidential medal in Jackie Robinson's name from President George W. Bush. Robinson's name is carried forward in schools across the country, in the works of the foundation with 275 students a year receiving college scholarships, and in the grants made in his name for educational purposes for minority youngsters.

"Only recently we endowed a lifetime scholarship funded in perpetuity from Derek Jeter. There are so many wonderful things happening in Jack's name," said Rachel Robinson.

It all began with his arrival in Brooklyn in 1947 and reached its baseball peak in that glorious World Series win in 1955.

"I can still remember sitting there with Dottie Reese and Joan Hodges in Yankee Stadium, hardly able to breathe, and finally the last out. We won. Fifty years ago. Is it really that many years? Sometimes I think it was last week," she said.

Rachel Robinson was off to her work at the foundation, off again to keep the historic name of Jackie Robinson alive, one of the giant figures of America in the 20th century or any century.

"I'll be at the 2005 reunion of the team," she said. "We are unveiling the statue for Jack and Pee Wee. That will be a special day. Every day in Brooklyn was a special day, especially that day in 1955."

₧ ₧ ₧

She was the girl from Brooklyn and remains so today, 59 years after Joan Lombardi married Gilbert Raymond Hodges.

The first baseman of the Brooklyn Dodgers and the tomboy from the East New York section of the borough, daughter of Francesco Lombardi, the neighborhood butcher and homemaker Olga, who raised two girls and a boy, were married December 26, 1948.

"Gil was going to Oakland City College out in Indiana," said Joan Hodges, as she sat on the white couch in her comfortable living room on Bedford Avenue in Brooklyn, about 15 minutes from the old location of Ebbets Field. "He wanted to be a physical education teacher or a high school basketball coach."

Hodges was signed by the Dodgers out of his hometown of Princeton, Indiana. He was born April 4, 1924, and joined the Dodgers as a third baseman for one game in 1943 before enlisting in the Marines. He fought in the South Pacific, won several combat medals and returned to the Dodgers in 1946. They saw those huge hands and that size—6-foot-2, about 195 pounds, and decided he could be their anchor catcher for the next 10 years.

Bruce Edwards was the Brooklyn catcher then, but his time ended when the Dodgers quickly moved up the catcher they had signed from the Negro Leagues, Roy Campanella. They decided that strong right-handed bat offered by Hodges would help in the lineup if they could find him a position. Those hands. Ah, thought skipper Leo Durocher, first base.

Hodges quickly accepted the position change and would remain the first baseman of the Dodgers for the next 14 seasons before finishing up again in New York after the Dodgers moved to Los Angeles with the New York Mets.

He was as successful and popular a player with the Dodgers from 1948 through 1961 as the team had. He had a lifetime mark of .273, slugged 370 home runs, had seven seasons with a hundred or more RBIs and played on seven pennant winners and two world-champion Dodger teams in Brooklyn in 1955 and in Los Angeles in 1959.

Ted Williams, a force on the Baseball Hall of Fame Veterans Committee throughout his lifetime, decided that Hodges was not a Hall of Famer and often talked him down at committee meetings. It was not so much Hodges' lack of Hall of Fame credentials as it was Williams' jealousy of Hodges who had been a popular Washington manager while Williams had been unpopular. Hodges became the Washington manager in 1963, moved back as the Mets manager in 1968, won a world championship there in 1969 and had another challenging club that would win a pennant again in 1973 when he was struck down in 1972.

Gil Hodges remains the name with the most Hall of Fame votes ever without gaining admission to the baseball shrine.

"I'm getting old," Joan Hodges said as she approached her own 80th birthday. "If it doesn't happen soon, I won't be around to enjoy it."

She has campaigned hard for Gil's election over many years. The frustration each winter when the votes are counted brings her to grief.

"Maybe the reunion of the 1955 team will be lucky for us," she said.

Joan Hodges graduated from Public School 235 and Girls Commercial High School before taking a job at Macy's department store in 1947.

"We were all fanatic Brooklyn fans. I used to cash in the soda bottles for money for the games. Every night I would say my prayers and ask God to help the Dodgers win," she said.

She was engaged in 1948 to a neighborhood fellow and was visiting a friend from Macy's, Peggy Chase, at her apartment on Hawthorne Street in Brooklyn, on a rainy spring night after work.

"Peggy knew one of the guys who lived in the building. He was Ed Miksis who played for the Dodgers. He was with his roommate. That was Gil.

"I'll take her home," Hodges announced.

He hailed a cab and shared the ride back to Joan Lombardi's East New York family home. Before he let her out he asked for a date.

"A few days later we went to see the singer Jane Frohman at the Riviera in New Jersey. The next date was a movie at the RKO Albee in downtown Brooklyn. We saw *The Bells of St. Mary's* with Bing Crosby. After that it was a date almost every night Gil was free. We married in December and celebrated our honeymoon at spring training in Vero Beach that next February in Florida," she said.

Gil wasn't sure about his Brooklyn job in the spring of 1949 so they visited Indiana before he left for spring training just in case they might settle there when he finished school.

"I met all the family and I loved them all," she said. "I wasn't concerned about Gil's future. I knew whatever he did we would be happy and successful."

Joan Hodges said she wasn't awed meeting Gil's teammates, Dee Fondy, Ed Stevens, Chuck Connors (later the famed *Rifleman* of television), all first-base competition for Gil or the stars, Pee Wee, Duke, Jackie and the rest.

"I was awed later meeting Leo Durocher, who had moved over to the Giants by then but was always a big Brooklyn name. He was a charmer, and then meeting the broadcasters Red Barber and Connie Desmond. They had brought the Dodgers to me for years. They were important guys in my life," she said.

Gil Hodges was concerned about making the team in 1949. After manager Burt Shotton settled on Campanella as his catcher and Hodges as his first baseman, the Dodgers settled in as the best team in the league. Gil and Joan Hodges bought a house in Brooklyn and began their family. They would eventually have four children, and Joan Hodges now brags of six grandchildren and two great grandchildren.

"It was such a wonderful group of people," Joan Hodges said of the Brooklyn Dodgers. "It was like having 20-25 brothers. I was so close to Dottie Reese, Rachel Robinson, Bev Snider, all of them. We used to play gin rummy when the players were on the road with the wives of Clyde King, Spider Jorgensen, Jack Banta. Once I had a big run and took everybody's money. Gil said it wasn't good for team morale. I had to give it all back."

Hodges worked in the off-season in those days selling cars, working in a television store or helping a pal who owned a clothing store.

"The salaries weren't much, but we managed," Joan said.

On October 3, 1951, she drove with Gil to the Polo Grounds for the third game of the 1951 playoff against the Giants.

"The Giants and Dodgers really hated each other. They almost never talked. That day we pulled into the players' parking lot and Bobby Thomson got out of the next car. He walked over to Gil and said, 'Well, one of us will be happy after the game. I just want to wish you a good winter.' They shook hands and then walked inside. It was like an angel passed by Thomson's head."

Joan Hodges sat on her living couch with a wry grin as she recalled that dastardly day more than 55 years ago. She had been a young newlywed then with a new baby and now she was a great grandmother. Her red hair was coiffed attractively. Her stylish dark sweatsuit and glasses made her appear as if she were preparing for a summer barbecue with other Dodger wives.

That home run Bobby Thomson hit a few hours after the meeting in the parking lot would still stick in the throats of Brooklyn Dodger players, their wives, their fans, their families and millions of Brooklyn sympathizers more than half a century later.

"A guy came over to us as we were sitting down that day, just some fan who recognized us as Brooklyn wives and he said, 'If Bobby Thomson hits a homer, you'll lose the game.' I'm a Catholic. I'm not supposed to be superstitious. I just looked at him. I wonder to this day who he was," Joan Hodges said.

She waited for her husband after the playoff game. Umpire Larry Goetz was the first person she saw. She burst into tears. He was very sympathetic and kind. "He told me it might be a while before Gil gets out of the clubhouse. He said there was a lot of crying going on in there," Joan Hodges remembered.

"There's no crying in baseball," Tom Hanks said in *A League of Their Own*. What did he know of October 3, 1951?

Gil Hodges failed to get a base hit in the 1952 World Series as the Dodgers lost again to the Yankees. He had a wonderful Series in 1953 with a .364 average. Pee Wee Reese was on the losing side of a Series against the Yankees again for the fifth time since 1941.

Would this torture ever end?

Gil Hodges drove to Ebbets Field for the team bus on October 4, 1955, in his green Mercury. Joan Hodges drove to Yankee stadium later with Gil's parents, Charlie Hodges, a retired miner, and Irene Hodges. They sat alongside other Dodger wives, Fern Furillo, Bev Snider and Dottie Reese.

"I sat with a rosary in my hands all game," Joan Hodges said. "I was emotional. Gil knocked in the first run with a hit and the second run with a sacrifice as Johnny Podres pitched that great game. Then Elston Howard was up for the Yankees with two out in the ninth. I talked to the sacred heart of Jesus. I just asked him not to let my husband be the goat of the game. That's all I could think of then. My head was down. The other wives gave me the play-by-play. I prayed Jesus would not abandon us."

Elston Howard hit that final roller to shortstop, and Reese's throw was low to Hodges at first. He leaned out toward the infield and caught the ball. It was over.

"We had always been the bridesmaid. Now we were the bride. We drove home afterwards and there were so many cops around the house. The fans, the kids, everyone was cheering and applauding as we drove up. The cops put a fence around the house so we could get inside," Joan Hodges said.

They later went to the Dodger team party at the Bossert Hotel, drank some champagne, danced to big band music and rejoiced with all the other Brooklyn families.

"I remember pulling up to the hotel and there were a couple of dummies hanging from the light poles. They had Yankee caps on them and a sign on their chest, 'Dead Yankees.' That was so funny. When we went inside we saw Fresco Thompson [the farm director] and he had a sign taped to his chest, 'We win it. We win it.' Gil was just so happy. It was such an emotional night," she said.

The Dodgers won the pennant again in 1956 but lost again to the Yankees. In 1957 they were beaten out of the pennant by the Braves. They moved west at the end of the 1957 season.

"I was so sad about that," Joan Hodges said. "Brooklyn was our home. Gil was from Indiana but he felt like a Brooklyn native by now. He loved everything about Brooklyn. It was such a wonderful neighborhood. I remember when the kids would come by on Halloween for trick or treat. One of them was a kid named Charles Schumer from down the street. He went to James Madison High School nearby and grew up to be a senator from New York."

Joan Hodges never enjoyed Los Angeles. They rented a house there and she traveled back to Brooklyn often when the team was on the road. They came home again in 1962 when Hodges was selected by the expansion New York Mets. He was 38 years old and didn't have much left. He batted .252 in 54 games for the Mets but did hit the team's first home run in history. After 11 games in 1963 without a home run, Hodges was traded to the Washington Senators and named the team's manager.

"I cried because I realized I would never see him play again," Joan said. "That was sad for me. I remember Gil trying to console me by saying, 'We won't have to worry about Willie Mays any more.' I just cried some more and blurted out, 'Now we have to worry about Mickey Mantle.' It was quite a change in our lives.

"We lived in the Shoreham Hotel in Washington and that was fun. The kids loved the big swimming pool there. It was an easy commute back and forth to Brooklyn when we needed to go home," Joan Hodges said.

Gil Hodges often pitched batting practice for the Senators as he would do for the New York Mets as their manager.

"One day he was hit in the head by a batted ball off the bat of outfielder Don Lock. He had constant headaches from then on. His eyes were often bloodshot. He suffered an embolism. I think that injury had as much to do with Gil's dying in 1972 as any heart trouble," she said.

General manager Bing Devine of the Mets called Hodges after the 1967 season ended. He asked Hodges to fly up to Boston from his Brooklyn home. The Red Sox were in the Series against the Cardinals that year. Hodges was offered the job of manager of the Mets and quickly accepted it. They were home again.

"We just loved every minute of that," Joan Hodges said. "The whole family was involved. My parents didn't know a baseball from an onion, but every so often my mother would look at Gil and say, 'I love you, but you left the pitcher in too long.' We just laughed," she said.

The Mets won the miracle pennant under Hodges in 1969 after a ninth-place finish in 1968 in his first season at the helm.

"It was so wonderful. You know what stands out in my mind about that win? Gil wouldn't do the Johnny Carson show because Carson had always made fun of the Mets and called them clowns. What a joyous day," she said.

Hodges had suffered a minor heart attack late in the 1968 season. Joan and Gil Hodges went south early the next spring and Gil felt well all that year. He was often told by doctors not to smoke but couldn't stop. He was often seen puffing on a cigarette in the small ramp next to the team's dugout.

"Gil really didn't smoke that much," Joan insisted. Most people around the team in those days disagree.

On April 2, 1972, Easter Sunday, after spending a few weeks in spring training, Joan Hodges was visiting at her mother's home on East 40th street. One of the guests was a family friend, Dr. Anthony Terranova. The phone rang. Dr. Terranova answered it. The blood rushed from his face. He almost dropped the phone. Joan Hodges looked at him.

"Terry," she shouted, "what's the matter? Is my husband dead?"

Hodges had succumbed to a massive heart attack as he walked off the golf course next to the team's hotel in West Palm Beach, Florida where the last spring game was scheduled against the Atlanta Braves.

The funeral was held at Our Lady Help of Christians with burial at Brooklyn's Holy Cross Cemetery.

Joan Hodges began her campaign to get her husband named to Baseball's Hall of Fame that year and hasn't let up since. He has more

Hall of Fame votes through the years than any other player in the game's history. It still hasn't helped to get him in.

There are other honors for Hodges, a bridge in his hometown of Princeton, Indiana, a bridge in Brooklyn, a school near their Bedford Avenue home and even the entrance to their street on Bedford Avenue now known as Gil Hodges Way, pushed forward by the Brooklyn-born former New York City Mayor and uncontrollable Yankee fan, Rudolph Giuliani.

Joan Hodges served on the committee that planned the 50th anniversary reunion of the 1955 Dodgers in a major Brooklyn event in 2005.

"It's all like it happened yesterday, that 1955 team and all that fun and satisfaction that we finally won it," she said. "It makes me feel young again. That team was such a wonderful family, so together, so much a part of the Brooklyn city history. I look forward to it all like a family reunion, all blood brothers brought together by that one wonderful event of winning in 1955, finally beating the Yankees. I know I'll cry, but I also know that I will feel so much joy. During that time, for that event I'll feel that Gil is back with us and they are all young and we are experiencing that joy together as we did that day in 1955. Is that wrong?"

Joan Hodges led me down to the family den. It was filled with baseball pictures of a young Gil Hodges, of many of his young Brooklyn teammates, of Gil and Joan Hodges as a young married couple.

It was over half a century ago. Those 1955 pictures showed something else for all of us connected to the Brooklyn Dodgers in one way or another. It showed that 1951 was not the end of the world. No it wasn't. There will always be 1955.

Sandy and Lasorda

"The Dodgers' gay dash *through the west came to an abrupt end tonight amid the thunderous cheers of 43,068, Milwaukee's second largest crowd of the year,"* New York Times sportswriter John Drebinger, on leave from his regular assignment with the Yankees, wrote on June 24, 1955.

"The Braves hit three homers in the first three innings. The third put Carl Erskine out, and from there Jolly Cholly Grimm's Milwaukeeans went on to win the opener of a three-game series 8-2.

"This gave the Braves their seventh victory in a row and enabled them to retain their slender hold on second place. They lead the Cubs by a single percentage point, though still trailing the Brooks by thirteen lengths," continued Drebinger's report.

Drebinger was famous as a *Times* writer and renowned press box eater who once downed an alleged grilled cheese sandwich with an added layer of yellow Western Union paper. A fellow newspaperman slipped the paper into the sandwich, which Drebinger ate without any reaction.

Drebinger's *Times* story continued, describing Milwaukee home runs off Erskine hit by future Hall of Famer Eddie Matthews, slugging catcher Del Crandall and future Hall of Famer Hank Aaron.

"That finished Erskine," Drebinger wrote. *"It marked the ninth time in his last ten starts that the trim little right-hander had been put to rout. The defeat was his fourth against eight victories."*

The Braves were on their way to their seventh straight win in the 8-2 victory over Brooklyn. Still, the Dodgers led in late June by that comfortable 13-game margin. Then again, these were the Dodgers. Only four years earlier they had blown a 13 1/2-game first-place lead to the Giants, resulting in the season-ending tie and the necessary playoff. Ouch. Manager Walter Alston decided this was the time to take a chance on the new kid.

"After that," Drebinger's story continued, *"about the only item of interest came in the fifth and sixth innings when manager Walter Alston decided to take the wraps off Sandy Koufax, Brooklyn's bonus left-hander. The one-time Lafayette High star, making his first professional appearance, got off in a hole when the Braves filled the bases with none out in the fifth."*

The kid, born Sanford Braun in Brooklyn, New York, on December 30, 1935 who became Sandy Koufax after his mother divorced Braun and remarried a gentle Brooklyn lawyer named Irving Koufax, was a Lafayette star, all right, as Drebinger wrote. Only he had the sport wrong.

Koufax was a star on the basketball team and was good enough to earn a scholarship in the game from the University of Cincinnati as a 1953-1954 freshman. His pitching in Brooklyn was mostly for sandlot teams.

His only serious year of competitive pitching before signing a bonus contract with the Dodgers was at Cincinnati in the 1954 freshman college season. He had a 3-1 record with a 2.81 ERA in 32 college innings. What drew attention were the 52 strikeouts and 30 walks, the blazing fastball and the inconsistent control.

The first batter Koufax faced that day in his professional debut was Milwaukee shortstop Johnny Logan, one of the wild men on a Braves team filled with talent and flakes—Warren Spahn, Matthews, Lew Burdette (he didn't even know how to properly spell his first name), Bob Buhl, Joe Adcock and several others. Only Aaron was all talent without neurosis on that team.

In Jane Leavy's intriguing and revealing portrait of the Jewish kid from Brooklyn, *Sandy Koufax: A Lefty's Legacy*, she illustrates the confusion of history. The pitcher, now 68, told her Logan hit a blooper off the end of the bat. Logan, now 77, said he hit Koufax's pitch for a line-drive double over first baseman Gil Hodges' head.

"A blooper?" Logan said. "You got to be kidding. It was a line drive over Gil Hodges' head. Hit the white line in right field for a double. A double. Crissakes, I remember that just like today is—what day is it? You tell Sandy Koufax it was a double."

The box score of the game reveals only one double. That was hit by Joe Adcock. Revisionist history. It is the best part of nostalgic baseball. The players all know and the sportswriters all remember that the further removed a guy is from playing, the better he was at the game.

Logan was on first base and Matthews, a slugger of such note that he would later that year become the first cover boy of the new *Sports Illustrated* magazine, surprisingly, bunted. Koufax threw the ball into center field. Two on. None out. First pro inning. Not much to write home about. All the doubters that a kid without pro experience could pitch for the Dodgers, a few of his teammates jealous at the money Brooklyn paid him to play in 1955 and some anti-Semites, just on principal, were bellowing their I-told-you-sos. Koufax walked Aaron, showing immediately just how smart he was.

"Sandy was really an insecure and immature kid at that time," said Mets owner Fred Wilpon, a boyhood pal of the Dodger pitcher from their days at Brooklyn's Lafayette High School. "I even played basketball in the fall just to hang around and help him. I wasn't very good at basketball. He was very good. Both of his parents worked, and after the schoolyard games he would come home with me almost every night and eat dinner with us."

Finally, in his first big-league game, less than two years out of high school, Koufax then struck out Bobby Thomson, well past his New York Giants glory, and got Adcock to bounce into a double play, Pee Wee Reese to Jim Gilliam to Gil Hodges.

Koufax retired Danny O'Connell, Crandall and Burdette in the bottom of the sixth. Manager Alston sent George Shuba up to hit for Koufax in the top of the seventh. Shuba singled. Then Clem Labine and Ed Roebuck finished up the pitching chores for Brooklyn.

Koufax allowed no runs in his first big-league game. He struck out two. He walked one. He gave up a single hit, A BLOOP SINGLE, in two innings. Box scores tell only the truth.

At the age of 19 and a half, Sandy Koufax had his name in a 1955 box score along with all of them—Reese, Hodges, Campanella, Furillo, Erskine, Snider and Gilliam. Even Johnny Podres got his name in the same box score as a pinch hitter for relief pitcher Jim Hughes that day.

The kid from 1104 83rd Street in Brooklyn's Bensonhurst section was forever part of Brooklyn lore.

He got his first start a couple of weeks later, had his usual early career walking problems in a loss to Pittsburgh and disappeared for seven weeks. Then he pitched two shutouts back to back against Cincinnati with 14 strikeouts in late August and against Pittsburgh with six Ks for Koufax in early September. The entire season was a 2-2 mark, 3.02 ERA, 30 strikeouts and 28 walks in $41\frac{2}{3}$ innings. Don't forget the World Series ring.

⚾ ⚾ ⚾

Fred Wilpon is the sole owner now of the New York Mets. He was a high school teammate and neighborhood pal of Sandy Koufax in the early 1950s. He was the best pitcher on Lafayette High School's team, with Koufax playing first base in an undistinguished way then. Wilpon tried out for the Dodgers several times. He was always a little short.

Wilpon graduated with a business degree from the University of Michigan, entered the real estate field, founded a company called Sterling Equities and made a fortune. He became close friends with a Long Islander, Nelson Doubleday, the publishing heir. Together they purchased the New York Mets in 1980 from the estate of original owner Joan Whitney Payson. In 2002 Wilpon bought out his partner and took over full control of the New York National League franchise.

Wilpon and Koufax remained close friends through the years as Sandy pitched into 1966 and Wilpon concentrated on business. Wilpon often entertained Koufax on his off days with the Dodgers. They remained friends through the 1970s and into the 1980s as Koufax remained aloof from public events.

When Wilpon bought into the Mets he got Koufax to make an annual appearance at their spring training camp even though Koufax remained loyal to the Dodgers. Wilpon often suggested that Koufax might join the Mets in some capacity, but the Hall of Fame pitcher never seemed interested in a full-time job.

Koufax broke diplomatic relations with the Dodgers when they were owned by Rupert Murdoch after an embarrassing gossip column item in a Murdoch newspaper. There were more rumors he might join his old pal in New York. It never happened. He still appeared at the Mets spring camp in 2003 and 2004. There were long discussions with the Mets' ace left-hander, Al Leiter.

Wilpon protects Koufax's privacy as part of their friendship. There is no ballplayer in baseball more private than Koufax. His shyness is legendary.

"I think he is a lot more comfortable in public now than he was years ago," Wilpon said late in 2004. "He has a lady friend who has really helped him in that area. In fact, only recently, we all dined together in a New York restaurant and nobody bothered him."

Wilpon brought Koufax to a dinner of the New York Baseball Writers Association in 2003 and encouraged Koufax to appear with other Hall of Fame pitchers Bob Gibson, Whitey Ford and Tom Seaver at Yogi Berra's Montclair, New Jersey Museum late in 2004.

"I remember one Lafayette High School game we played together at Ebbets Field," said Wilpon, as he stood on the field at Shea Stadium in the summer of 2004. "We were playing the city championship game against Grady Vocational High School. I was pitching and Sandy was playing first base. Sandy batted right-handed and he was up in a big spot. He got this high outside pitch, swung hard and broke his bat. But the ball sailed out to right field and it went over the outfielder's head and hit the wall. It was a double and it was the biggest hit of the game. Sandy actually won the game for me with a hit. Can you imagine that? Sandy was more of a basketball player than a baseball player. He could really jump. I played a little basketball with him. I always thought I would be a pro baseball player and he would be a pro basketball player. It didn't quite work out that way."

ßßß

Sandy Koufax didn't exactly take the game by storm. He snuck up on it. He was 2-2 in his first pro season of 1955, 2-4 in his second season and 5-4 in his final Ebbets Field season of 1957. Too many damn walks. Walter Alston kept him around, though others in the Dodgers organization suggested it was time for some minor-league rehab for the left-hander.

"I never sent him down because I always knew he could pitch," Alston told me in the early 1960s after Koufax became KOUFAX. "I also didn't want any other manager changing anything about him."

He was 11-11 in 1958 as he started 26 games, 8-6 as the Dodgers won their first Los Angeles pennant in 1959 and 8-13 in an injury-filled 1960 season. He struck out 197 hitters but walked a hundred.

He was still only 24 years old at the end of the 1960 season. His record for six big-league seasons was 36-40 in the big leagues. Nobody talked Hall of Fame then when they talked about Koufax.

The frustrations grew. His right-handed pal, Don Drysydale, about a year younger than Koufax, won 17 games in 1957 in Brooklyn at the age of 21, and then 12, 17 and 15 in the next three seasons. He was intimidating at all times and never walked more than 93 hitters in any one season.

Koufax moped at times, hung back in the shadows of the clubhouse, and grew more frustrated while his career moved as if in quicksand. The talent was always there. Everybody saw that. But baseball is a cruel game. The numbers stare you in the face. Talent, schmalent. What was his won-loss record? In 1960 it was 8-13. Any schmo could turn in those numbers.

There was talk around the Dodgers that Koufax and Alston didn't connect. Alston was tight-lipped, rarely expressive about his feelings, rarely verbalizing his own frustrations that the magnificent arm wasn't doing more for the team. Some Dodgers even whispered to the press that the kid from Brooklyn might just hang it all up. Six years. That was enough for any baseball player to find out if he could cut it.

Norm Sherry caught 186 big-league games and hit .215. His little brother, Larry Sherry, was a flashy relief pitcher for a few years. They were the rarest of baseball tandems, a Jewish brother battery. Norm Sherry had another co-religionist as part of another tandem—Sandy Koufax. Norm Sherry was with the Dodgers as the backup catcher behind John Roseboro from 1960-1962 and finished up with Casey Stengel's Mets in 1963.

When Koufax started overwhelming baseball in 1961 for those six glorious years, it was Norm Sherry who started him on that trail.

"We sat together on a team bus going to some Florida exhibition game," Sherry once told me. "We just started talking about his frustrations, his control problems, why he couldn't be more consistent with that stuff he had. I just said, 'Throw softer instead of harder.' It was like a lightning bolt. Something stuck. Softer, more control, more command."

Koufax eased off from 98, 99, 100 miles an hour to 96 or so. The ball danced as always. The curve ate up air space. He hit the corners. He sliced the ball at the knees, on the letters, as it crossed the edge of home plate, which is called for no known reason *the black* in baseball lingo. He did all this with the smoothness of a ballet dancer. The arm went up. The arm came down. The ball whizzed across the plate on its unreachable path.

The sportswriters began noticing him. They were writing about him extensively. They made him, reluctantly, into a baseball personality. Those fingers, those long, thin, delicate, beautiful fingers. What those fingers could do with a baseball.

"Trying to hit Sandy Koufax," Pittsburgh Hall of Fame slugger Willie Stargell would later say, "was like trying to drink coffee with a fork."

Koufax was 129-47 in the last six seasons of his career—perhaps the most dominant force ever in the game's history over a similar run. He collected three Cy Young awards and an MVP title. He had four World Series wins, four no-hitters, a perfect game, 40 shutouts—including 11 in his 1963 25-5 season, five straight ERA titles. He ended his career with an ERA of 2.76 over 12 seasons, four strikeout titles and the ultimate standing as the standard of pitching excellence. There was Sandy Koufax and then there were all the other pitchers in baseball history.

Maybe it was the inconsistency of the early years. Maybe it was the over activity of those six years, a pennant to be won on two days' rest, a World Series game pitching out of turn, all those strikeouts, 2,396 of them—nothing compared to Nolan Ryan, Randy Johnson and Roger Clemens, the four thousand clubbers, but the elbow always hurt. Koufax giving interviews to the press after another winning game with his elbow soaking in ice was a common picture of the baseball 1960s.

They pumped cortisone into him on a regular schedule. Here, have a shot, Sandy. Go pitch another shutout. Strike out 15. Win, win, win. The Dodgers wanted something out of him early and got little. They wanted so much out of him late and got so much. Was it enough? When Koufax and Drysdale held out together for their 1966 contracts in an attempt to crash the artificial $100,000 barrier (Ted Williams, Joe DiMaggio, Hank Greenberg, Stan Musial made that much and no more) it got ugly. Koufax and Drysdale. Who the hell do they think they are? Well, maybe the best pitchers in the game. Pay pitchers more than $100,000 when they work maybe 30-35 times a year, and Maury Wills and Steve Garvey and Ron Cey go out there 160 times.

Koufax finally got $125,000 and Drysdale got $110,000. Bitterness lingered, not so much over the money but over the public embarrassment, humiliation and emotional whirl the pitchers were put through.

Koufax was 27-9 in 1966 at age 30. His ERA was 1.73 with 317 strikeouts in 333 innings. He lost his only Series start to the Orioles and Jim Palmer.

He was calm as he sat on a steamer trunk after the Dodgers had been swept. I got the sad story from the other Dodgers and walked up to him for the final time that year.

"See you in the spring, Sandy, have a great winter," I said.

That was sportswriter ritual. Keep those contacts. Always stay connected with the Jewish kid from Brooklyn. Who knows? He might come to the Mets at the end of his career like Hodges and Snider and even Willie Mays.

Koufax smiled wryly. I hardly noticed. I said I would see him next spring in Dodgertown at Vero Beach, Florida. He said nothing. On November 18, 1966, he announced his retirement. The arthritis in the elbow had gotten him. The cortisone shots were getting to be an unpleasant habit. Twelve seasons in the big leagues. He was not yet 31 years old.

ßßß

The Jewish kid from Brooklyn. He was the hero of all of the Jewish kids from Brooklyn, me included, and the kids from everywhere—every kid who wanted to be a big leaguer at the age of 19.

Sandy Koufax was 19 years old that spring of 1955, tall, thin and so darkly handsome. He was living out the dreams of all of us. He had actually made it to the Brooklyn Dodgers and was dressing in the club-house with Pee Wee and Duke and Jackie and Carl and Campy and Newk and Erskine and all the rest of them, the guys whose faces we cut out of the *Daily News* and pasted into our scrapbooks, the guys we had on baseball cards taped against the apartment wall. As kids growing up, we would never bring those cards to games, fearing we might lose them.

Years later, when I became a sportswriter for the *New York Post*, I would sit in the corner of the Dodger dugout with Koufax at the Polo Grounds or Shea Stadium or the Coliseum or Dodger Stadium when he wasn't scheduled to pitch and kid about the places in Brooklyn we all knew as playing fields—the basketball courts at the Jewish Community House, the Hotel St. George with the low roof, the fields at Prospect Park, Kelly Park, Dyker Park, Lafayette High where he played first base and James Madison High where I tried to play base-ball.

Harry Eisenstat, a big-league pitcher for Brooklyn, the Tigers and Cleveland, had made it out of Madison High. Marty Glickman had been there before he was robbed of his 1936 Olympic medal by Olympic boss Avery Brundage who didn't want the Jewish kid from Syracuse University embarrassing Herr Hitler in his own Berlin stadi-um. Fuzzy Levane had starred on the basketball team and Frank Torre had starred on the baseball team. Nobody heard of anybody from Lafayette until Koufax made it to the Dodgers in 1955.

He was animated about those memories when we talked in the early 1960s, less so about the no-hitters he was pitching, his 1965 per-fect game, and the strikeout records he seemed to set every time he walked to a mound.

Now, after the 1966 retirement, Koufax did some broadcasting for NBC, showed up at Los Angeles spring training camp, worked as a representative for the team in many ways, married and divorced twice, and stayed under the radar screen. There would be a spring training picture of him in Dodgertown or later with the Mets under pal Wilpon. He would appear at a BAT dinner (Baseball Assistance Team) or some favorite charity event.

In 1972 he was elected to Baseball's Hall of Fame. He showed up again in Cooperstown when former teammates or other baseball pals walked that cherished line to immortality. He was around baseball but not really around. Sandy Koufax marched to his own drummer. He was the drummer.

He was crushed by the death of Don Drysdale in 1993 at the age of 56 while still broadcasting baseball. He retreated even more. He could never really talk about it. They were as tight as two guys from Brooklyn and California could be.

He was restored to the Dodger family again in 2004 when a Boston real estate construction developer named Frank McCourt completed a deal for the team, ending the disastrous tenure of Rupert Murdoch's News Corporation ownership. He walked through Dodgertown again, scanning those pictures on the lounge walls of himself in a younger time, the left arm following through on the pitch to the plate in poetic symmetry.

⚾ ⚾ ⚾

Sandy Koufax had just returned from a Caribbean vacation with his lady friend to his home in Vero Beach in the late spring of 2004. He played golf and basketball in the area, still graceful on the court, as he neared the age of 69. He listened to music or caught a few innings of baseball as he lounged around his home. He ate dinner in a modest restaurant just out of town with former Dodger radio boss Tom Villante and they would talk a little of the old days and a lot of the new ones. He moved north as soon as the weather warmed to his summer retreat near Easton, Pennsylvania. He enjoyed long walks, a jog once in a while and even a fishing trip in a nearby lake with friends like former

St. Louis Cardinal and New York Giants pal Bill White, once the National League president.

"I didn't have much to do with it," Koufax said when asked of his memories of that 1955 Brooklyn championship season.

He was asked to clear up a Koufax legend, the discovery of the kid from Brooklyn after he started pitching in college in Cincinnati. As John F. Kennedy once said, "Victory has a thousand fathers. Defeat is an orphan." When a ball player makes it big, especially Hall of Fame big, dozens come forward as the guy who saw him first or pushed him or encouraged him or created him with the right word, the right letter, the right phone call to the key guy.

Jimmy Murphy was a schoolboy sports writer for the hometown paper, the *Brooklyn Eagle*, and he had mentioned Koufax's name in several articles about Brooklyn sandlot baseball in the summer of 1953. He had also mentioned Koufax to Bill Zinser, a full-time schoolteacher who picked up a few dollars and some free tickets for Dodger games while looking for undiscovered kid prospects in the glorious days before baseball drafts and free agency.

Zinser watched Koufax pitch in Prospect Park a couple of times and watched him again the following summer of 1954 after he had some experience in college at Cincinnati.

Word got to the Dodgers' chief scout, the main man for untapped talent, Al Campanis. Later Campanis became the Dodgers' general manager and was an unfortunate victim of racial misspeaking with thoughtless statements on Ted Koppel's program that there were no black managers because "blacks didn't have the necessities."

"Zinser was the first scout to see me," said Koufax when asked about the founding fathers of the Koufax legend. "Then Al Campanis."

Koufax worked out on a cloudy day in Ebbets Field in August of 1954. Rube Walker, the backup catcher to Roy Campanella and later a Mets coach under Gil Hodges on the 1969 champions, caught him for 15 minutes. Walker just raved about the kid lefty to everyone around. Manager Walter Alston and farm director Fresco Thompson watched Koufax throw off the mound—he had played first base there but only watched as Wilpon threw from the Ebbets Field mound a year earlier—and were enthralled by his speed.

Other teams, notably Pittsburgh and the Milwaukee Braves, had eyes out for the kid. It is easier to hide the Hope Diamond than a left-hander of 18 with a 100-mile-per-hour fastball.

The Dodgers locked the deal up with a $14,000 bonus and $6,000 salary. Irving Koufax shook hands with Campanis and the deed was done. Pittsburgh and Milwaukee offered more money, but half a century ago a handshake was worth more than a contract.

"I knew about the bonus rule," Koufax said. "I had to stay with Brooklyn two years. That was something that made my family happy."

He went to Cincinnati in September and the deal was announced in December. Koufax would finish the next semester and report to Vero Beach in March.

"I thought I was ready to pitch in the big leagues. I figured the Dodgers thought so, too, or they wouldn't have signed me under the bonus rule and kept me," he said.

Even in his darkest big-league days in the first six seasons, Koufax never doubted his baseball skills. He never thought he was as wild as others suggested. He never thought he couldn't win. He never thought others were better.

"I just didn't get enough work," he insisted.

When asked 50 years later, his memories of the participation on that Brooklyn team, Koufax bit off the words.

"I thought I could have pitched more," he said.

He was never overwhelmed by being on a team with all those legendary names. He was mature enough to keep his anger at being ignored to himself. He did get those five starts, 12 games and the two wins out of Brooklyn's 98 in 1955.

"Billy Loes was my first roommate. He was fun," said Koufax. "Then I roomed with Carl Furillo. I learned a lot from him. It was a wonderful year. We won. Of course, I wished I had pitched more."

Koufax would pitch on the Los Angeles winner in 1959 and anchor the team in the 1963, 1965 and 1966 titles. He would be immortalized in baseball lore by the time he saw it all end in 1966.

"With all the Dodger teams I was on, that was my first winner. So of course it is very special to me, even today," he said. "I was very glad

I was a member, even an unimportant member, of the 1955 Brooklyn Dodgers."

And he wishes he had pitched more.

ßßß

He isn't in the 1955 Brooklyn Dodgers World Series team picture, but he did start a game that year in Ebbets Field. He had four innings pitched in that season, made it into four games and was on the Brooklyn Dodgers of 1955 until June 9, 1955.

Tommy Lasorda also now wears the 1955 Brooklyn Dodgers World Series ring as a gift from former owner Peter O'Malley. He only had to wait 48 years to get it.

"Peter wanted me to have it just before he sold the Dodgers," said Lasorda. "He had it made up special for me and presented it on the field before a game."

Lasorda had been an outstanding minor-league pitcher, but his fast ball was always a little short in the big leagues and his curve—no Koufax curve—had a slow trajectory, just nice enough to line off the wall.

He had that same confidence, the same aggressiveness he would show later as a big-league manager, in his early playing days out of the Philadelphia suburb of Norristown, Pennsylvania.

He had no won-loss record in his eight games with Brooklyn in 1954 and 1955 and was 0-4 with Kansas City in 1956. He turned to scouting and coaching after that before being named the manager of the Los Angeles Dodgers on September 29, 1976.

He succeeded future Hall of Fame manager Walter Alston and built his own Hall of Fame credentials over 20 years as the Dodgers skipper from 1976-1996. He won two World Series titles, four pennants and eight division titles.

More importantly, he became one of the game's great ambassadors, the Casey Stengel of his time, with rollicking stories about the game, exaggerated tales of his time and constant chatter with press and fans. One spring training he put me in the passenger seat of his spring train-

Tommy Lasorda, manager of the Dodgers and a fringe pitcher on the 1955 Brooklyn Dodgers World Championship team had to wait almost half a century for his World Series ring. © Los Angeles Dodgers, Inc.

ing golf cart as he toured the grounds of the Los Angeles training facility at Vero Beach. It was like riding with the Pope of Baseball.

Lasorda has been a Los Angeles vice president since his 1996 retirement after heart problems. His pace has not slowed a bit.

"Peter never said a thing to me about the 1955 ring," Lasorda said one day in the summer of 2004 as he sat in the Los Angeles team offices in Chavez Ravine. "We got a call at home and my wife, Jo [they were married April 14, 1950 while Lasorda was pitching in the Dodger organization at Greenville, South Carolina] said Peter had called. He just said, 'They got the mold.' Now I wear the same ring that Duke and Newk and Erskine and Labine and the rest of them wear. The ring that Pee Wee and Jackie and Campy wore. Isn't that something? What a thrill."

Lasorda's thrills—from Kirk Gibson's most dramatic Series homer off future Hall of Fame pitcher Dennis Eckersley in 1988, to the win over the damn Yankees in 1981 to dozens of emotional triumphs—pale next to sharing his newly acquired 1955 championship ring.

"I had been in the organization so long by then. I started in 1945, went into service and started pitching regularly in 1948. I had so many great minor league seasons. I always expected to make the Dodgers as a regular starter every year. I finally got up there in 1954 and made it out of spring training in 1955," he said.

If the truth be known, the kid pitcher, Koufax, injured his ankle and didn't count on the roster until he was ready to pitch in June. That probably gave Lasorda his Dodger shot for two months.

He made the 40-man roster that spring, survived the cut to 28 and was kept around when the team went down to 25 active players with kid Koufax on the disabled list.

"Then Buzzie [Bavasi, the GM] called me into the office one day and told me I had to go back to Montreal. Go back to Montreal? I had won 21 games there the previous season. Why would I go back to Montreal? Buzzie looked ashamed," Lasorda said.

Bavasi tried to make it as easy as possible for Lasorda, then 27 years old, as he informed him of his demotion.

"What can I do? I can't cut Koufax," said Bavasi.

"He can't hit a barn door," bellowed Lasorda.

Half a century later, through all those successes, accolades, honors and Olympic Gold acquired with the USA team in Sydney, Australia in 2000, that demotion still stings.

"I could pitch. There were others, besides Koufax, to send out. It just wasn't fair," Lasorda said.

Lasorda knows that Bavasi was only doing his job that June day in 1955. They had been longtime friends by then and remain so now more than 57 years after they first met.

"Buzzie was running the team in Greenville when Jo and I got married. I didn't have any money. I asked Mr. Rickey for an advance. He wouldn't do it. Somehow Buzzie came up with $500 to pay for the wedding. Then he sent Jo flowers. Every year since, he has sent Jo flowers on our anniversary with a little note reading, 'I'm sorry.' I love Buzzie but he shouldn't have sent me out," Lasorda contends.

Lasorda said he was proud that he was on the greatest Brooklyn team ever, the only World Series winner, and he remains close to many of the 1955 Dodgers to this day.

"I was close to a lot of the guys then—Gilliam, Jackie, Pee Wee, Erskine, all of them. [Don] Zimmer and I used to run around together, go to the track, have a lot of fun. One time we went to the track in the daytime and were driving back to Ebbets Field for the night game. The traffic was very heavy. Zim was driving and he saw a funeral line starting near a corner. 'Let's get in the funeral. We won't have to stop at the lights.' We jumped right in behind the hearse, went through all the lights, peeled off near the ball park and made it just in time," Lasorda said.

The Dodgers were a generous bunch and even counted Lasorda in for a quarter share of the Series money, a few hundred dollars.

"I should have paid Bavasi back. I never did. The Dodgers didn't need it. I took it as a bonus for sending me out like Koufax got a bonus for them sending him in," Lasorda said.

The 1955 Brooklyn World Series championship ring is on Lasorda's finger. The stories that go with it come along free.

Erskine and Roebuck

"Carl Erskine gained his ninth triumph *of the year and first in nearly a month as the Dodgers flattened the Pirates tonight in the first game of a twilight-night doubleheader, 10-5,"* John Drebinger wrote in *The Times* on July 6, 1955, *"but that was as far as Walter Alston's Brooks were to go on this sultry evening."*

Drebinger reported that the Pirates won the second game behind tall right-hander Vernon Law, a future 1960 star for the World Series winning Pirates over the Yankees, in a 4-1 win.

"Law fanned 10 Dodgers amid the lusty cheers of 20,174 and brought the Bucs home in front in this one," Drebinger's report from Pittsburgh said.

"Ed Roebuck, after nailing down the opener for Erskine with two innings of neat relief work, was the victim in the nightcap. Replacing Sandy Koufax in the fifth inning with the score tied at 1-all, Roebuck held the deadlock into the eighth when the young Bucs suddenly erupted for three runs," Drebby wrote.

It was Koufax's first big-league start, and it was Erskine's attempt at his first complete game in nearly a month. Home runs by Jerry Lynch, Frank Thomas, later a memorable Met and Dale Long, made it close.

"When the trim little Hoosier, plagued for weeks with a sore right elbow, threatened to run into another squall in the eighth, Alston, despite

a three-run lead, decided to bring in Roebuck," Drebinger continued. *"The tall young right-hander quickly brought matters under control while the Brooks went on to win in a romp."*

They were now 12 ½ games in first place ahead of the Cubs and 28 ½ ahead of the last-place Pirates.

℘℘℘

Carl Erskine is probably the most famous pitcher never to get out of a bullpen. On the memorable New York afternoon of October 3, 1951, Erskine was warming up alongside Ralph Branca when bullpen coach Clyde Sukeforth told manager Charley Dressen, "He just bounced his curve ball."

Dressen chose Branca for the face-off against Bobby Thomson and the tears flew all over Brooklyn.

"When I was pitching to Campy he had this expression, 'Bury the curve.' When I really had the good curve and it dropped sharp and hard, Campy would yell from the plate, 'You buried that baby.' The idea was to keep it low so nobody could hit it. He wasn't worried. He was quick as a cat behind the plate. He'd stay with the pitch. No passed balls on *that* buried curve. You know what? Sukey never asked me about it that day in the Polo Grounds. Just as the phone rang, I buried that baby," Erskine said.

Carl Daniel Erskine was born December 13, 1926, in Anderson, Indiana. His father, Matt, worked as an inspector on the General Motors plant line in Anderson and his mother, Bertha, was a home-maker.

"I was raised in the 1930s at the bottom of the Depression and things were tough. But they kept the plant going. Some people could still afford cars, so we always had a meal on the table," said Erskine.

In basketball-mad Indiana, he played that game smoothly but quickly came along in high school in Anderson as a baseball pitcher. He stood only 5-foot-10 and never weighed more than 165 pounds but he could throw hard. He also had that biting curve ball. He could bury it. He buried it well enough in his career to pitch two no hitters and to set a World Series strikeout record of 14 against the Yankees on October 2, 1953. He struck out Mickey Mantle four times in the game and also got left-handed-hitting first baseman Joe Collins four times as he beat the Yankees 3-2 with Campanella hitting the winning homer in the eighth inning.

Erskine pitched 12 years in Brooklyn and Los Angeles from 1948 through 1959 with an impressive record of 122-78. He won 20 games in 1953, 18 in 1954 and was 11-8 in the championship season of 1955 despite constant arm problems.

"I suffered an arm injury in my first year of the big leagues, 1948, and I never really pitched without pain from that time on," he said.

He was sitting in the den of his family home in Anderson as he approached his 78th birthday in 2004. He was still handsome and trim, his hair a little thinner and a lot grayer than when he pitched in Brooklyn. He and his wife, Betty, have now been married 59 years. They have four children, five grandchildren and one great-grandchild. Their last child, Jimmy, 45, a mentally challenged youngster from birth, still lives with them and works in Anderson in a local department store.

"Every time I think about the 1955 Brooklyn Dodgers, I think about the wonderful friends we made there on the team and around the community. We lived in the Bay Ridge section of Brooklyn and we car pooled to Ebbets Field, three or four of us every day so the gals could have the cars. It was almost as much fun riding in the cars with Rube and Pee Wee and Zim and the rest as it was in the ball park," Erskine said.

His closest friend on the team was Duke Snider, and they remain constantly in touch. Erskine was on the phone often in the late part of 2003 and early in 2004 as Snider fought through some physical problems.

"Duke is pushing 78 now, and he never thought he would get there. All those stories about Mickey Mantle thinking he would die young. Duke was the same way. His mother died young, and he would talk about her all the time. 'My mother died and I'm gonna die.' Especially after a game when he struck out a few times. He was a little bit of a hypochondriac. He'll probably outlive all of us," Erskine said.

"I was Duke's roomie for a lot of years. I went through a lot of his ups and downs. He's a Hall of Famer, but he had a lot of bad days, maybe seven out of 10. Isn't that the way it works in baseball—even if you hit .300? We started out as kids together, grew up together and now we are old men together," Erskine said. "What a tremendous talent he was."

A scout named Stanley Freezie, who signed Gil Hodges and later Bob Friend out of Indiana, came a-calling on Erskine in 1945. He loved that curve ball.

"He was really looking at the catcher on our team, Jack Rector, and he caught me on a good day. I had a lot of strikeouts and when the game was over, he asked me a couple of questions. I wasn't sure why," Erskine said.

"How old are you, kid?"

"Eighteen," I said.

"How much do you weigh?"

"Oh," I stammered, "about 140 pounds."

"Freezie shook his head but said he liked both of us and would pay our way to New York City so that Mr. Rickey could meet us and talk to us. Mr. Rickey was always looking for great players, of course, but he was specifically looking for great players with great character. He especially liked pitchers with character. There was something about character, Mr. Rickey believed, that helped a pitcher in those tough games with the 3-2 count and the winning run on third."

Freezie put Erskine and his catcher on the Pullman train out of Anderson, Indiana, headed for New York City.

"He said there were reservations for us near Grand Central Station in the New Yorker Hotel. We were to call the offices of the Dodgers as soon as we got into New York City. Then he gave us two brand-new $100 bills each and said we didn't have to call the Dodgers after we got into town until the next morning. We were thrilled beyond words. We got to the hotel and got a room on the 28th floor. Then we stood by the elevator and watched it go down, whoosh, whoosh, those 28 floors. We were from Anderson, Indiana, population 60,000 without a building over three or four stories high in those days."

Rector agreed to sign with the Dodgers, but Erskine decided to hold off.

"I was about to be drafted and I didn't want to make any deals until I figured that part of my life out," he said. "Soon I was in the Navy and on my way to the Sampson Naval Air Station up in the Finger Lakes in New York. A few weeks after I got into the Navy they dropped the bombs over Japan. I knew I would be out of the service before too long."

Erskine had heard from the Boston Braves and the Pirates by then. His parents had even been invited with him to Boston by the Dodgers for the 1946 All-Star game.

"Mr. Rickey met my parents, and all he talked about for an hour was farming in Indiana and Ohio. Then my dad finally said to him, 'The boy wants a bonus.' Rickey said that was fine. 'How much does he want?' We were sitting in the lobby of the Kenmore Hotel in Boston. The Braves had already talked about $2,500. My father said, 'How would $3,000 be?' Mr. Rickey said, 'Let's just make it $3,500.' That was good enough, and my father and Mr. Rickey shook hands on it," Erskine said.

Three days later Erskine was separated from the Navy and prepared to take a train to Danville, Illinois, for the start of his professional career when he received a call from the office of baseball commissioner Albert B. (Happy) Chandler.

"The assistant on the phone said the Dodgers signed you before you were out of service. That is a violation of baseball rules. We want you tomorrow here in Cincinnati at the Carew Building and we'll explain all the details."

"I just wanted to play for Brooklyn," Erskine said.

The Red Sox had already made inquiries about Erskine's services in a $10,000 bonus package. The Hoosier right-hander decided he still wanted to sign with the Dodgers. The price was raised to $8,500 by the Dodgers. Erskine signed his second contract with Brooklyn and took off for Danville.

Erskine pitched at Danville; Pensacola, Florida; Havana, Cuba; and Fort Worth, Texas, before getting the call to Brooklyn.

He made his first relief appearance for the Dodgers in Pittsburgh on July 25, 1948. He relieved Hugh Casey. He hit his first batter in the bigs, Johnny (Hippity) Hopp.

"The next batter was Ralph Kiner. He hit a hard drive to left. George Shuba came in for the ball and caught it. The umpire called

Kiner out. I walked off the field with the third out. Shuba passed me as I moved towards the dugout. 'I trapped it.' He just smiled at me," Erskine said.

Erskine beat the Cubs 6-4 in his first big-league start on August 5, 1948, with Gene Hermanski hitting three consecutive home runs.

Erskine went from 13 to 37 starts from 1950 through 1954. He led the league in percentage in 1953 with 16 complete games. He was 122-78 in his 12 seasons in the big leagues despite constant shoulder problems.

"I really injured my arm in my first start in 1948," Erskine said. "I was halfway through the game and I told [manager Burt] Shotton, 'My arm is killing me.' He wouldn't take me out. That was his first year back with Brooklyn after the '47 season when Leo Durocher was suspended. Durocher started the '48 season and then went to the Giants. Shotton took over again and I guess he thought he had to show he was tough, so he forced me to stay out there. I think it damaged my career," Erskine said.

Despite his relatively small size, Erskine could throw hard, had a wonderful curve ball (when he tried to bury it as Campanella suggested), had an effective changeup, always had more strikeouts than walks as a starter and showed real guts on the mound.

"There were times I was passed over because my shoulder was aching," he said. "But there were other times the managers used it as an excuse. I could have pitched in the 1951 playoff when Dressen started Labine in the second game. I certainly could have pitched in relief when Dressen chose Branca. I told Charlie on the bus to the Polo Grounds that day I was ready and well rested."

Erskine won 14 games in 1952 and had that great year in 1953.

"Those teams in 1952 and 1953 were a lot better than the 1955 team. It was ironic that we won everything in 1955 and beat the Yankees when we had a much better Brooklyn team in 1952 and certainly 1953," he said.

Erskine said the Dodgers were all getting old by the 1955 season. He was only 11-8 in that championship season in 31 games.

"Pee Wee had been around since the beginning of the run in 1941, and Jackie had been there since 1947. He was getting all gray by then and really getting heavier and slowing down. That gray hair looked almost comic on him. We all started calling Jackie 'Uncle Remus' after that comic book character. He didn't like it much but he took it. By then we all had crazy names for each other. When they wanted to needle me they just called me 'Oisk,' the way the Brooklyn fans pronounced my name," he said.

Erskine said he will always remember that seventh game of the 1955 Series.

"Podres was just pitching so great and keeping the Yankees under control. He was talking a lot on the bench between innings and then he got lucky with the Amoros catch on Yogi's fly ball. That seemed to quiet him down. He didn't talk much after that. He just sat there and went out to pitch each inning. I think he was pretty silent that half inning before the last one," he said.

Podres retired Elston Howard for the final out, and there were a lot of congratulatory handshakes and the Dodgers hustled into the visiting clubhouse at Yankee Stadium.

"There was almost a reverence in there," Erskine said. "It was awfully quiet. It was as if we all looked over at Pee Wee and tried to figure out how he would react after all those years of frustration. Once he looked like it was all going to be tears but then he collected himself and started laughing and guys began rubbing his head and everybody busted out the champagne and then the joy just took over."

Erskine said the bus ride back to Brooklyn after the final game and the crowds in the streets and the massive celebrations were all poignant memories half a century later.

"There was so much going on, so much to see, so much in the streets that it was impossible to capture it all. I think if we won 10 in a row after that it would not have been the same. This was the first, the best. The win over the Yankees and everybody just covered up by the happy feelings," Erskine said.

Erskine pitched no-hitters against the Cubs in 1952 and against the Giants in 1956 and had that incredible 14-strikeout game in the 1953 Series. It was all personal highs. But that series win, that 1955 group therapy always held such a vital place in his life.

"I don't know. It is just hard to explain. Brooklyn was such a special place and that victory was as much for the fans as it was for us," he

said. "We had so many friends in Brooklyn and kept in touch for so
many years."

After moving to Los Angeles in 1958 with the Dodgers, Erskine
hung on for a while before his shoulder just gave out. He went back
home to Indiana.

"I had stayed in the banking business all the years I was pitching in
Brooklyn," Erskine said. "I always recognized that baseball careers were
short and there would be plenty to do afterwards."

He moved up in the local bank, served on many community com-
mittees, visited often with old Dodger fans at fantasy camps, appeared
at special events at Dodger Stadium. In 2000 he returned for the first
time in years, played the National Anthem on his harmonica and
received a standing ovation from Los Angeles fans who remembered
him as an anchor of the Brooklyn teams.

"There are always people originally from Brooklyn at a Dodger
crowd in Los Angeles. I was sure I heard a few of them yelling, 'Oisk,'
that day. That always happens," he said.

"I have the ring and a few pictures from the 1955 Dodgers. I did-
n't save much. I guess I thought there would be a lot more World Series
wins in Brooklyn after that. It didn't quite happen that way, did it?"

There are only 11 members of that 1955 Brooklyn World Series
champions still around, eight pitchers and three non-pitchers, Duke
Snider, Don Zimmer and George Shuba.

"I hope we can get together in 2005 and celebrate the victory,"
Erskine said. "That was a very special group of guys who did a very special thing. Imagine if there was never a Brooklyn winner. Wouldn't that
be a sad thing to look back at 50 years later?"

🐻🐻🐻

Ed Roebuck was a relief pitcher in the days before that craft was
defined specifically as "short men" or "long relief" pitchers.

"You pitched whenever the manager called for you," said Roebuck.
"It could be in the first inning or it could be in the ninth inning."

He won five games and saved 12 for the 1955 Brooklyn Dodgers,
the highlight of his professional life and couldn't prevent the Phillies

from blowing the 1964 pennant in the last week of the season, the low point of his career under panicked skipper Gene Mauch.

"I look back at that 1964 season with the Phillies, and it still sickens me," said Roebuck. "Mauch whipped us into a frenzy and then we lost 10 in a row to blow the whole damn thing. [Jim] Bunning and [Chris] Short, Bunning and Short almost every day. What a tragedy."

Edward Jack Roebuck was the ninth child of Jacob and Caroline Roebuck. He was born in East Millsboro, Pennsylvania, on July 3, 1931, the baby of the family with five brothers and three sisters.

"My father was a coal miner for 40 years," said Roebuck. "Then he died. My father was from Poland and thought the mines were a sacred duty. When I started playing ball and told him I never wanted to go into the mines he thought I had committed a religious sin. I got a $3,000 bonus to sign and my father never made more than $25 a week. I was so afraid of his reaction when I decided to sign with Brooklyn. I was afraid my father would disown me."

The Roebuck family lived on a 170-acre farm and leased it for $10 a month. All the children helped out on the farm, and Jacob Roebuck went about his chores on the farm until sundown when he returned from his chores in the mines.

"They had a lot of teams around there in Western Pennsylvania, and I was pitching for them when I was 13 or 14 years old. I was a big kid and always played with older guys. I think that helped my career. I went to the West Bend Grade school, a one-room schoolhouse in East Millsboro and then on to the Brownsville High School, which had three or four rooms. I walked a mile and a half to school each day and that's why I had strong pitching legs. I graduated at 16."

The Red Sox had scouted him in local games with coal miner teams but hadn't offered a contract.

"Then I found out the Dodgers were having a tryout camp in Washington, Pennsylvania. This was 1948 and the Dodgers seemed to be signing everybody to build up their farm system. I had turned 17 by then and was about full grown. The Dodgers said they would be in touch in a few days. One afternoon while I was doing my farm chores this big, black Buick pulls up in front of the farm. This Dodger scout, Rex Bowen, gets out and walks to the house. He tells my mother that the Dodgers want to sign me and he would give us $3,000 just for my signature. She said that would have to wait until her husband got home, so Bowen just sat around on the front porch, drank some iced tea and waited for sunset. Then my father came home and he listened to Bowen. I think all he really heard was that $3,000. He signed everything and I was on my way to Newport News, Virginia."

Roebuck was sent to Elmira, New York, for the 1950 season. He was 0-8 in his first professional games as a starter.

"I think I was in over my head," he said.

By 1951, still at Elmira, he began pitching better and settling down as a professional player. He had a teammate from Cincinnati, an outgoing cocky kid named Don Zimmer. They have been friends for almost 55 years.

"Zim decided to get married to his girlfriend, Soot. I was thinking of getting married to my hometown gal, Janice. He said he would do it on the field and I agreed that I would, also. Janice wasn't too keen on it since she was a church-going lady. She insisted we get married in the local church in Elmira, so that's what we did," Roebuck said. "That was August 16, 1951, the same wedding date as Zimmer but at a different place."

They have two sons and two grandchildren, all of whom live nearby the Roebuck family home in Lakewood, California.

"In 2001 we had our 50th wedding anniversary. Zim was still with the Yankees then and he brought us in from California. We had a grand old time celebrating our anniversaries. That was some fun. Zim is a little heavier and a little lighter in the hair than he was when we were pals at Elmira, but he is still the same kind of entertaining guy to be around," Roebuck said.

Roebuck moved up to the Dodgers top farm team at Montreal in 1953. The manager was Walter Alston.

"I had a good year there, and Alston decided I might even do better as a relief pitcher. I wound up 15-13 with a lot of the victories in relief. Everybody wanted to be a starter in those days, but Alston convinced me it would increase my chances for a run at the Brooklyn club. I went along with that. The idea was to get to the big leagues where you could make some real good money, maybe four or five thousand dollars a year," Roebuck said.

Joan Hodges in the basement of the Brooklyn home she shared with husband Gil Hodges.
Photo by Maury Allen

Roger Craig at his California retirement home in 2004.
Craig Family Photo

Johnny Podres (left), Joan Podres and author Maury Allen in 2004 at Podres's home.
Photo by Janet Allen

Willie Mays (left) and author Maury Allen in 2002 during a visit to Cooperstown.
Photo by Janet Allen

Ed and Janice Roebuck at their California home in 2004.
Roebuck Family Photo

Clem Labine at his Florida home in 2004.
Labine Family Photo

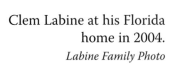

BROOKLYN

Pee Wee Reese (left) and author Maury Allen at 1993 Cooperstown Hall of Fame game.
Photo by Janet Allen

Carl Erskine in 2004 at his Anderson, Indiana home.
Erskine Family Photo

Joe Pignatano, Brooklyn native, as he hits the golf course in 2004.
Pignatano Family Photo

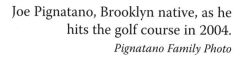

EMEMBERED

Duke Snider (left), Willie Mays, and Mickey Mantle as they share a laugh at a New York Baseball Writers Dinner in 1995.
Photo by Jackson Pokress

Sandy Koufax (left) and author Maury Allen at the 2003 New York Baseball Writers Dinner.
Photo by Jackson Pokress

Carl Erskine (left) and all-time home run king Hank Aaron at the New York Baseball Writers Dinner in 2000.
Photo by Jackson Pokress

Rachel Robinson (left) honors former New York Mets star Tommie Agee at the 1992 New York Baseball Writers Dinner.
Photo by Jackson Pokress

Rusty Staub (left) honors Don Zimmer at the 1999 New York Baseball Writers Dinner.
Photo by Jackson Pokress

Two big-time New York shortstops, home run hitter Bucky Dent of the 1978 Yankees (left) and Don Zimmer of the 1955 Dodgers.
Photo by Jackson Pokress

Longtime Dodger broadcaster Vin Scully goes back to the Brooklyn days with the infamous 1951 defeat and glorious 1955 triumph.
© Los Angeles Dodgers, Inc.

Al Campanis, worked as a player with Jackie Robinson with the Montreal Royals, and later led the Dodgers farm system for many years.
© Los Angeles Dodgers, Inc.

Three Yankees who opposed the Brooklyn Dodgers in the 1955 Series, Don Larsen (left), Whitey Ford, and always dangerous Yogi Berra who hit into the famous double play—Amoros to Reese to Hodges.

Photo by Jackson Pokress

Two great shortstops, Cal Ripken Jr., the Iron Man of Baseball, with his Brooklyn nemesis, Phil Rizzuto, the Hall of Fame Yankee shortstop at a New York Baseball Writers Dinner.

Photo by Jackson Pokress

Yankee executive Gene Michael (left) and Duke Snider at the 1999 New York Baseball Writers Dinner.
Photo by Jackson Pokress

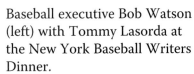

Baseball executive Bob Watson (left) with Tommy Lasorda at the New York Baseball Writers Dinner.
Photo by Jackson Pokress

From left to right: Jeff Wilpon, the Mets chief operating officer; Valerie Wilpon; Sandy Kofax; Jody Wilpon; Fred Wilpon, chairman of the Mets; Betty Howe; and Art Howe, manager of the Mets at the 2003 New York Baseball Writers Dinner.
Photo by Jackson Pokress

He was 18-15 in 1954 as Alston moved up to the Dodgers. He was on the spring roster in 1955 but with the pitching depth of the Dodgers with Newcombe, Erskine, Podres, Loes, and Russ Meyer as starters and Labine, Jim Hughes, veteran minor league star Tommy Lasorda and that bonus kid locked into the team, Sandy Koufax, Roebuck's chances seemed slim.

"I had a real good spring and Alston knew what I could do from our days together at Montreal. He decided to bring me north and see what I could accomplish at the start of the season. Koufax had a bad ankle anyway, so there was going to be a spot open on the roster. I was throwing hard, I was getting my curve over, and my control was exceptional. All of a sudden I was in Brooklyn with a job next to Labine in the bullpen," he said.

Roebuck contributed early as the Dodgers ran off with a ten-game winning streak and a 21-2 start that opened up a huge lead into May.

"When Koufax was ready in June I wasn't worried. I knew the Dodgers needed me to give Labine some rest. I figured I would make the club. That's how it worked out. They decided to send out another left-hander, Lasorda, to make room on the roster for the kid left-hander, Koufax, that they had to keep," he said.

Roebuck got into 47 games for the Dodgers in that 1955 season. He was 5-6 but saved a dozen games before that save rule was put into baseball as an official statistic.

"I got a lot of those saves early when we busted up the race, so I always felt that I was an important contributor to the title even though I slowed down later in the season," he said.

Roebuck admitted that he always felt a little shaky around those famous Dodgers on that team.

"I had been in the minors until 1955 and the Dodgers, Duke and Pee Wee and Jackie and Campy and the rest had been winning all those pennants. Sure I was awestruck. Who the hell wouldn't be?"

Roebuck and his wife rented a home from an old Swedish couple in Brooklyn from May until September of that year.

"It wasn't all that nice but it was pretty close to the ball park. That made it easy for Janice to get to all of the games," he said.

Roebuck said he and his wife would shop in the local stores, bring the car in to the local gas station and picnic in nearby parks on off days.

"People started recognizing me after a while. It was all in fun. Once in a while a guy would hang over the dugout at Ebbets Field and tell me he was our butcher or our garage guy and the wife had been in only that morning. Everybody was real friendly," Roebuck said.

By 1955 Jackie Robinson was one of the league's biggest stars. Campanella, Newcombe and Amoros were also on the team.

"I grew up in Western Pennsylvania and played ball with guys from all nationalities and all colors. That was no big deal for me. I just enjoyed playing ball with Jackie. He was such a marvelous player. They all were. And he was a terrific card player. We used to play contract bridge on those train trips. I played with Pee Wee and Zim. Billy Herman, one of our coaches, was the official kibitzer. He would just make funny remarks as we were playing a hand. It was pretty hard to concentrate on the card game with Herman around," Roebuck said.

Roebuck said that Robinson was always very encouraging, especially when he had a bad day.

"I don't know why, but he took an interest in me. He would always talk to me about the game or about the hitters or how I should throw a pitch. What a great manager he would have made. But Jackie liked to argue a lot, especially with Pee Wee. One time when Pee Wee told Jackie, 'A lot of guys hate you and not because you're black,' I had a tough time not laughing at them. This was the captain and the team's big star, and they were carrying on like a couple of high school kids," Roebuck said.

Roebuck pitched two scoreless innings in the sixth game of the Series won by the Yankees behind Whitey Ford, setting up the final, dramatic seventh-game ending to the 1955 baseball season.

"I didn't feel any pressure in the Series even though I was a rookie. I had been around a lot by then. I threw a little in the seventh game with Podres out there, but I knew I would never get in. This was Podres' game—win or lose. I just turned around at the end and saw Pee Wee throw that little humpback throw over to Gil at first for the last out. Then we started drinking champagne out of the water fountain," Roebuck said.

Roebuck stayed with the Dodgers in Brooklyn and Los Angeles through the 1962 season when he went to Washington. He pitched for the Senators and the Phillies before calling it quits after the 1966 season.

"That 1964 season, at the end, with Mauch and the Phillies, that was like dying," he said.

He pitched in Saint Paul and in the Dominican after that but was hurting. He went to see the Dodger doctor, Bob Kerlan, and Kerlan said he was finished.

Roebuck scouted for the Braves, the Dodgers, the Reds, the Pirates and the Red Sox in the California area before retiring from baseball.

"I like to go out to the race track and watch the horses run. Zim got me into that, and when he comes out here we still try and get together for an afternoon before he has to get out to the ball park," Roebuck said.

He never made more than $20,000 as a big-league pitcher but with his scouting salaries and baseball pension, he and his wife live in a comfortable home in the beautiful area of Lakewood near Los Angeles.

"What can I say about the 1955 Dodgers? Well, was it 20 million light years ago? I can't conceive that it was 50 years ago and there are still some of us around to enjoy it. I know I enjoyed it and it was the best year of my career. I am anxious to get back to Brooklyn and see if anybody remembers that I was on that team. I'll flash my World Series ring and then they'll know," Roebuck said.

Ralph Branca

He won 21 games at the age of 21 in 1947 for the Brooklyn Dodgers, the most incredible feat of its kind until a 20-year-old named Dwight Gooden won 24 games for the New York Mets in 1985.

Ralph Branca isn't really remembered for that. He is remembered for one errant pitch in the 1951 playoff game against the Giants, a fastball that Bobby Thomson floated into the seats in left field. "The Giants win the pennant, the Giants win the pennant . . . " Ahh, forget it.

Branca was 88-68 in 12 big-league seasons, starting as an 18-year-old from New York University out of Mount Vernon, New York, and ending with his second shot with the Dodgers in 1956 after late career spots with Detroit and the 1954 Yankees.

"I was in the stands for every one of the seven games of that 1955 Series. I knew a lot about the Yankees since I played with them the year before and gave that information to the Dodgers as part of a scouting report. I had pitched against them in the 1947 and 1949 Series. I was injured and didn't pitch in the 1952 series. That 1955 Series was satisfying to me."

Branca was born January 6, 1926, starred as a basketball and baseball player at A.B. Davis High in Mount Vernon, signed with the

Dodgers during World War II and stayed with the team through early 1953. He married the boss's daughter, Ann Mulvey. They have two daughters, one of whom married Bobby Valentine, who later managed the Mets to a 2000 Series loss to the Yankees.

He still attends Dodger fantasy camps and has stayed close to the organization for all these years. He ran an insurance business in White Plains, New York, and was one of the key founders of BAT (Baseball Assistance Team), an organization that helps destitute ball players and their families. He can often be found on golf courses for charity events in the New York area.

"People hear about the big salaries of today, but there are a lot of ball players from the old days whose families can't even afford to bury them," Branca said. "We take care of that."

Branca was one of the leading committee members of the 1955 Brooklyn Dodgers reunion set for the fall of 2005. He knows what that team meant to Brooklyn and the world.

"There was so much frustration with the Dodgers of those days not being able to beat the Yankees," Branca said. "When they finally won in 1955 it took the monkey off their backs. I think it helped take a lot of the pressure off the franchise and contributed to lots of titles later on. Look at the Red Sox and the Cubs. The players of today don't know their history, but they still can't seem to win, so the defeats are stressed and repeated year after year. If Brooklyn didn't win the Series in 1955 it would have been harder for them to win later on in 1959 and 1963. There were still guys like Koufax and Podres around from those 1955 Brooklyn teams."

Branca was determined to make the 1955 reunion in 2005 one of the great New York happenings of all time.

"Maybe kids today around New York don't know the history, don't know what that victory meant to the people of the city. There have been a lot of New York sports victories. Lots of them. Nothing like the 1955 Dodgers. Nothing. I was just sorry I couldn't make it until then."

Branca probably lost his chance to stay with Brooklyn through 1955 after a severe back injury he suffered in 1952.

"We were playing monopoly at my home, Ann and me against Clyde King and his wife, Norma. I got out of my chair to get a soda. I had put another soda bottle down near the chair. When I came back the chair slipped on the bottle and I slipped off the chair and fell to the ground. It damaged my back severely, and I never could really throw hard again," he said.

Branca started the 1955 season with the Giants farm team at Minneapolis. He was released in July after pitching with a tender arm. He pitched some batting practice that year and was signed by the Dodgers late in 1956 after his arm seemed to come back.

"It was still tender, so I knew I was finished," Branca said.

He also pitched lots of batting practice as late as 1969 for his former Brooklyn teammate, Gil Hodges, as he led the 1969 Mets to a championship.

He is hopeful the memories of the 1955 title for those players still around from that team will be something special—even for those old Dodgers like himself who just missed it.

"I played with all of those guys on the 1955 Dodgers. I want them to enjoy this as much as they can at this late stage of their lives," he said.

The Duke and Clem

"You want a story? I'll give you a story," bellowed Duke Snider after a tough Dodger loss in July of 1955. "These are the lousiest fans in baseball.

"I hope you print it. You better print it," he screamed.

Dick Young licked his chops. He printed it, all right, with the details of Snider's explosion and a suggestion that the handsome center fielder from California was one big baby.

Snider always wore his emotions on his sleeve. A home run in a key spot would produce that Hollywood handsome grin. A strikeout with the bases loaded and the Brooklyn fans booing his very name announcement the next day would result in a week of sulkiness.

He was a great center fielder, really better than Willie Mays or Mickey Mantle, because he had to do it all in the tight confines of Ebbets Field while they sauntered to the depths of the Polo Grounds or Yankee Stadium for their show catches. Babe Ruth never played a night game or faced a 100 mph relief pitcher or took a night flight to California after a day game in New York. Times change. Conditions are often the factor of success.

Snider was just the most emotional of baseball players on the 1955 Dodgers. Robinson, of course, had to hold it all in. Hodges naturally did. Pee Wee eased through life. Carl Furillo was angry most of the time. Erskine was pleasant all the time.

"I'd say there was a perception of Duke as a loner," said Erskine, who roomed with Snider for many years after their arrival in Brooklyn. "I didn't see him as a loner. He didn't drum up groups to go and have a drink, but he didn't sit in a bar by himself, either."

"He was an only child growing up, a mama's boy," Carl Furillo once said. "A lot of the guys called him that. He admitted it himself. 'California fruit' we used to call him. But don't get me wrong. He was a good ball player, God bless him."

"He was thrust into the limelight early in life, like a lot of pro athletes are," said Erskine. "He had difficulty taking criticism. Who doesn't? But he always had to respond."

෧ ෧ ෧

The Los Angeles Dodgers lost the 1962 playoff for the pennant to the San Francisco Giants, something the Dodgers seemed to specialize in after their postseason failures in 1946 and 1951.

The wailing was loud from the Dodger clubhouse. There *is* crying in baseball, Mr. Hanks. Lots of it. Especially when pennants are blown, especially when they are blown on walks as that one was.

We wretches from the press, collected outside the Dodgers dressing room to write the team's 1962 obituary, waited for an open door to the scene. No chance.

Then one guy walked out. He was dressed in a sweatshirt, baseball pants, and sandals. He held on to a cigarette. His eyes were glazed and his graying hair was matted. He looked as if he had been on the Titanic. He had at least been on the baseball version. Duke Snider faced the music.

"One thing I remember from the 1951 playoff," he began, as hard-bitten reporters were too nervous at the 1962 situation to even think of a question, "was that when I got home after we lost to the Giants my wife, Bev, said to me, 'At least you won't have to live through that again.' I wonder what she'll say today."

ßßß

"Yeah, I remember that," said Snider, as he sat in the den of his California home in Fallbrook late in 2004. "I think the other guys were too busy crying to talk to the press."

Edwin Donald Snider was born in Los Angeles on September 19, 1926. His father, Ward, worked in the nearby shipyards and his ailing mother, Florence, cared for him alone at home.

"My father liked baseball and pitched to me as a kid. I was naturally right-handed, but he turned me around to hit the other way. He saw that most fields favored left-handed hitters. When I was young, maybe six or seven years old, I came in from outside after playing with the neighbor kids and my father just said, 'Here comes the Duke.' I never remembered whether he thought I looked like the Duke of Windsor or what. It was just a name that stuck. My mother died when I was 10 years old. She was 44 years old. My father made it to 65. He saw me play ball."

Snider played and watched every sport. One day he was walking along with a UCLA baseball player as he crossed a field from his game to broad jump on a distant field in a track meet.

"That was the first time I saw Jackie Robinson. He was a childhood hero of mine. It was amazing how our careers were linked in a way," Snider said.

After signing with the Dodgers in 1944 and serving in the Navy, Snider played at Newport News, Fort Worth, Havana, Cuba and Saint Paul before making the Dodgers in 1947. On April 15, 1947, he sat on the Brooklyn bench at Ebbets Field as Jackie Robinson played in his first game for the Dodgers at first base.

"They came around that spring of 1947 when I was trying to make the club and asked me if I would sign a petition that I wouldn't play with Jackie and didn't want him on the team. Me sign that? I was just trying to make the club and Jackie was a famous California athlete, a hero of mine. It was so ridiculous."

Manager Leo Durocher caught wind of that deal and quickly killed it with his tart tongue.

Snider swung very hard, struck out 24 times in 40 games in 1947 and batted only .241. He was shipped back to Montreal and rejoined the Dodgers for 53 games and a .244 average in 1948.

His Hall of Fame credentials began accumulating in 1949 as he became the regular center fielder, Carl Furillo moved to right field and the Dodgers won the pennant. Snider hit .292 with 23 homers and 92 RBIs that season.

The Dodgers were mostly a right-handed-hitting team with the power coming from Campanella, Robinson, Furillo, Hodges, Pee Wee and whoever the left fielder of the moment happened to be.

Snider would beg out of games against tough left-handed pitchers on occasion and sometimes grow angry when he was seated against left-handers he thought he could handle. Warren Spahn, fast and tricky, drove him nuts. No matter. Spahn, the winningest left-hander in base-ball history with 363 triumphs, drove almost everybody nuts.

He reached his peak in 1953 and 1954 with a .336 mark and a .341 average and the beginning of five straight years with 40 or more homers.

Snider played 18 years in the big leagues with a final season with the Mets in 1963 and 91 games with the Giants in 1964. He hit .243 and .210 in his last two years and finished with a .295 career average and 407 homers.

A youngster named Ed Kranepool, then 18 years old, was taking batting practice with the Mets in 1963 after Snider, a future Hall of Famer, joined the team. Snider offered a couple of hitting suggestions.

"What do *you* know—you're hitting .220," bellowed Kranepool.

It was the kind of reaction Snider might also have had in his younger days. A lot of Brooklyn teammates whispered to Dick Young and others that Snider only cared about Snider, that he was a little pompous, a little standoffish with other Dodgers.

The real explanation was that he was a California kid. Most of them are affected by too much sun. He was just one whale of a baseball player, the best of the Dodgers. He carried the team, with some help, to half a dozen pennants.

"It's funny that you're asking about the 1955 Dodgers, the only Brooklyn winner," Snider said. "I was walking through my garage the

other day where I have a big colored picture of the 1955 Brooklyn
World Champions. Only 11 of us are left—just 11. That's sad. There's
Zim and Shuba and me who aren't pitchers, and then Newk, Erskine,
Podres, Labine, Loes, Roebuck, Craig and Sandy. Only 11. But I guess
50 years will do that to a team."

⚐ ⚐ ⚐

Snider laughed when we started talking about the most remembered Brooklyn game of all time, the 5-4 loss to the Giants in the Polo
Grounds on Bobby Thomson's wimpy home run.

"You know, I never really thought that game was in doubt when
Charlie [Dressen] made the change and brought in Ralph [Branca] for
Newk. He just gave Ralph the ball, said, 'Get 'em out,' and left the
mound. They didn't have those long discussions like they have today. I
watched that thing sail and my heart sank with it. What a horror. It's
all hindsight now, a lot of years later, but in some funny way it really
helped us. It made us a better team. We won the pennant again in 1952
and 1953. Even though we lost to the Yankees, everybody agrees we had
the better teams. Then came 1955. We won easily and stuck together
to win the Series."

Snider said the Brooklyn lineup pretty much stayed the same in
those years of 1952 and 1953. It changed often in 1955.

"After we got [Andy] Pafko to play left field in 1951, Charlie could
make out the lineup on Christmas morning. It was always the same. We
won the two pennants, got fooled by the Giants with Mays back in
1954 and won again with that great start in 1955. We knew it
wouldn't be a memorable year if we didn't beat the Yankees," Snider
said.

Snider always had that love-hate relationship with Brooklyn fans
because of his huge home runs and frequent strikeouts. He batted .309
with 42 homers and a league-leading 136 RBIs in 1955.

"When I made an out they booed me, and when I homered they
cheered me. It was tough to deal with them. Some guys like Pee Wee
and Jackie and Erskine just ignored all that. Me? I took it home and got
worked up over a booing," he said.

Snider said the Dodgers were pretty loose riding that bus from Ebbets Field to Yankee Stadium for the seventh game on October 4, 1955. Guys were yelling at Podres, 'How many runs do you need, Johnny?' He laughed back at us and held up his finger, 'Give me one.' After it was all over and he beat them 2-0, I laughed with him and said, 'We gave you twice as many as you needed.' It was all in fun."

Snider said he could still see that ground ball final out off the bat of Elston Howard, the rookie Negro outfielder of the Yankees, bouncing over to Pee Wee at shortstop.

"Then there was the big crowd of guys at the mound around Podres and everybody running off the field. I got in there at the Stadium clubhouse and it was awful quiet. You would have thought it was just another game in June. Not much noise, not much emotion. Guys just staring into their lockers. Then it all opened up. It got wild and stayed wild on the ride back to Brooklyn, that ticker-tape parade as we crossed the bridge and one amazing party that night at the Bossert Hotel."

Snider was one of the few Dodgers who appreciated the move west to Los Angeles after the 1957 season. He was returning home and he was getting away from the conflict with the fans and the media.

His hair was almost all gray by now and he had earned the moniker of The Silver Fox. He had proven his talent after some shaky early years and he was one of the league's premier players by the time he switched the B on his Blue Dodgers cap for the L.A.

He talks often to several of his Brooklyn teammates—Erskine, Podres, Zimmer and Branca and has made several appearances at the Dodgers Fantasy Camp in Vero Beach.

He broadcast baseball in Montreal for many years and did some scouting for the Expos and Dodgers. He has had some health and financial problems through the years but seems content and comfortable now. He is a frequent visitor to the Hall of Fame inductions in Cooperstown, though the journey from California becomes more wearisome each year.

Snider and his wife, Bev, have four children and nine grandchildren, many of whom live in the California area near their Fallbrook home.

"It is hard to say the 1955 team was my favorite because we won the Series over the Yankees. All the winners were fun, even the first one in Los Angeles in 1959. The great thing about the passage of time is that we remember ourselves as better players as the years pass. I like that. I never struck out. I always hit a home run."

Snider said he would make it to Cooperstown again in the summer of 2004 for the induction of the latest members of the game's most exclusive club, Dennis Eckersley and Paul Molitor.

"Molitor is a right-handed hitter, but he always said I was his favorite player and that is why he wore number four on his uniform. That was flattering and touching for me. I want to be in Cooperstown for his induction. That will be something special," said Snider.

The Duke of Flatbush was the power base for those old Brooklyn teams and certainly the most volatile of all the Dodgers during that era.

"It was just such great fun playing on those teams and winning as much as we did in those days," said Snider. "That's what it's all about—just winning. That's why you play the game. Losing just makes you unhappy. I have to have a special place in my heart for the 1955 team. We won. We won everything. We beat the Yankees. There weren't any boos from the fans in Brooklyn that day."

Clem Labine was the great relief pitcher of the Dodgers who seemed always ready for the emergency start. In 1955 he was in 60 games for Brooklyn, winning 13 games against five losses, saving 11 and pitching 144 innings.

He won 77 games and saved 96 in 13 big-league seasons with Brooklyn, Los Angeles, Detroit, Pittsburgh and the New York Mets.

"I had been through the disappointment of 1951, and we didn't beat the Yankees in 1952 or 1953, so that 1955 Series was pretty tense for us," said Labine.

He is sitting on the patio of his winter home in Vero Beach, Florida, before traveling back north to his Woonsocket, Rhode Island, home with his second wife, Barbara, a native of nearby Lincoln, Rhode Island.

"After his first wife, Barbara, died in 1976 I saw Clem on a golf course near home. I knew he needed a partner so I played with him. Then we became life partners in 1987," she said.

Labine has five children, including his son, Clem Jr. who lost a leg in Vietnam and now has an important government job, and five grandchildren. He and Barbara spend the winter months in Florida and the summer months in Rhode Island, golfing and fishing.

฿ ฿ ฿

"I went to Braves Field when the Dodgers were in town for a try-out. That's how it all started," said Labine. "I was at Woonsocket High and I played baseball and ran track. Branch Rickey was looking to sign everybody then. He signed me and I couldn't play because I was going in the Army. They sent me to Fort Benning, Georgia, and when I got out they gave me $500 as a bonus and sent me to Newport News, Virginia."

Labine said he was making $250 a month at Newport News and paying $125 a month in rent for a nearby apartment.

"The manager there was a guy named 'Fitz' Fitzpatrick, and one day he asked me my weight. They couldn't afford a scale in the locker room. I had started at 175 and now I was down to 155. He knew I had just gotten married so he said, 'It's all the fault of your wife. Send her home.' He said she wasn't feeding me right. He also said that I wasn't concentrating on baseball. I was concentrating on Barbara. That's the way managers were in the minors in those days. They wanted you to be on the field—just thinking and talking baseball 100 percent of the time."

Labine was sent to Asheville, North Carolina, where he met up with another manager, Bill Sayles, who was different than his Newport News skipper.

"He encouraged me all the way. He really helped me. He even set us up in a hotel and when I told him I couldn't afford the $8 a night rent when it was 10 days from pay day he pulled out a $100 bill and gave it to me. He never let me pay him back," Labine said.

He went to spring training for the first time with Brooklyn in 1949 and returned in 1950. He got into one Brooklyn game that year and impressed the new Brooklyn skipper, Charlie Dressen, in 1951. He made the club as a relief pitcher and part-time starter.

"We lost the first playoff game that year with Ralph Branca pitching and it was up in the air who might start the second game. Duke Snider just went up to Dressen and said, 'Start Labine. He has the best stuff.' So Dressen started me, the team scored 10 runs and I pitched a shutout."

Labine couldn't pitch the next day, so Branca and Erskine were in the bullpen. Dressen chose Branca for Thomson and "Taps" was sounded all over the Borough of Brooklyn.

"We loved those days with the Dodgers," Labine said. "What a great bunch of guys. We had so much fun together. We just enjoyed each other. The big thing was, the wives got along so well. If wives of players don't get along, if you are dealing with all those petty jealousies, then you aren't going to be too successful. We rented a house on 75th Street in Bay Ridge and went to Ebbets Field with the other guys. The wives and kids would all come down together later in the day. We were one big, happy family."

Labine said he approached the 1955 Series with a lot of hostility.

"The Yankees had beaten us so many times and it was getting real frustrating by then. Also, they showed their arrogance by the way they talked and the way they walked on the field. You know—*we're the Yankees and you're the losing Dodgers and why are you bothering to show up when you know at the end we'll get you?* That was why we were so anxious to win, to finally put an end to that stuff."

Labine pitched in the first two Series games, watched as Podres got the first Brooklyn win in the third game and pitched again in the fourth game. He went 4 ⅓ innings as the Dodgers rallied for an 8-5 win. Labine came back the next day to save Roger Craig's win as the Dodgers held a 3-2 lead in games.

Brooklyn lost the sixth game and Podres closed it all out in the seventh game.

"Alston just had a lot of confidence in me," said Labine. "He knew I had good stuff and he knew that I could throw strikes. If you could make good pitches against the Yankees you could beat them like you beat any ball club."

Podres with his two wins, Craig and Labine became linked in Brooklyn history as the winners of the four Series games in 1955 and have often appeared together at special baseball events and card shows as the winners of the 1955 Series for Brooklyn.

"I don't say we could have done it without the hitters," said Labine, with a laugh, "but we did get those four important victories in the book."

Labine got into the losing 1956 Series for the Dodgers against the Yankees, pitched for the 1959 Dodgers with one appearance and closed out his Series career against the Yankees again in 1960 as a member of the winning Pittsburgh Pirates.

Labine was one of the familiar faces in the first spring training of the Mets in 1962 in St. Petersburg, Florida. The crew cut was the same as in his Dodger days, his body was still lean and rugged and his sinker was still fooling hitters.

"I remember when Charlie Dressen saw me for the first time. He said, 'Kid, keep throwing that slider. That's a hell of a pitch.' The only thing was I didn't have a slider. I just had a good curve ball that would sink hard," Labine said.

After the Mets decided in 1962 that Labine's arm was no longer up to the low standard they had set, he went home to Rhode Island.

"I opened up a sports apparel store that was pretty successful and we had a lot of time for golf and family activities, so it all worked out well," he said.

Several years later he sold the clothing business and took a job as the branch manager of a Woonsocket bank.

"Mostly my job was to meet with the business people around town on the golf course and see if I could convince them to put their investments in our bank. It worked well, so we had some very happy years," he said.

The cold New England winters began bothering Labine's back and knees, so he and his new wife bought a home in Vero Beach where he could play golf, enjoy a fishing trip on occasion and visit with old baseball pals around the Dodgers in February and March.

"We get together with Duke when he comes down here and Erskine and even Lasorda once in a while. Sandy lives around here and I see him once in a while, but he moves around a lot so he's hard to pin down. The idea of seeing all the guys from the 1955 team in 2005 is real exciting. I think it won't take very long before the stories begin rolling and a lot of kidding each other starts. That was quite a bunch of needlers on that club."

Labine said he isn't resentful of the new role of relief pitchers as specialists nowadays or with the huge salaries they earn for so little work—an inning at best maybe once or twice a week.

"More power to them. We did all right for our time. I made the $30,000 level, and 45 years ago that was considered a big salary. We didn't play baseball to get rich in our day. We played because we loved it, because we loved the competition, because we couldn't imagine doing anything else that was more fun."

There were so many stars on that 1955 team and Clem Labine had to be one of the most important. He played in 60 games that year and led the league in appearances. He had a 3.24 ERA and he seemed to pitch only when it mattered.

It certainly mattered in October in that World Series of 1955 and Walter Alston had enough confidence in the tall, crew-cut right-hander that he sent him out there in four games.

"I know that people always bring up the 1955 Series whenever I make any kind of appearance," Labine said. "That was something that all of us will remember until our final days. I think by the letters and emails I get, there are millions of people out there who remember it as much as the players do. *The Dodgers beat the Yankees in the World Series. Finally.* Fifty years later and I still get a charge out of it."

Dodger Roger and Shuba

There was that history they could never escape, the blown lead to the Cardinals in 1942, the 1946 playoff loss to the Cardinals, the 1950 loss to the Phillies on the last day of the season that prevented a tie for the pennant, the 1951 blown pennant, a 13 ½-game lead in August that evaporated to the Giants in the September sun. Then the painful play-off and a blown 4-1 ninth-inning, final-game lead. The Brooklyn 1951 pennant. R.I.P.

The Dodger victories in 1952 and 1953 didn't really ease the pain because they lost to the Yankees again each time in the Series. All of a sudden rookie manager Walter Alston was in charge on the field and finished second by five games in 1954 to the hated Giants.

There was edginess around the Dodgers in the July heat of 1955. Don Newcombe, blazing fast with a 17-1 record, was showing arm trouble. Johnny Podres couldn't win. Carl Erskine's chronic shoulder was acting up again. Billy Loes, the Spaceman before Bill Lee of Boston ever thought about it, was in his own cocoon. Russ Meyer, an early-season winner, had disappeared from the rotation for unexplainable reasons. Was there a panic yet? Not really. Was there serious concern? No question about that.

The 14-game lead over Milwaukee had slid to a manageable 10 ½ games. The Dodgers needed steadier pitching if they weren't going to let another one slip away. It was time for GM Buzzie Bavasi to supply

Alston with a new pitcher, two if he had them. The prayers of Dodger fans were answered on July 17 when Roger Craig and Don Bessent came up from the minors and pitched the Dodgers to a doubleheader victory (ahh, those doubleheader days with one admission price) over the Cincinnati Reds.

ⱷ ⱷ ⱷ

Roger Craig has just returned to his home from 18 holes on the Ramshill Golf Club in Borrego Springs, California, near San Diego. He is 6-foot-4, a little heavier than his pitching weight of 185 pounds but still lean and trim enough with that weathered face of a Hollywood cowboy to earn the nickname of Slim.

He and his still lovely wife, Carolyn, have four children, seven grandchildren and two great grandchildren. They have been married 56 years. She offers Craig a cool drink after the hot morning on the course and he laughs when questioned about the 1955 Brooklyn Dodgers.

"I came in July that year but they gave me a full Series share, $9,000. I have that 1955 World Series ring in my safe deposit vault. That is too precious to wear around a golf course," Craig said.

He had three seasons in Brooklyn from 1955-1957, four more with the Dodgers in Los Angeles, two more back in New York with the Mets, then three more pitching seasons with the Cardinals, Reds and Phillies.

"I came up in July of 1955 with the Dodgers with Don Bessant, and we helped win that pennant. I was cut with Ed Roebuck, a Dodger teammate, when I was with the Phillies in 1966 and that ended my pitching days. I guess I had a lot of Brooklyn connections," he said.

He helped stabilize the Brooklyn staff that summer of 1955 with a 5-3 mark in 21 games, won 12 games in the pennant-winning season of 1956 and slipped to six wins in 1957. His overall big-league mark was 74-98 with a 2-2 World Series mark, including one of the 1955 victories.

"I guess people remember my time with the Mets more than my time with the Dodgers," he said.

Craig was 10-24 and 5-22 with the Mets in his two seasons there and hardly ever pitched a bad game. The Mets didn't often help their pitchers win.

"I pitched the last game ever for the Brooklyn Dodgers in 1957 in Philadelphia and the first game ever for the Mets in 1962. That's some kind of distinction," he said.

Craig lost 18 straight for the Mets in 1962 but never seemed troubled by the losses. He always gave his best and became a fan favorite because he kept the Mets in almost every game he pitched. It all ended when center fielder Jim Hickman hit a grand-slam home run off the low Polo Grounds overhanging scoreboard for the victory. The clubhouse celebration matched a World Series victory party.

After he retired as an active player, Craig coached and managed the San Diego Padres and the San Francisco Giants. While working with the Detroit Tigers he began teaching the split-fingered fastball, the pitch that probably revolutionized the art of pitching in the 1990s.

"There were other guys who threw it before I started teaching it. Bruce Sutter probably had the best one, but after I picked it up a lot of pitchers asked about it and a lot of teams hired me to teach it," he said.

Roger Lee Craig was born in Durham, North Carolina, on February 17, 1930. He was one of 10 children of John Thompson Craig and Irene Craig. His father was a shoe salesman who never made $50 a week.

"We used to sleep three in a bed when I was a kid. Sometimes my father would come home after a long day of work and just tell my mother, 'I think I'll skip dinner.' That's because we just didn't have enough food for all the kids and anything left for him at night. My father passed away when he was 61. Later on my mother took part-time jobs around town just to keep the family together. She was always so proud that we never got any handouts from the government during the Depression. Somehow we made it ourselves and I grew tall and thin and played basketball and baseball at Durham High School," he said.

He got a $6,000 bonus to sign with the Dodgers in 1950 and was sent to Valdosta, Georgia. He pitched at Newport News, spent two years in the Army and was ready to pitch again in the spring of 1954.

"The day before spring training started I fractured my left elbow playing basketball. Then I pitched at Elmira, New York and Newport News before the Dodgers sent me to Montreal. I was pitching in Havana and we won a doubleheader. Tommy Lasorda pitched the other game. When the doubleheader was over I was told I would be pitching Sunday for Brooklyn. Lasorda went wild when he wasn't called up," Craig laughed.

Craig won the first big-league game he ever saw and when it was over he was dressing in front of his locker. He planned to get a cab to pick up his wife at La Guardia Airport. She had stayed back in their North Carolina home while he went on the road with the Royals.

"Jackie Robinson came up to me. He had heard that my wife was coming in. 'C'mon, kid, I'll take you to the airport.' What a thrill that was. I was just in awe of all these guys, especially Jackie and what he had gone through. That was really the greatest team I ever played with," Craig said.

He settled into an apartment on Colonial Road in Bay Ridge, car pooled to Ebbets Field with other Dodgers each day and pitched in turn. He won his five games with a 2.78 ERA as the Dodgers won the pennant and was told by Walter Alston with the Series tied at two games each that he would start the fifth game of the Series.

"The newspaper guys really ripped Alston for that. They couldn't understand why he would start me, a rookie, when he had Carl Spooner or Newcombe or Loes or Russ Meyer available.

"Alston just gave me the ball and I went out there. I wasn't scared. I knew all I could do was my best. I had a great team behind me," he said.

He allowed the Yankees only one run in six innings with Clem Labine finishing up and joined that historic threesome—himself, Labine and Podres as 1955 winning pitchers for the Dodgers.

"I got on the *Ed Sullivan Show* after the Series was over and I got a free dinner at Jack Dempsey's restaurant on Broadway. The party was something special after we won at the Hotel Bossert. I can still see Johnny Podres dancing with Fresco Thompson's young daughter," Craig said.

Craig moved back to New York as a popular figure with the expansion New York Mets in 1962 and remained one of the heroes of the team despite 46 losses in two seasons.

"I think the old Dodger fans forgave me for having won a game for Brooklyn in the 1955 Series. I lost 24 games in 1962, but I was shut out 11 times. I think that helped," he said.

After his playing days ended he coached and managed until his retirement after leaving the Giants. He still gets an occasional call to work with a talented pitcher on that split-fingered fastball.

"A few years back I was going to camp with the Tigers to work with their kids. We have a place in Hilton Head, South Carolina, and I fell down some stairs and broke my ankle, which ended that spring for me," he said.

Craig pitched on pennant winners in Brooklyn in 1956, with Los Angeles in 1959 and as the grizzled vet on the World Champion Cardinals in 1964, a team that beat the Yankees in seven games.

"I made a necklace out of those other Series rings for my wife," he said. "But nobody touches that Brooklyn championship ring. I know how important that was and even now, 50 years later, I am still very proud and very emotional about it."

☞ ☞ ☞

As the Dodgers closed in on the 1955 pennant all thoughts turned exclusively to October. Could they beat those damn Yankees?

"I must have talked about it every day," said Robert Merrill, the famed operatic baritone who played all the houses from La Scala in Italy to the Metropolitan Opera in New York.

"I did more than 500 performances at the Met but singing the National Anthem before the World Series with the Dodgers in 1977 in Yankee Stadium was my greatest thrill," said Merrill. "I remember one time at the Stadium I walked out on the field with Joe DiMaggio. He was to stand right next to me as I sang. He said, 'Sing loud so they won't have to hear me.' He joined in with all the fans as we sang the Anthem and when we finished he just smiled at me and said, 'Thanks, maestro.' He was really a great fan of opera."

Merrill had two passions in his life that he was still emotional about as he approached his 87th birthday in 2004—the operatic singing he did with such skills for more than half a century and the Brooklyn Dodgers.

"Ahh, 1955, the Dodgers beat the Yankees. How can we ever forget that? When you are from Brooklyn and a wild Dodger fan like me that part of your life never leaves you," he said.

Merrill was born and raised on South Second Street in the Williamsburg section of Brooklyn. His mother, Lillian Miller Merrill, was a singer on Yiddish radio stations in the New York area, a popular form of entertainment for the Jewish immigrants crowding into New York from Eastern Europe in the early part of the 20th century. His father, Abraham Merrill, was a dress manufacturer who rose early each morning to catch a subway train before 6:30 to get to his Manhattan factory.

Merrill graduated from Public School 19 and attended New Utrecht High School with a neighborhood pal, Tommy Holmes, who became a member of the Brooklyn Dodgers and played with them in the 1952 World Series after 10 years with the Boston Braves. Holmes had a lifetime .302 average and later coached and managed in the big leagues.

"We used to play punch ball and stick ball together in the streets around our house," remembered Merrill as he sat in the den of his New Rochelle, New York home in the Westchester County suburb. "We were street kids like all the kids in those days. In the 1930s, a car would be second base and maybe a woman standing and gossiping with a neighbor across the street would be third base as we hit the red Spalding—a Spall-dean we called it—as we played together."

Holmes and Merrill would take the subway from their neighborhood stop for a nickel to the Prospect Park stop near Ebbets Field.

"We'd stand near the gates and just ask everybody if they had an extra ticket. There was always someone who would take us in. I must have seen 10 Brooklyn games a year in those days and never paid for a ticket."

When he was 15, Merrill was taken aside by his mother one day and asked to sing. He had this marvelous baritone voice and his mother worked with him for several weeks. She had been a noted singer in Yiddish and was heard on several stations. She quickly realized her son's voice was exceptional.

"She took me to a teacher. She paid him eight dollars a week. I loved it. Before I knew it I was singing Figaro from *The Barber of Seville* before hundreds of people in the Brooklyn Opera Company," Merrill said.

None of this impacted on his love of the Brooklyn Dodgers. He read the newspapers every day, listened to Red Barber and Connie Desmond on the radio and caught an occasional game in a newsreel clip in a movie theater.

"I followed all my favorites—Dixie Walker, Pee Wee Reese, Pete Reiser, all of them in the early 1940s. Then Jackie came along. Wow. He was something. Each day he would do something more spectacular and we talked about him all the time. Tommy Holmes was playing in the big leagues around then and he told us about playing against Jackie. Then in 1952, I think, Tommy joined the Dodgers and he had some clubhouse stories about Jackie and Pee Wee and Duke and the rest of them."

Merrill was singing around the world by then, in Italy, France, Spain, Germany and all through the United States. He was heard regularly on radio on the Saturday opera programs and his fame grew.

"Everybody knew I was from Brooklyn and fans around the world would start a conversation about the Dodgers," he said.

By 1955, Holmes had ended his playing career and he and Merrill went together to several of the World Series games.

"We had good seats in Ebbets Field on the third-base side. We were both so excited when the Dodgers finally won. You know, two kids from Brooklyn getting their revenge on the Yankees after all those years," Merrill said.

Merrill and his wife of 50 years, Marion, a professional pianist for him for more than 20 seasons, have a daughter and a son and often attend Yankee games together.

"I was performing at the Met one year and George Steinbrenner heard me sing in the early 1970s. After my performance he came by to say hello. We started talking about baseball and I told him I missed the

Dodgers in Brooklyn. He asked if I would like to come out to Yankee Stadium. I went to the game and met all the Yankee players and had a great time. Then George asked me to sing the National Anthem. I got to sing it at the opening of the World Series in 1977 and 1978. You could imagine how that brought back memories," Merrill said.

On a few occasions the microphone would be set up on the field near second base so the entire Stadium could watch the performance rather than behind home plate.

"I think I sang it that way the time I was on the field with Joe DiMaggio. I've looked up at the full house at the Met or La Scala and it was thrilling. But looking up at the full house at Yankee Stadium with Joe DiMaggio standing next to you, that's an experience no one can ever forget."

Merrill said he has never been asked to sing at Dodger Stadium and doesn't even think about that.

"That's not Ebbets Field. That's not the Brooklyn Dodgers. I would have liked to be on the field at Ebbets Field in 1955. But it is still pretty nice to think about the Brooklyn Dodgers all these years later. We won in 1955 and no matter how many George wins with the Yankees, I don't think it will ever equal the joy we all felt when the Brooklyn Dodgers won in 1955."

Robert Merrill isn't performing in public any more but his voice has that same baritone resonance it had for so many decades, especially when he thinks back to 1955 and the triumph of his Brooklyn Dodgers. "The Brooklyn Dodgers beat the Yankees," he said in that beautiful, classic baritone sound. "The Brooklyn Dodgers won the World Series."

(Editor's note: Merrill died late in 2004. He was 87.)

ß ß ß

It was just a baseball photograph, the kind that appears in your favorite newspaper every day, the home-run hitter shaking hands with the next batter as he crosses home plate. No big deal. This *was* a big deal.

This was early in 1946 in Montreal, Quebec, Canada. The batter, the home-run hitter, was the much-discussed rookie the Dodgers had signed the previous October, Jackie Robinson.

The next batter, greeting him routinely as the tradition goes, was George Shuba, the hard-hitting, left-handed slugger the Dodgers thought might be another Duke Snider, a power hitter of note who could hit home runs over the short wall in Brooklyn's Ebbets Field.

"The picture ran all over the country," remembered Shuba. "It probably got more play than any home run any other rookie ever hit. I wonder why."

Shuba is 82 years old and his hearing is about gone. Some of the conversation over the phone from his home in Youngstown, Ohio, had to be transmitted to him through his wife of 48 years, Kathy. They have three children and six grandchildren living in the Youngstown area.

Shuba said he never thought anything of the impact of the historic photograph until many months later.

"I started getting letters about shaking Jackie's hand. Can you imagine that? Some people were mad at that. People even suggested that Jackie's skin color would rub off me. I would turn black because I shook his hand," Shuba said.

Like most young ball players, especially those in the competitive Brooklyn organization of the 1940s, Shuba wasn't interested in a teammate's skin color. He was interested in a uniform with Dodger blue.

"I was a Dodger fan as a kid growing up in Youngstown, and I always wanted to play for Brooklyn, play with Pee Wee Reese and all those great Brooklyn stars," he said.

He signed in 1943 with the Dodgers after an outstanding high school career in baseball and basketball, spent the next two years in service and went to spring training in Daytona Beach with the Dodgers in 1946.

There were just too many good outfielders in the Brooklyn organization for Shuba to make the team then. He was sent to Montreal, played with Robinson there and was a star on the 1946 Minor League champion Montreal Royals.

Shuba spent another season at Montreal as Robinson made his big-league debut in 1947 and joined his former teammate in 1948 at the new Brooklyn training facility Dodgertown in Vero Beach, Florida.

Shuba was a curious and talkative fellow when he joined the Dodgers in 1948 at the age of 23.

"George was one of those guys," Pee Wee Reese once said of him, "who could ask you for the time of day and then spend the next half hour telling you how to build a watch."

Gene Hermanski, Carl Furillo and speedy Movin' Marvin Rackley got most of the playing time in the Brooklyn outfield in 1948 with kids like Duke Snider, Dick Whitman and Shuba waiting their turn.

Snider's home-run power got him a full-time job on the Brooklyn club, while Shuba's occasional home runs (he hit only four in 1948 with 32 RBIs) made him a part-timer, a pinch hitter and an occasional outfield replacement.

Snider took over center field the next season, Furillo moved to right and Hermanski became the more or less regular left fielder, a position that the Dodgers never really filled permanently in all the glory years of the 1940s and 1950s.

Shuba hit only .207 in 1950, so he escaped being a member of the disastrous playoff-losing 1951 Dodgers. He joined the team again in 1952, played in the World Series against the Yankees and stayed with Brooklyn through the 1955 World Championship season.

He had seven years in the big leagues with 355 at-bats and a lifetime .259 average and three World Series seasons, not a bad mark for any big leaguer. Ernie Banks played 19 years in his Hall of Fame career for the Chicago Cubs with 512 homers and not a World Series at-bat. That's the way it goes in baseball at times.

Shuba never made more than $16,000 in any season in his Brooklyn days and returned home after the 1955 title with his World Series championship ring and no job.

The Dodgers let him go because they had younger talent coming up, and Shuba's running speed and strong arm were no longer at a big-league level.

"I took the government test for the Post Office and spent the next 20 years doing that," he said. "I moved up to administrative work so my salary level was pretty decent when I retired."

As soon as baseball fantasy camps evolved, Shuba became a regular. He appeared at Brooklyn fantasy camps in Florida, organizing reunions of some of his Brooklyn teammates for card shows and chatting on the phone with old teammates.

"George would see something in the paper that interested him. It could be about baseball, but not always. He would call me to discuss his latest subject for quite some time," said Carl Erskine. "He just seemed interested in everything."

Shuba wore thick glasses as he aged and looked more and more like Superman's alter ego, Clark Kent, as he maintained a strong, athletic physique into his 70s.

"He gets a little frustrated now when he can't hear well enough to carry on a conversation with his friends, especially something connected to the Brooklyn Dodgers," said Kathy Shuba.

In the final game of the 1955 World Series, Shuba, indirectly, made one of the most important at-bats in Brooklyn history.

The Dodgers had scored a run in the sixth inning for a 2-0 lead behind Johnny Podres. Manager Walter Alston decided he had a chance to blow the game open and sent up Shuba to pinch hit for second base-man Don Zimmer with the bases loaded. Shuba hit a hard ground ball to Moose Skowron at first base to end the inning. It was offensively dis-appointing for the Dodgers if the Yankees rallied.

Alston moved left fielder Jim Gilliam (oh, that left-field Brooklyn problem again) to second base and sent the faster Sandy Amoros to left field. The Yankees got two on in the top of the seventh off Podres. Yogi Berra then hit that infamous Yankee fly ball to left field that Amoros caught on the run and converted into a double play as he caught the drive with his outstretched glove on his right hand.

The Shuba pinch hit, the Zimmer substitution and the Amoros catch became as memorable a positive Brooklyn historic feature as the Erskine bounced curve ball became a negative feature in 1951.

As he sat in the living room of his tasteful Youngstown home, Shuba recalled the at-bat leading to the change.

"I wish I had hit a double down the line so we would have won eas-ier," he said.

He was asked his favorite memory of that illustrious season. There were none in particular for Shuba. What he remembered most, half a century later, was simply being a member of the only Brooklyn Dodgers World Series championship team.

"These were just wonderful men to play baseball with," he said, with a small catch in his voice. "They were smart, fun to be around and exceptionally talented. Remember we had to beat those great Yankees with Mickey Mantle and Yogi Berra and Whitey Ford, Hall of Famers, and all the rest to get that championship. That is quite an achievement."

Shuba said the 1955 Brooklyn World Series ring is his favorite possession and rests in its case in his local bank's safety vault.

"You don't wear something like that and flash it all around so somebody can hit you over the head for it," he said. "You just keep it protected so that it remains in the family with your children and your grandchildren. They can look at it and think about you after you're gone."

Every member of that 1955 Brooklyn team was important to the legend in his own way. Shuba hit .275 that year in 44 games and only had that one at-bat in Game 7.

Still, he was a member of the only Brooklyn Dodger team to win a World Series and to do it against the New York Yankees. That is enough glory for any ball player in a lifetime.

Ernie Banks may enjoy his Hall of Fame standing and recollect many of the 512 home runs he hit in his legendary career. But a World Series ring? No way.

George Thomas (Shotgun) Shuba was a member of the 1955 Brooklyn Dodgers, and that makes him one of the 11 living figures of the greatest, most beloved Brooklyn team of all those exciting Ebbets Field seasons. Enough honor for anybody.

Buzzie and Smokey

The Brooklyn Dodgers beat Milwaukee 10-2 on September 8, 1955, and wrapped up their fifth pennant in nine years. The Yankees were actually tied for first around that time with the 1954 pennant winners, the Cleveland Indians, but blew it open in the last two weeks for Casey Stengel's sixth pennant in seven seasons. Stengel had not lost a Series in the previous five tries at the October Classic.

It was to be a Brooklyn-New York World Series again with all the experts—that means the newspapermen with outlets—calling for another Yankee triumph. Even the bookmakers, more objective than newsmen, went along with the Yankees despite the huge Brooklyn win by 13 games in making them a 6-7 favorite.

Joe DiMaggio, who had been retired for four seasons by now, was on a vacation in Rome without Marilyn Monroe, his recently divorced wife, and was caught by a wire service reporter. He was asked his opinion of the upcoming Series.

"The Dodgers can't beat the Yankees," the media-shy DiMaggio predicted. "I guess the only thing that can cure them is a brainwashing. It has gotten so bad in Brooklyn that they can't even say the word, 'Yankees.'"

DiMaggio's comments were a rarity coming from the by-now legendary Yankee Clipper, but Dodger defeats in October had become so routine that his statements shocked nobody.

It was the Curse of the Yankees, as manifested in the 1941 Mickey Owen gaffe, the 1947 loss, the defeats in 1949, 1952 and 1953, that kept the Dodgers down.

Was there anything different about the 1955 Dodgers that indicated that this could, finally, finally, finally, be the year the World Series victory flag would fly in Brooklyn?

Most observers saw the 1955 Dodgers as a team in decline. Age was catching up to that old gang of theirs. The pitching was shaky. The defense was uncertain, the easy win had melted away some of the fierce competitiveness that was typical of earlier Brooklyn teams in life and death struggles for baseball supremacy with the vaunted Yankees. Series flags flew in the Bronx—not in Flatbush.

⚐ ⚐ ⚐

Buzzie Bavasi is 92 years old now, as sharp as ever. He can be found sitting in his den at the La Jolla, California, home outside of San Diego, writing e-mails on his computer to old pal Dodgers, Clem Labine, Duke Snider, Maury Wills, Ralph Branca, among others.

Snider had an avocado farm for years. Bavasi saw something on a web site about avocados and immediately got into an electronic communication with Snider about the best way to raise them.

He regularly phones many of his former Brooklyn teammates when he's not writing his e-mails, sends computer printed letters out to some and handwritten notes to others. And he entertains an occasional visitor.

Bavasi was the general manager of the 1955 Brooklyn Dodgers, the man who put that team together, who filled all the holes, who made sure that this pitcher could work with that catcher, that this hitter could lead off and that batter could bunt. He was the man who collected the 25 men that manager Walter Alston could connect in winning ways.

"Gee, is it 50 years already since we won in Brooklyn? Most of us thought it would never happen. I never gave up. We had Podres going in that last game and he was my man. You want to get one hitter out? You want to win one game that matters? Get Podres out there," he reminisced.

Emil Joseph Bavasi was born in Astoria, Queens in New York City on December 12, 1914. His father, Joseph, delivered newspapers, and his mother, Sue, a native of Jersey City, New Jersey, was the homemaker.

He picked up the lifelong nickname of Buzzie from his older sister, Iola, who saw her little brother moving and darting around the house as soon as he could walk.

"She just said I buzzed around like a bee and I was underfoot everywhere in the house. She started calling me Buzzie and my parents picked it up. Then friends started with the name. I have lifelong friends who have no idea that 'Buzzie' is not the name on my birth certificate," he said.

He was an active athlete and a very good student in school.

"Education was very important in my home," said Bavasi. "My parents knew that I could go as far as my education would take me."

The newspaper delivery business prospered, and by the 1930s the Bavasi family could move from Queens to the fashionable New York City suburb of Scarsdale. Ford Frick, the former sportswriter who became the president of the National League and later the commissioner of baseball, was a neighbor.

Frick was best known for being close to Babe Ruth, the great Yankee star he had covered for so many years for the *New York Journal American*, and for his mishandling of the 1961 home-run chase of Roger Maris and Mickey Mantle.

In protecting Ruth's record, Frick ruled that the new mark of 61 home runs or more (Ruth had hit 60 in 1927 for the record) would not be accepted unless Maris or Mantle did it the first 154 games of the expanded 162-game season. The pressure on both players was enormous. The greatest performance under pressure in a baseball game may have been the attempt by Maris to hit home runs 59 and 60 in that 1961 season in game 154 in Baltimore. He got number 59 but just missed number 60 with a long fly ball out.

"My parents were very friendly with Ford and I would sit around while they talked baseball and other things in our Scarsdale house. He was a real great story teller and he often told stories about Ruth I never heard anyplace else," said Bavasi.

Bavasi graduated from Fordham Prep in the Bronx but decided against going on to Fordham University. He attended DePauw University in Greencastle, Indiana, and graduated with a major in English in 1935.

"Larry MacPhail was running the Dodgers by the late 1930s and through Ford, who knew MacPhail, I got an interview with the Dodgers at their famous office downtown at 215 Montague Street. They offered me a job as the business manager of the Dodger farm at Americus, Georgia. I took it because I wanted to be in baseball. I wasn't sure where it would lead or if it would lead anywhere," he said.

Bavasi dealt with the southern heat, the slow life of rural Georgia, and the shock of removal from the action of New York City.

"What mattered is that I was in baseball," he said. "It didn't take me long to realize that this was really what I wanted to do with my life."

The Dodgers moved Bavasi to Valdosta, Georgia, and later to their club at Durham, North Carolina. World War II was on by then and Bavasi served in the infantry in Sicily and Italy.

"Mr. Rickey had taken over the Dodgers by then and he sent me up to Nashua, New Hampshire, where we had a couple of Negro players, Don Newcombe and Roy Campanella. I was supposed to watch over them because they were great prospects and I had to send back reports about whether I thought they could handle being on the Dodgers. Brooklyn had already assigned Jackie Robinson to Montreal for the 1946 season."

The manager of that Nashua team was Walter Alston, later to be reunited with Bavasi in Brooklyn under very exciting circumstances.

Bavasi said he remembered embarrassing himself one time in conversation with Rickey about Jackie Robinson in Montreal and about his potential as a Dodger.

"I asked Rickey why Robinson was in Montreal and not in Saint Paul, where the Dodgers often sent their better prospects. I was trying to learn his thinking," Bavasi said.

"I wanted him with the Canadian club," said Rickey.

"I forgot that Rickey didn't drink. I thought he was referring to the booze he could get in Canada," said Bavasi.

Bavasi scouted Robinson in Montreal, wrote glowing reports about the two kids, Newcombe and Campanella, he had in Nashua, learned how to operate a franchise successfully and quickly rose up in the Dodger organization.

In 1951, under new Brooklyn owner Walter O'Malley, the attorney who gained control of the team, Bavasi became the general manager of the Brooklyn Dodgers.

He thought his first year as Brooklyn boss would be a great success as the Dodgers jumped out to a 13 ½-game lead over the hated New York Giants.

It all ended in that tragic finale for the Dodgers on October 3, 1951.

"That was my mother's birthday," said Bavasi. "We had to call off the party. How could we have a birthday party for my mother after something like that?"

All these years later, the pain is still there. Bavasi was told that Gil Hodges met Bobby Thomson in the players' parking lot of the Polo Grounds before they played the final playoff game. The players shook hands and wished each other well.

"Too bad Gil didn't break his thumb," said Bavasi.

Bavasi said he was very proud of how the Dodgers came back and won pennants in the next two seasons, 1952 and 1953, after the Polo Grounds debacle.

"The 1955 team won it all, but the best Dodger team was the 1952 team," Bavasi said. "All the big stars were at their peaks that year. I still can't understand how we didn't beat the Yankees in that Series."

Bavasi made some changes on the team in the two years leading up to the 1955 season. One of his best moves, most criticized at the time, was the signing of the left-hander from Brooklyn, Sanford Koufax, out of Lafayette High School.

"The price was big, $14,000, and the fact that we had to keep him on the big club all season, was even more important in the decision making. We knew he wouldn't help us much that year but we thought we could win it with, really, a 24-man roster and then have a great pitcher in the future. Walter went along with it and I shook hands with Sandy's father on the deal," Bavasi said.

Bavasi recalled one other factor in the signing of Koufax, the biggest move in his Brooklyn days as the team's GM.

"A lot of guys had seen him and liked him—Al Campanis, Rube Walker when he caught him on a tryout, a couple of other guys in the organization. Our head scout in the area was Arthur Dede. He was overwhelmed by the kid. Here was this pitcher with so little experience and we had just paid him this huge bonus for that time—$14,000. I asked Arthur if Sandy was worth that kind of money. He just looked me in the eye and said, 'Buzzie, I'll mortgage my house to pay for this kid.' That was good enough for me."

Bavasi thought about Koufax, maybe the greatest pitcher of his time or all time in baseball, and offered his unique perspective. Sandy's problem in his earliest days was his lack of control. He would walk as many hitters as he struck out and was always high and wide in batting practice.

"All through those years, I never discussed this with Sandy, but I always felt I knew what the problem was. Sandy threw so hard and struggled so much with control that he was really concerned about hitting or killing somebody. The more he worried about it, the wilder he got. Al Campanis and Charlie Dressen always suggested he wouldn't make it unless he was sent out for experience after the two bonus years ended. Alston and Pee Wee went the other way. They wanted to keep him around and have him learn on the job. I think it all worked for Sandy when our catcher in Los Angeles, Norm Sherry, got Sandy to throw easier. That way he didn't have to worry about killing anybody."

Bavasi had the famous holdout battle with Koufax and Don Drsydale in 1966 before the two pitchers broke through the artificial salary ceiling of $100,000. Koufax wound up with a $125,000 contract and Drysdale settled for $110,000 in the tandem holdout.

"Sandy often talked of quitting, so I wasn't terribly shocked when he left after that season because of the elbow trouble. I remember once in 1959 when we were still playing in the Los Angeles Coliseum. Sandy was down after a couple of bad outings. He said, 'I'm quitting.' I just said, 'What time do you want to leave? We'll have your ticket ready.' The talent was always there. I knew that someday he would put it together and make us all happy if we stayed with him all those years," Bavasi said.

Bavasi said he recalled that Podres was real loose on the team bus going from Ebbets Field to Yankee Stadium for the final game of the 1955 World Series.

"All the guys were pretty loose and relaxed. I wasn't. Johnny just walked up to me and said, 'You worried? I'll pitch a shutout.' Damned if he didn't."

Bavasi, like all of the on-field and off-field members of the 1955 Brooklyn Dodgers, recalled the party at the Bossert Hotel after the team's triumph.

"Everybody talks about how Johnny went after Fresco Thompson's daughter and threw her his hotel key. Did they tell you she was about 15 years old? At least he didn't throw her any money," said Bavasi.

The Dodgers won again in 1956. One of the additions Bavasi picked up for the pitching staff was Sal (The Barber) Maglie, the great New York Giants curve-balling right-hander and famed Dodger killer.

"He had been sent by the Giants to Cleveland. He was about 40 years old. We still thought he could help us back in the National League where he knew the hitters and the hitters knew about him," Bavasi said.

The Dodgers only had to give Cleveland $100 in a waiver deal and they picked up a guy who would win 13 games for them, pitched a no-hitter and was on the losing end of Larsen's famous perfect game in the 1956 World Series.

"I think [Hank] Greenberg and [Bill] Veeck started talking about $100,000 for Maglie when we inquired about him. Then they came down to $10,000. They just wanted to get rid of him and his big salary. That was certainly the best $100 the Dodgers ever spent for a guy," Bavasi said.

After the 1956 season ended, tales of a Dodger move west were becoming more frequent. Bavasi had a conversation with owner Walter O'Malley about Jackie Robinson. Robinson had batted .275 in 117 games for Brooklyn in 1956 at the age of 37. He had played mostly at third base, some second, even a little first base and a couple of games in the outfield. He was slowing down and growing heavier. His Dodger future was clouded.

"There had been some personal things between Walter and Jackie that I don't want to discuss even now. They had just come to a parting of the ways. Walter just said, 'Get rid of him,' so we made that trade with the Giants. Then Jackie decided to retire. He had already given the story to Tim Cohane in *Look* magazine about his retirement, so I always thought no matter what we did he wasn't coming back to play for Brooklyn in 1957. I think that was a great mistake by Jackie. I always thought of him as a possible assistant who could some day become the general manager of the Dodgers. If he had gone to the Giants I think he would have become a field manager there or one of their higher-ups in the organization. Everybody had great respect for Jack's knowledge and status in the game by then. I guess he wanted to go in another direction, so he accepted that business deal, got into politics and did other things the rest of his life. I've never talked to Rachel about all this, but I have to think there is some element of regret in the Robinson family that he didn't stay in the game."

Bavasi, a New York guy all his life, reluctantly went along with O'Malley when the team moved west after the 1957 season. There was no choice. He wore his favorite bow tie, a white shirt, a light sports jacket, a dark fedora and a wry smile as he boarded the Dodger plane for a flight west with O'Malley, Fresco Thompson, broadcaster Vin Scully, public relations director Harold Parrot and other Brooklyn executives as they flew to California in October of 1957.

Years later Bavasi said he remembered a mock vote in the Brooklyn front office about the move.

"The vote was 8-1 against the move, but the one pro vote was O'Malley's," Bavasi said. Those were the same kind of 'democratic votes' conducted by Stalin, Hitler, Castro and Saddam Hussein.

"After all these years I would have to say it was a good move, money-wise," Bavasi said.

The Dodgers were Bavasi's team and his life. They were no longer in Brooklyn. He wouldn't be there, either.

"I was happy in Los Angeles. We won again in 1959 as Sandy started showing that talent, and we beat the Yankees again in 1963 with Sandy, Drysdale and Podres again. That was very satisfying because they were guys we had signed as kids and the three of them developed into great pitchers. Two Hall of Famers and the one guy, Podres, I would pick for my one win I had to have," said Bavasi.

Bavasi left the Dodgers for San Diego in 1968 and moved to the Anaheim Angels in 1978. He retired from baseball after the 1984 season with three of his four sons becoming active in the game.

"I still stay in contact with a lot of the old Dodgers. I talk to Vin Scully all the time and he keeps me up on the current Dodgers. I talk on the phone. I e-mail maybe six or seven of the players from that era. Zimmer was one of our guys in 1955, and I always kid him when I talk to him how we won twice because we got him out of the lineup. In 1955 Walter [Alston] pinch hit for Zimmer and had to send Amoros out to left field as Gilliam moved to second and Amoros made that great catch. Then in 1959 Zimmer broke his toe and we had to replace him as the regular shortstop with a kid we had at Spokane, Maury Wills. He led us to the pennant and the World Series that year. So we won twice because Zimmer couldn't play. That's something, isn't it?"

Bavasi shows no signs of slowing down at the age of 92. Perhaps part of his secret is staying so connected with the people from his past. He was the Brooklyn boss in the most successful run by the team. He was a legendary executive in the history-making era of the Brooklyn Dodgers, the Jackie Robinson, Don Newcombe, Roy Campanella Brooklyn Dodgers, the Pee Wee Reese, Duke Snider, Carl Erskine Brooklyn Dodgers, the 1955 Brooklyn Dodgers, the Dream Team for millions then and millions even now.

⚾ ⚾ ⚾

In the spring of 1964 the Dodgers played an exhibition game against the New York Mets at Holman Stadium in Vero Beach, Florida. A visit to Dodgertown was always a highlight for any sportswriter. There was the comfortable press room, free-flowing booze, great food, wonderfully warm treatment and the nostalgic walk past the old Brooklyn photos on the wall.

Casey Stengel's Mets, as bad as they were, remained the best beat in baseball. Interest was high and Casey made it so. My career was zooming upwards, partly because the Mets drew so much attention for any sportswriter.

I walked across the field on this delightful spring day. A fellow veteran sportswriter, Barney Kremenko of the *New York Journal American*, walked up to me near the Dodger clubhouse.

"Alston wants to see you," he said.

"Alston wants to see me?"

"He asked if I could send you into his office as soon as I see you," Kremenko said.

In the final weeks of the 1963 season I had written a tongue-in-cheek column about the slumping Dodgers as they played the Mets in New York. The Dodgers had lost the 1962 pennant to the Giants in a tragic playoff.

"You'll never have to live through this again," Duke Snider quoted his wife outside that losing locker room.

Now their lead was sliding away again. There were several former 1962 Dodgers on the 1963 Mets, including Duke Snider, Larry Burright and Tim Harkness. I asked them if they thought the Dodgers would blow the pennant again as they had in 1962. All agreed they would. All, now removed from the Dodgers, put the blame on manager Walter Alston.

Snider told me a story about Alston blowing up late in the 1962 season because the payment count for soft drinks in the clubhouse did not match the drinks taken. When that happened the Dodgers had to make up the difference. The players were supposed to put a check mark next to their names when they took a soft drink from the cooler.

It sounded ridiculous and reminded me of the trauma caused by Captain Queeg over the missing strawberries in the movie classic *The Caine Mutiny*.

I wrote a funny column about it. Snider laughed at it. So did Harkness and Burright. So did all of the Mets as they played the Dodgers that series. They thought I had captured Alston in print as he was—a little tight, a little panicky in the tough pennant race without a bit of a sense of humor. Baseball was serious business for this guy.

I interviewed Alston over the next couple of days as his team played the Mets. He never mentioned my column and I quickly forgot it. The Dodgers went on to win and with Koufax, Drysdale and Podres, they swept the Yankees in the 1963 World Series.

Maybe Alston or friends of his read the column over that winter after the glow of the Series triumph had disappeared.

I marched comfortably into Alston's office. I got the message that something was up when he slammed the door shut behind me. Then he began howling. He screamed about how unfair the column was and how he had won the World Series. I told him that this column had been written in late September, well before the season ended. I reminded him that most of the embarrassing statements came from Snider, Harkness and Burright, former players on his Los Angeles team. He tried to bury the messenger.

He grabbed me by the shirt collar and began pushing me towards the clubhouse wall. Oh, by the way, I stand 5-foot-9 and weighed about 170 pounds then. Alston was a growling 6-foot-3, weighed about 215 pounds and had a collar size of 18. He seemed to be turning purple as he screamed.

Lee Scott, the handsome, debonair, mustachioed traveling secretary of the Dodgers, happened on the scene. He heard the shouting and the scuffling. He had experienced this routine with other writers before. He marched into the room as Alston was preparing to stuff me into one of the lockers. Scott came between Alston and this writer and escorted me out without a fare-thee-well.

Alston was never one of my favorite managers. He was a bland, introverted, suspicious gentleman, but he did manage the Dodgers to seven pennants and World Series titles in 1955, 1959, 1963 and 1965 so he rightfully earned his Baseball Hall of Fame honors in 1983. He died in 1984 at the age of 72.

Walter Emmons Alston was born December 1, 1911, in Venice, Ohio. He was signed by the St. Louis Cardinals during their Gashouse Gang era and made it to the club for only one game in 1936. He played an inning of first base and struck out in his one at-bat. He earned the nickname of "Smokey" for his hot temper.

Alston went back to the minors and failed to move up as a player, so he turned to coaching and managing. Branch Rickey, who had known Alston while he was building the Cardinals farm system, brought him to the Brooklyn organization in 1948 and assigned him to manage at Nashua, New Hampshire in 1949. He brought along two

Negro youngsters, Don Newcombe and Roy Campanella, who would go on to Brooklyn fame under him in 1955.

Alston managed in the Brooklyn organization at Nashua, Trenton, Fort Worth, Saint Paul and Montreal before being named the team's skipper in 1954. Charlie Dressen had won two straight pennants for Brooklyn in 1952 and 1953. Pushed by his wife, he bellowed about not being truly appreciated. A two- or three-year contract would prove he was loved by the Dodgers.

Owner Walter O'Malley, the Brooklyn Boss long before George Steinbrenner ever dreamed of the title with the Yankees, found the chatty and not-so-humble Dressen an abrasive personality.

"Do you realize how important it is to have a manager who doesn't irritate you?" O'Malley responded to the press when asked about his comfort level with Dressen.

On October 24, 1953, the unsigned Dressen was out of the Brooklyn picture, and Alston agreed to a one-year contract for $17,000. About 15 Dodgers were making more.

Alston was unknown in Brooklyn, and the press quickly made fun of the selection of the quiet man from Ohio. He won four World Series titles for the Dodgers before retiring.

About 40 years later a well-known player from Brooklyn named Joe Torre was named the manager of the Yankees. The press greeted Torre in print the same way, because he had failed as a manager with the Mets, Braves and Cardinals. He was called "Clueless Joe" in a huge headline. It was something like "Genius Joe" after four World Series titles in his first eight years in the Bronx.

Alston learned his trade in 1954 as the Giants, with Willie Mays back in their lineup after Army service, won the pennant and swept Cleveland in the World Series.

Not much more was expected of the aging Dodgers in 1955 as rumors began that veteran Pee Wee Reese, a Dodger since 1940, would soon be named the player-manager of the team.

Alston had an uncomfortable spring. Jackie Robinson's biting comments were causing him much grief.

Fellow manager Casey Stengel had a brilliant comment on the subject. He noted that 15 regulars on a team, starters and pitchers, will always like the manager. The next five, playing occasionally, will be unsure. The last five, almost never playing, will always hate the manager. "The secret of successful managing," Stengel said, "is making sure you keep the first five extra guys away from the last five."

Stan Williams, a 19-year-old Brooklyn rookie, remembered Robinson's last season with the Dodgers at his first spring training in 1956.

Williams pitched 14 seasons in the big leagues with a 109-94 mark. He later served as a pitching coach in the big leagues and a longtime scout. In 2004, as an advance scout for the Tampa Bay Devil Rays, he sat in the pressroom at Yankee Stadium.

"The Dodgers won the Series in 1955, but this was really an old team when I joined them for my first look at all these great stars," Williams said. "I think I remember Jackie the best of all. He was such an imposing, historic baseball figure by then. Sort of Brooklyn's answer to Babe Ruth. And he was so big. I think he weighed 240 or 245 pounds by then. I was 6-foot-5 and weighed about 235 myself, but he was much bigger than I was. He could still move. I was shocked when he covered ground in the infield or ran the bases. He was so graceful and quick. It was still a thrill being on the same field with Jackie. He was gone after that year, so I never really played with him. I was sorry about that," the former right-handed pitcher said.

A 10-game winning streak and a 21-2 start in 1955, just about locking up the pennant by May, solidified Alston's standing on the team.

The World Series triumph, triggered by Alston's selection of young Johnny Podres for Game 7, locked the Ohio farm boy into Brooklyn lore.

Alston, despite great success in Brooklyn and Los Angeles, would never get more than a one-year contract with the Dodgers. He always said he never needed it as long as he kept winning.

After 23 seasons from 1954 through 1976 and his last Series title in 1965, Alston was asked to go gently into the night. Tommy Lasorda took over in 1977 to begin his Hall of Fame managerial career with the Dodgers.

Lasorda had actually played for Alston in Brooklyn. They were as different as apples and cabbages. Still, Lasorda admits he picked up some managerial tricks from Alston.

"Everybody manages in their own style," said Lasorda. "Still, you are combining what you gained from all the managers you played for."

Other big-league managers who played for Alston included Gil Hodges, Bobby Valentine, Don Zimmer and Maury Wills.

During his playing days and through his early managerial years, Alston spent a good deal of time in the winter as a substitute teacher in local schools around his home in Darrtown, Ohio.

"It kept me busy, I made a few extra bucks and I learned a lot about taking care of immature youngsters," he once said. "Baseball players often fall into that category."

After his success with the Dodgers in 1955 and 1956 and later on in Los Angeles, Alston bought a huge farm, gave up teaching and enjoyed the quiet life around his Ohio home.

Alston was always proud of the 1955 title but as a laconic fellow it was difficult through the years to get much emotion out of him regarding the famous Brooklyn title. He seemed as excited about the victories in 1959, 1963 and 1965.

"Walter did a good job for us and we felt he handled some difficult situations as best he could on the field," said Buzzie Bavasi. "There was a lot of turnover of the team during his time, and that is about the most difficult job any manager can have."

Alston inherited an aging team in 1954 and won with it in 1955. He won the Series three more times and left Lasorda a young team when he left in 1976. Lasorda was able to win two pennants in a row in 1977 and 1978 with those damn Yankees beating the Dodgers again in those two years.

Whether or not Alston was clearly a Baseball Hall of Fame manager is debatable to this day. The seven titles and the four Series victories give him the statistics for a strong case. Personality, a Casey Stengel personality, a Lasorda personality, a Sparky Anderson personality, do not come into play in measuring Walter Alston's standing in the game.

He was an Ohio farm boy, a schoolteacher, a big leaguer for one at-bat, a successful minor-league manager and a four-time World Series winner.

More importantly he was the manager of the 1955 World Champion Brooklyn Dodgers. He was the guy, with or without help from the front office, his coaches or his veteran players, who wrote the name of Johnny Podres as starting pitcher in that immortal seventh game.

The Dodgers won only one World Series title in Brooklyn, that 1955 championship, and Walter Alston was the leader of that team. He deserves commendations for that accomplishment and he deserves gratitude from all of us who rooted and cheered for Brooklyn Dodger titles.

Traveling secretary Lee Scott saved me from an Alston beating. Alston saved Brooklyn from the ignominy of never winning a championship crown.

Down But Not Out

The Dodgers motored up to Yankee Stadium in a Greyhound bus from Ebbets Field over the Williamsburg Bridge about 9:45 on the crisp Wednesday morning of September 28, 1955.

In Bensonhurst and Boro Park, in Flatbush and Flatlands, in East New York, Crown Heights, Dyker Beach, Manhattan Beach and Brighton Beach, at Lafayette, Madison, Lincoln and Boys High schools, the students came equipped with their portable radios. Red Barber, Connie Desmond and Vin Scully would soon be bringing the World Series message to anxious Brooklynites. Toots Shor was gathering pals at his 52nd Street eatery for a limousine ride up to Yankee Stadium to root for Joe DiMaggio's team. They were feeling little pain when they arrived at River Avenue and 161st Street.

"We were confident," Joan Hodges, wife of Brooklyn first baseman Gil Hodges, remembered. "We had been through so much by then. After all, it was four years after the tragedy of '51."

Whitey Ford was the Yankees' starter in Game 1 and Don Newcombe would be Brooklyn's pitcher.

Pulitzer Prize columnist Arthur Daley, who walked around batting practice with a clipboard jotting down the ramblings of players, suggested in his pregame column that this was Brooklyn's best chance for a victory over the Yankees in all the Series match-ups since the first one in 1941.

"The Yankees stopped scaring people when DiMaggio retired," he quoted an unnamed source as saying. Whether or not Daley created the quote or some Yankee hater in a different uniform actually said it hardly mattered now. Daley was setting the tone. Without DiMaggio, who left after the 1951 season, the Yankees were not the invincible team they once had been. Although New York beat Brooklyn without him in 1952 and 1953, these were not the 1927 Yankees who had scared the Pirates in batting practice with long home runs and their large physical presence in a Series sweep. Mickey Mantle was less than six feet tall, and even he couldn't make the opening-day lineup because of a hamstring injury.

Carl Furillo skipped the team's last workout with a severe cold but promised manager Walter Alston he would be ready for the Wednesday opener.

Pitchers Russ Meyer and Ed Roebuck went into the Stadium stands during the Tuesday workout to sit in the seats assigned to the Brooklyn wives. They had a good angle on the field.

"If my wife isn't happy, I'm not happy," said Roebuck in 2004. "That's what I had to be sure about."

While the Dodgers worked out Tuesday afternoon at Yankee Stadium the Yankees went over to Ebbets Field in Brooklyn.

"It's the same old cracker box," said Billy Martin as he took the field again after damaging the Dodgers in 1952 and 1953.

Fans filled the two team hotels at the Concourse Plaza in the Bronx, a pleasant walk away from the Stadium and the Bossert Hotel in Brooklyn, a nickel subway ride to the Prospect Park stop for Ebbets Field in Brooklyn.

Fourteen thousand bleacher tickets were available at $2.10 each, and a smaller number of grandstand tickets at $4.20 were also available for customers. The two first-in-line bleacher fans, Ralph Belcore of Chicago and Charles Kierst of Auburn, New York, complained to police that their valuables had been stolen from outside the bleacher gate Monday night. They had made the mistake of stepping off line for a while, leaving their luggage behind them. New York was ready for the World Series.

The Series began at Yankee Stadium. The Dodgers had a loose batting practice before the first game against two minor-league pitchers, Chuck Templeton, a left-hander, and Wally Singer, a right-hander, brought in for the occasion. They also batted against one of their own left-handers, Sandy Koufax, indicating that Alston had no plans to put the 19-year-old bonus kid into the World Series.

Pee Wee Reese and Phil Rizzuto were in the starting lineups for their respective teams, the 35th time the two would be against each other in World Series games, some sort of a rivalry record.

The Brooklyn lineup, carrying the hopes and dreams of millions, was the same as always—Gilliam, Reese, Snider, Campanella, Furillo, Hodges, Robinson at third base, Zimmer and Newcombe.

The Yankees would have Bauer leading off, McDougald, Irv Noren in center field for the ailing Mantle, Berra, Collins, Howard, Martin, Rizzuto and Ford as the starter.

The Dodgers jumped off to a quick 2-0 lead in the second on Furillo's homer, a triple to deep left center by Robinson and Zimmer's bloop single.

Robinson's weight, a constant source of controversy around the Dodgers, gained attention before the Series even started. John Drebinger of *The Times* noted that Robinson had lost about ten pounds in the weeks preceding the Series. He also pointed out that Robby would be playing his fourth World Series position in five Series starts after being at first base in 1947, at second in 1949 and 1952, in left field in 1953 and now at third base.

Whenever the Dodgers played from 1947 through 1956, Jack Roosevelt Robinson would be the center of interest on and off the baseball field. His middle name was in honor of former president Theodore Roosevelt, who died the year Jackie was born, and like Roosevelt, wherever he went, all eyes were on him. That's just the way it was.

Even in the 6-5 opening-day Brooklyn Series loss, Robinson was the center of attention.

ßßß

Joe Collins walked in the second inning. That brought up the left
fielder, rookie Elston Howard, the first African American to play for the
bigoted Yankees. They had a first baseman named Vic Power in the
organization earlier. He was slated to be the Jackie Robinson of the
Yankees. When GM George Weiss found out that Power had white girl-
friends, he told others in the organization, "He doesn't fit the Yankee
image."

Weiss probably didn't fit the Yankee image, either. When he was
fired by the Yankees with Casey Stengel after the 1960 season, he stayed
home for a year. Then he was hired to build the New York Mets. At the
press conference announcing his return to baseball, his wife, Hazel
Weiss, announced, "I married George for better or worse—but not for
lunch."

Howard caught Newcombe's high fastball on a 0-1 count into the
lower left-field seats for a two-run shot and a tie ball game.

Snider homered for Brooklyn in the third for a 3-2 lead. The
Yankees quickly came back when Newcombe walked Ford, the former
first baseman from Queens, in the third. Bauer singled him to second.
McDougald advanced the Yankee lefty to third on a grounder and he
scored on Noren's grounder.

Collins, an unappreciated Yankee in his time, homered in the
fourth for a 4-3 Yankee lead. After Berra singled in the sixth, Collins
homered again for a 6-3 Yankee lead.

Radios were shut off in Bensonhurst. Salesmen, home early in
Brooklyn Heights for the game, decided it was time for paperwork.
Mothers, ignoring the uncooked chicken for an hour while the Dodgers
played, decided to get that roaster into the oven. Again. It looked like
it would be another long winter while Yankee fans zinged us all winter.
Would this pain ever end?

There was one moment of glory that afternoon, a joyous Brooklyn
memory, which has lasted half a century.

The Yankees led 6-3 into the eighth inning. Furillo singled to start
the Brooklyn eighth and Hodges flew out to center field. Then
Robinson hit a hard ground ball to McDougald at third base. He got
his glove on the ball but the spin carried the baseball under his glove

and down the third-base line. Furillo hustled all the way to third base, and Robinson made it easily to second base.

Casey Stengel stayed with the tiring Whitey Ford. Weak-hitting Don Zimmer lifted a long fly to center, deep enough for Furillo to tag up and score the fourth run for the Dodgers and for Robinson to make it to third base with two out. Now the score was 6-4 for the Yankees with four outs to go for a first-game victory.

Frank Kellert, who batted .325 that year as a backup to Hodges at first, was called on to pinch hit for pitcher Don Bessent with Robinson on third.

Ford, with his back to Robinson at third as he went into his stretch motion, did not see Robinson take a few steps off third base in his daring base-running routine.

Ford threw a high outside fastball for a 1-0 count as Robinson electrified the crowd with his antics. No man in the history of the game ever made the distance between third base and home seem shorter or more exciting.

Ford took the sign from Berra. He called for a low inside fastball. The lefty went into his stretch. Robinson danced down the line four or five steps. Ford let the pitch go. Now Robinson was roaring down that 90 feet. His loose shirt was flapping in the breeze he created. Currents of air rippled his baseball trousers. His cap remained firmly on his head. Berra moved up a step toward the plate as he anticipated Robinson's arrival. Home plate umpire Bill Summers bent over low to get a better look. The ball arrived on its level trajectory. Robinson's right foot, stretched out far from his compact body, made contact with home plate as Berra's glove came down with the ball for the tag. Summers never hesitated. He spread his arms wide, flat to the ground, in the classic baseball safe sign. Robinson had stolen home! The Dodgers were down only one run.

As if twisted by a corkscrew, Berra spun around and howled at Summers. He bawled and bellowed, never using a curse word, but suggesting that Summers did not see his tag. "He's out! OUT," Berra screamed. Ford moved toward home plate but never got closer than 30 feet. Manager Stengel, gimpy-legged since his own playing days ended more than three decades earlier, arrived on the scene. Berra was holding his mask and walking after Summers as he turned from the plate.

Summers never lost his cool. He gave Berra enough rope. Then he waved to Stengel that the game go on.

"Out, out, brief candle," Shakespeare wrote in *Hamlet*.

"Out, out," howled Berra for half a century after the act.

When reporters gathered around Robinson after the game, despite a Yankee victory, Robinson's play was the center of attention.

"Jackie interpreted some question as adversely critical of the move," John Drebinger wrote in *The Times*.

As noble as he had been in his first couple of years in the big leagues against the most pressure any player ever had to contend with, Robinson always had a severely sensitive side in his later years. He bristled over any suggested criticism of his weight, his race or his baseball ethics. He saw the questioning after the steal as second guessing his judgment in a 6-4 game with only four outs to go.

"It's easier to get one run than two," barked Jackie, "and when they give me the run I'm certainly going to take it. The only ridiculous thing about that play was the Yankees squawking about me being called safe. There wasn't any question about it," Drebinger quoted Robinson as saying in the Brooklyn clubhouse after the game. *"I was over the plate before Berra got the ball on me."*

Robinson is gone now but the memory lingers on with Berra, Ford and all who witnessed the play. It is on television at almost every All-Star game or World Series buildup as one of the most dramatic plays in baseball history.

In the summer of 2004, Berra sat in front of a picture of the play in the Yogi Berra Museum at the campus of Montclair State University in New Jersey.

"He was out then and he is out now," insisted Berra, when pressed on the legendary play. "He was out. I tagged him before he reached the plate."

A few weeks later Berra was doing a television interview with former Cardinals star catcher and longtime broadcaster Tim McCarver. McCarver said the magic word.

"On the play with Jackie . . . " McCarver began.

"Out," Berra smiled.

"The replay isn't conclusive," said McCarver.

"Out," said Berra.

Ford takes a different approach with the same conclusion.

"I was moving in towards the plate as I caught Jackie trying to steal home. I had the best view. I was looking at the play head on. Summers couldn't see it as good as I did. He was blocked by Yogi. There was a lot of dirt flying," the Hall of Fame pitcher said in the summer of 2004.

Ford looked out at the Yankee Stadium Monument Park, where a plaque for him and so many Yankee legends, are examined daily by fans. He shares space out there with Berra, among others.

"Yogi said Jackie was out. I said Jackie was out. He was out," Ford laughed.

Ford then added a new piece of information on the famous old play.

"[Phil] Rizzuto was talking about it one day and said he could see it from shortstop. He didn't know what the fuss was all about. He thought Jackie was safe. Well, that made me start looking at the old films closer and talking about it with other guys," said Ford.

Another former Yankee, Irv Noren, heard Ford discuss the play and talk about Rizzuto's impression on a sports show. He called Ford.

"Whitey, forget what Scooter said about it," Noren said. "He wasn't even in the game."

In the bottom of the sixth inning, Stengel had sent Eddie Robinson up to bat for Rizzuto in hopes of breaking open the game. Billy Martin was on third base, and Bessent was the new Brooklyn pitcher replacing Newcombe. Martin tried to steal home and Campanella tagged him out. He also sat on him at home plate after the play, something Martin, an aggressive player, resented. Jerry Coleman went to shortstop in the seventh.

"When I told Rizzuto that Noren reminded me he wasn't even on the field for the play, Phil backed off. He said he remembered seeing it from the bench, but that's too far away to count," Ford said.

The play stood. Berra and Ford have had a lot of fun and good conversation with sportswriters and fans over the decades. Duke Snider simply said, "If Jackie tried to steal home he almost always made it."

The Dodgers loved Ebbets Field as their home park. Except for
Snider, all of the starters were right-handed hitters, and left-handed
pitchers rarely pitched against them in Ebbets Field, save for a Warren
Spahn. Snider feasted on those righties but so did the Dodger right-
handed hitters. Nobody gets to the big leagues if they can't hit right-
handers.

Casey Stengel never cared about record books. He remembered
everything, but when he didn't he would howl, "You could look it up."
He didn't bother looking anything up about right-handed hitters
against left-handed pitchers when he sent out left-hander Tommy
Byrne against Brooklyn in the second game of the Series.

Byrne was 35 years old, a retread who had bounced around baseball for a dozen years by 1955, with turns on the St. Louis Browns and
Washington Senators, the dredges of the game. "Washington," the fans
in the nation's capital would say, "First in war, first in peace and last in
the American League."

Byrne picked up a screwball and had a big year in 1955 with 16
wins. Stengel decided he could be as effective as Ford, the other lefty,
against the right-handed-hitting Dodgers, especially in the wide-open
confines of Yankee Stadium.

As almost always, Stengel was right. Byrne pitched a sparkling five-
hitter and the Yankees won the second game 4-2. They were up two
games to none in the 1955 World Series. The curtains were being
closed early all over the borough of Brooklyn.

Billy Loes started that second Series game for the Dodgers and
matched Byrne for the first three innings in a scoreless game. The
Dodgers got a run in the top of the fourth on a double by Reese and a
single by Snider.

That inspired the Yankees. They scored four runs in the fourth for
a 4-1 lead. The Dodgers picked up a run in the fifth on a walk to
Robinson, a single by Zimmer, a double play and a single by Gilliam.

After the 4-2 Yankee win, the teams left the Stadium for home.
Each Dodger was encouraged despite the deficit with a scheduled

return the next day to Ebbets Field. None of the Yankees thought they would play another game in the Stadium that year.

Hundreds of fans waited outside the players' entrance for the Yankees to jog across the street for the parking lot. Rizzuto was first out and he signed several autographs as he chatted with the kids, some taller than he was, before getting into his Cadillac. His wife, Cora, was at the wheel as they soon drove off for their New Jersey home.

Mickey Mantle signed a couple of autographs as he limped across the street. His hamstring, which had kept him out of the first two games, was still tender.

Byrne finally came out of the entrance. He had won the game, talked to the press, taken his shower and now was marching to his car.

"Tommy, Tommy, sign this," a kid yelled as Byrne, his head down, walked rapidly across the narrow street.

"Get out of my way," said Byrne.

"Ahh, you're a Bum. You were just lucky," said a young fan wearing a Brooklyn cap.

Kids and adults were already lining up outside Ebbets Field for tickets for the Friday game in Brooklyn. They would go on sale at 8 a.m.

                                 ℞ ℞ ℞

On July 10, 2004, the Yankees played their 58th Old Timers Game at Yankee Stadium. The memory of Hall of Fame pitcher Red Ruffing, the winningest right-hander in Yankee history, was honored with a plaque in Monument Park.

Catcher Thurman Munson, who died in a 1979 private plane crash, had a plaque in Monument Park in memory of his sterling Yankee career. His son, Michael, who was three years old when his father died, chose that day and that event to ask his girlfriend, Michelle, for her hand in marriage. She accepted.

"I wanted my father to be part of it," Michael Munson explained later to the press.

Before all this drama transpired at the Stadium, three Yankees who played on the 1955 New York Yankees World Series losers to Brooklyn, recalled that feeling after the two Stadium wins that year as they approached the third game in Brooklyn.

Don Larsen, who pitched the only perfect game in World Series history in 1956, Bill "Moose" Skowron, the platoon first baseman that season with Joe Collins and Charlie Silvera, one of only 11 Yankees to play on the five straight champions from 1949-1953, recalled those days half a century ago. They sat outside the Yankee clubhouse in a ramp leading to the field.

"We really knew each other real well in those days," said Silvera. "We used to play three or four exhibition games in Florida in Dodgertown or at our place at St. Pete, then the three games before the season started and a game in the summer at Ebbets Field or the Stadium for a city charity. Then we matched up again with them in the Series in 1949, 1952, 1953 and now 1955. Two teams couldn't know each other better than we did."

"I loved going over there to Ebbets Field," Skowron said. "I used to kid Hodges that if I played in Brooklyn I'd hit 40 or 50 homers [his home-run high was 28 with the Yankees in 1961] every year. You could piss and hit the wall there it was so close. I guess that's why Hodges didn't make the Hall of Fame. Nobody believed his home-run numbers were real because he played in that little Brooklyn park."

"Even the bullpens were close," said Larsen. "I remember warming up in one Series game and somebody hit a line drive down the left field towards our bullpen and we all jumped. That would have been something if we lost one of our guys to a foul ball."

"I'd never see a game from that position," said Silvera. "When you sat on the bench down there you couldn't see home plate and when I got up to warm up a pitcher my back was to the game. I was always asking the other guys, 'Who's up? What's the score?' I always knew we were winning."

Silvera said that he was friendly off the field with several of the Brooklyn players.

"This was the World Series, and you know you would be making a big series check, $7,500, $8,000, $8,500, something like that," Silvera said. "It was a guarantee. That's how Weiss would get away with the low salaries he paid us. He would always say, 'Don't forget to add the World Series check to your salary numbers.' That was his scam. Anyway my best pal on the Dodgers was Furillo. We would see each other once in a while when both clubs were home during the season and we attended a lot of events together in the winter. After the first time we played against each other in the 1949 Series we always made up to exchange tickets. Players had to buy the tickets then. We both had big families. I spent around $2,000 on tickets in 1955. I don't think I got paid back for all of them. I probably was making $10,000 that year. The tickets were $6 for box seats and $4 for reserved seats. I got tickets for Skoonj [Furillo's affectionate nickname] in Yankee Stadium and he got tickets for me in Ebbets Field."

"We had won those first two games and Turley was going in the first one at Ebbets Field. I was scheduled for the next one and I figured I could end it all in Brooklyn. This was my first Series experience. I lost 21 games with Baltimore the year before. The Yankees made a deal for me anyway. I won nine games and then I was getting a start in the Series. I had seen Ebbets Field in the spring. I wasn't worried about the small park. My best pitch was a sinkerball. I knew they would hit a lot of grounders," Larsen said.

It was time now for these three former Yankees to walk out on the Stadium field again, hear the cheers of the crowd, enjoy the annual ritual, get the attention they deserved as parts of the Yankee legend and forget that 1955 disappointment. Sure, they almost always won in October. ALMOST.

⚾ ⚾ ⚾

Johnny Podres had been named by Alston as the starting pitcher for the first game at Ebbets Field. Podres had started a game in the 1953 Series, so he wasn't overly concerned about the excitement or drama of the Series start. He had a special incentive for the next afternoon. It was his 23rd birthday.

"I was staying with my aunt in Staten Island and she promised me a big party Friday night if I won. My father was down from Witherbee and we sat up late the night before when I got home from the Stadium. We talked and laughed and played cards and drank a little beer. It was exciting, but it really wasn't any different than any other start I had made. Sure, we were down, but we knew how good a ball club we had so there wasn't really a great deal of pressure on me. When you are playing with Robinson and Snider and Hodges and Furillo you know you are going to get a lot of runs. I figured if I pitched my normal game I would be fine. My last outing before this was in Pittsburgh and I had thrown the hell out of the ball. I kept thinking about that. I figured the Yankees had scouted me there and I would tell Campanella we might go more with the changeup."

Podres leaned back on the couch in his Queensbury home in New York. He rubbed a baseball and threw it in the air, catching it with his left hand.

"It didn't matter because we were playing the Yankees, and the Dodgers had never beaten them before. This was a different team in a different year with a lot of different guys. I felt good and I was sure I would have a good game. Hell, I had beaten the Giants and the Cardinals and the Reds and they all had good ball clubs. This was just another game as far as I was concerned. If I had good stuff I'd beat 'em. If I didn't, they'd beat me. That's the way it always worked. Remember this was only the third game. Hey, we aren't talking about the seventh game here, are we?"

Podres drove alone from his aunt's Staten Island home early the next morning for the one o'clock game. The family would come to Ebbets Field later. He listened to music on the car radio and hummed a few of the songs. He made the turn on to Bedford Avenue and turned off at Sullivan place. He pulled the car into the garage across from Ebbets Field and walked across the street.

A lot of kids were still lying in the street before the gates to the bleachers were open. They spotted him quickly and yelled out his name. "Hey, Johnny, we're witchya," yelled one kid.

"I'm witchya, too," Podres responded in his best Brooklyn accent.

There were, oh, maybe, two or three million other people with the Brooklyn left-hander that day. Happy birthday, kid.

The Series in Brooklyn

On September 30, 1955 *The New York Times* reported in an article with a Princeton, New Jersey dateline, *"Brooklyn Dodger fans will have a topic for endless debate if plans for a domed-over, indoor stadium in the borough are realized.*

"Preliminary details of the project were made public today by R. Buckminster Fuller, well-known architect of self-supporting domed structures. He has been retained by Walter O'Malley, president of the National League champions, to make initial studies of such an indoor stadium.

"Mr. Fuller, a visiting professor in Princeton University's School of Architecture, described the proposed arena as circular in shape and covered by a thin plastic dome 750 feet in diameter. The dome will be supported by a lightweight aluminum truss structure."

It never happened.

Mickey Mantle homered in Ebbets Field that September afternoon off Brooklyn left-hander Johnny Podres in an 8-3 Brooklyn win. Nine years later, in Houston, Texas, Mantle hit the first homer ever in baseball's first indoor stadium—the Houston Astrodome. The Astrodome was similar in design to Fuller's proposed stadium for Brooklyn that never got off the drawing board.

Before the third-game Brooklyn win *The Times* reported, *"Not since 1921 has a team, after losing the first two games, gone on to win the title. That year John McGraw's Giants did it as they conquered a Yankee team of another mold. But that was in the best five-of-nine game series. Never has it been achieved since the present four-of-seven system was restored the following year."*

The inference was clear as the Dodgers played the first Series game that October at Ebbets Field. It would take more than a miracle for the downtrodden Dodgers to pull this classic out.

Whitey Ford, winner of the opener for the Yankees, was the only one of the Bombers before the third game willing to predict a Series sweep.

"We'll win two out of three at Ebbets Field, maybe the first two," Ford told reporters after the second game and before the move to Brooklyn for the third contest. "I need the money."

Half a century later, Ford kidded about his 1955 prediction.

"I said we would win two out of three," said Ford. "I didn't say it would be the *next* two out of three."

In 2004, Podres remembered his approach to that third game.

"I didn't think we were up against it," he said. "I thought if our guys started hitting we would win. I really felt strong after being out the last few weeks."

On a cloudy, gloomy Friday afternoon in Brooklyn, Podres began his birthday bash with a great fastball and an even better changeup. It turned out to be one of the best pitching performances turned in by the lefty in his 15-year career.

"Campy saw early that I really had that great change," Podres recalled. "He started calling it early in the game and I was able to throw it for strikes all the way. A lot of the Yankee hitters seemed to be swinging off balance all afternoon."

Carl Erskine, who had been a candidate for the third-game start and was pushed back a day as Alston went with the lefty, remembered how much he admired Podres' performance half a century earlier.

"There's pitching and there's throwing," Erskine said from his Indiana home. "That was Pitching—with a capital P."

The Dodgers jumped ahead on the Yankees and Bullet Bob Turley in the first inning when Reese walked with one out and Roy Campanella, who would win his third Most Valuable Player title announced after the Series ended, slugged a long run into the upper left-field seats for a 2-0 Brooklyn lead.

The Yankees came back in the second with two runs and a 2-2 tie, the only time the Dodgers really worried about the game. Mantle led off with a huge home run to the highest part of the left center-field stands.

"I challenged Mickey with a good fast ball and he unloaded on me," Podres recalled. "I decided I wouldn't throw him any more hard stuff. If he was going to hurt me that day again he would have to do it against my best pitch. That day it was the changeup."

Moose Skowron followed with a hard double down the left-field line off Podres.

"Casey was platooning me with Joe Collins in that Series. If I didn't hit the lefty I wasn't going to be in there at all," said Skowron in 2004. "[Karl] Spooner was the only other lefty Brooklyn had, so I knew I wouldn't have a lot of work."

Skowron was on second with two out when Rizzuto hit a sharp single to left.

"The ball got out there fast and I didn't," laughed Skowron. "The throw beat me by 20 feet. I just continued to run hard to the plate. Campy was standing up when I hit him. The ball just flew out of his glove and I was in."

The bulky crew-cut former Purdue football player hit Campanella with all his might and Campy couldn't handle the jolt. Skowron was safe and the game was tied 2-2.

An edgy crowd of 34,209 at Ebbets Field began showing signs of discomfort. Hilda Chester rang her bell in center field to stir the Dodgers. Shorty Laurice and the Dodgers Sym-Phony marched through the lower stands to some cheers and a few boos from the Flatbush Faithful. They wanted Brooklyn runs, not alleged music.

The Dodgers went ahead for good 4-2 in the bottom of the second, mostly on the fleet feet of Jackie Robinson. He singled with one out, went to second when Amoros was hit with a pitch and went to third on a bunt single by Podres. Gilliam walked to force in a run as Robinson danced off third and threatened a steal home several times. Reese walked to force in another run after Stengel replaced Turley with Tom Morgan.

The inning really turned on Robinson's base-running antics. He never stopped moving all inning until he scored the lead run on the bases-loaded walk.

"Robinson was magnificent," Dick Young, never a Jackie promoter, wrote. *"He was the spark that the discouraged Brooks needed. For those two hours, and a little more, he was young again. His cap covered his gray hairs and his spirit disguised the age in his legs. On the bases, he taunted the pitchers till they hated him the way they used to.*

"He suckered outfielder Elston Howard into an extra base hit. He smacked a single and a double. He handled seven grounders, some of them toughies, in a busy day at third base. And all the while, he kept chattering encouragement to the kid on the mound, who was spending his 23rd birthday working hard on his first World Series victory."

A big birthday cake with several layers of chocolate and a creamy topping awaited Podres as he walked into the clubhouse after the game with the 8-3 win on birthday number 23. He blew out the candles and cut the first piece off the "Happy Birthday Johnny" cake for his teammates. Unlike a generation later, when New York Yankees pitcher and clubhouse comic Sparky Lyle sat on a creamy birthday cake, no one went near the cake until Podres cut the first slice.

"I drove home after the game and we had another little party with the family," Podres recalled as he sat in his Queensbury, New York living room. "I'll tell you what I remember most about the day. That was what Alston said to me after the game. He just walked up as I was going to the showers after all the interviews and said, 'If we have a seventh game, you're my pitcher.' With Newk and Erskine and all the others that was a thrill."

Podres hadn't won a game since August 29, hadn't pitched a complete game since June 14 and was as close to being off the roster after the batting-cage injury as he was to pitching that game.

"I was good and I was lucky," he said. "Lucky helps a lot."

Energized by the Podres performance, the Dodgers came back to tie the Series at two-all the next day with an 8-5 victory and a strange scoring decision.

Snider, Campanella and Hodges homered for Brooklyn and Clem Labine won the game in relief after starter Carl Erskine and reliever Don Bessent struggled for order. Bessent's 1 ⅔ innings of relief could hardly compare with Labine's 4 1/3 of tight relief even though Labine entered the game with Brooklyn ahead 4-3. If a relief pitcher's stint is described as "brief and ineffective," the victory can be awarded by edict to any other pitcher in the game. That's the way it worked.

"I was glad about that," said Labine from his Florida home in 2004. "If I didn't get the win I couldn't go to these card shows with the other two winners, Podres and Craig, for special appearances. I've made more money in card shows from that game than I ever made in World Series shares."

Labine, the crewcut sinkerball expert, got the victory by shutting down the Yankees and restoring order to the Series.

Snider's homer made it a 7-3 game for Brooklyn in the fifth. Even though the Yankees came back with two in the sixth on hits by Howard, Martin and Eddie Robinson, Alston stayed with Labine. He really had no choice as the Yankees closed to 7-5.

Carl Erskine, Billy Loes and Don Newcombe were all suffering arm woes after a long, weary season of pitching and would be unavailable the rest of the Series. Labine was the key guy out of the bullpen with Ed Roebuck and Russ Meyer now as backups. Alston had more confidence in Labine.

Brooklyn got another run in the seventh on hits by Campanella, Furillo and Hodges. Labine protected the 8-5 lead with a scoreless Yankee eighth. Then the right-hander closed out the win for the 2-2 Series tie with a perfect ninth inning, retiring Noren on a line drive to Hodges at first base, Gil McDougald on a fly to Furillo in right and the dangerous Mantle, still hobbled with a hamstring pull, on a dribbler back to the mound. Labine threw to Hodges at first and the game was over.

"I remember that like it was yesterday," Joan Hodges said 50 years later. "Gil said if the Dodgers could sweep the three games in Brooklyn they would surely win the Series with a victory at Yankee Stadium. Now all we had to do was win tomorrow."

"I was pretty embarrassed by that game," Don Larsen said half a century later on a visit to Yankee Stadium for the 2004 Old Timers Day events. "I had a good year and I was anxious for a World Series start. Casey gave me the start and I didn't deliver. The Dodgers hit me hard. I just vowed to myself if I got another chance at them I would do a much better job. I didn't get a chance again in the 1955 Series, but I did pitch against them in 1956. I pitched one pretty good game. I don't think they got a guy on."

Larsen's perfect game remains the best performance in World Series history, though a lot of Brooklyn fans would argue the best game ever was still to come, a seventh-game Podres performance.

Manager Casey Stengel, grumpy but funny as always after the loss, said baseball was the strangest game there is.

"Lefties won the first three games and now the righties can't win," said Stengel, referring to victories of his own by Ford, Byrne and the Dodgers' Podres.

One right-hander, Labine, did get the victory, so the Series would be settled with a two-out-of-three showdown starting the next afternoon.

Alston immediately announced after the game that the starter for Brooklyn would not be any of the struggling threesome of starters—Newcombe, pounded in the first game, Loes, hit hard in the second game or Erskine, sore armed as he often was, who was the fourth-game starter.

"It will be Roger Craig," he announced to the press in a corner of the Yankee clubhouse. "We think he is ready for it."

The Dodgers thought all signs were now pointing in their direction. They had come back from two games down. They had hit the Yankee pitchers hard. They were loose on the bases and strong at the plate. One other thing:

The Dodgers thought the baseball gods were with them. Yankee co-owner Del Webb, partner of playboy-owner Dan Topping, was hit by a foul ball off Mickey Mantle's bat. It curved into the stands as Brooklyn catcher Campanella chased it, bouncing off Webb's head as Campanella ran out of room for the play.

"Maybe that was the turning point of the Series," Campanella said.

Roger Craig was told he would start the fifth game as soon as the fourth game ended.

"I knew I would get the shot," Craig said from his California home in 2004. "I had pitched well since they brought me up. A lot of the other starters were hurting. I wasn't afraid of pitching against the

Yankees. I just figured if I had my stuff it would be no different than pitching against anybody else."

Alston had a lot of confidence in Craig. He told the press after the fourth game that he was sending Craig out there because he could throw hard, he wasn't a guy who would be frightened and he was well rested.

"The only problem with a young pitcher like Roger is you worry about his control. He has had some games when he battled his control, but he has also had some games when he didn't walk anybody. I think if he has his control he'll do a great job," Alston said.

Craig was only 24 years old that October 2 afternoon in Brooklyn when he started the fifth game of the 1955 World Series. One year earlier, to the day, he was starting a game in the Piedmont League.

A lot of the press made a fuss over Craig's age. They suggested 24 years old was young. He was a lot older, by more than a year, than Johnny Podres was that fall.

Craig retired the Yankees in the first inning without a score despite an error by Reese on a McDougald ground ball.

Hodges singled in the second inning, and little Sandy Amoros, who spent his winters in his hometown of Havana, Cuba, pulled a curve ball offered up by Bob Grim over the right-field wall into Bedford Avenue for a 2-0 Brooklyn lead.

Grim was from Brooklyn and his father still owned and operated a small Brooklyn bar called Grim's in the Park Slope section of the borough. Grim won 20 games as a Yankee rookie in 1954 but slipped to a 7-5 mark in 1955 with signs of arm trouble.

The big blows for Brooklyn that day were the home runs hit by Amoros and the two hit by Snider, called "incomparable," in John Drebinger's report of the game. Even Dick Young, who always seemed to have a running feud with Robinson and Snider, suggested the Duke of Flatbush belonged now in that hallowed pantheon of Series stars, Babe Ruth, Lou Gehrig and John DiMaggio for his World Series homer highlights.

Only Reggie Jackson, with three homers in the final 1977 Yankee World Series game against the now-Los Angeles Dodgers, would threaten that company with homer heroics.

Snider's second homer of the game in the fifth inning gave Craig a 4-1 lead and the confidence that this game was his.

"I really felt strong," he recalled 50 years later. "All my pitches were working and Campy really had the Yankees off balance the way he changed his calls that they might have expected."

Craig allowed the Yankees only one run and three hits through six innings. The Dodgers led 4-1 when Bob Cerv hit a pinch-hit home run in the seventh batting for Grim.

"I thought the kid [Craig] was tiring, so I went all the way for a big one," Cerv said in 2004 from his Nebraska home. "I caught a fast ball and I thought that would start a rally so we could tie the game."

Elston Howard walked and so did manager Walt Alston, to the mound. The scheduled hitter was Irv Noren.

"I can get this guy out," said Craig. "Let me pitch to him."

Alston said after the game that he allowed Craig to make his case but was determined to go with his best and that was Clem Labine, despite his long outing the day before.

Craig got a huge hand from the Brooklyn fans, 36,796 for the largest Series crowd ever at Ebbets Field, as he walked off the field. He tipped his cap as he reached the dirt in front of the dugout. Many of the Dodger players on the bench, including Sandy Koufax, stood up to shake his hand as he walked down the stairs to the bench.

Labine threw his warm-up pitches and then faced Noren. He got a strike over, missed with a curve and came back with a sinking fastball. Noren pulled a hard grounder to first base. Gil Hodges, as smooth a glove as ever the game did see, picked up the ball, fired to Reese at short for the force and hustled back to the bag for the return throw on the double play. McDougald grounded out to Labine to end the inning with the Dodgers up 4-2.

Berra homered in the eighth to close the game to 4-3 but a single by Furillo, a sacrifice by Hodges and a single by Robinson made the score 5-3.

Andy Carey, pitcher Tommy Byrne, a frequent pinch hitter for Stengel, and Howard each grounded out in the Yankee ninth inning to end the game, give Brooklyn a 5-3 victory for Craig and give the Dodgers a 3-2 Series edge.

A celebrating Brooklyn fan threw a July 4th smoke bomb on the field after the Dodger win, covering most of the area near home plate in a cloud of dirt and dust. The Brooklyn fans could smell that historic fourth-game Series victory instead of all that smoke.

"It's all my fault," growled Stengel later in the Yankee clubhouse. "Those home runs were my fault."

It simply meant that Yankee catcher Berra was getting a little help from his manager's pitch selection—a rare occurrence in the 1950s and now a regular baseball event in the 21st century.

The Dodgers tried not to be too cocky in their locker room after the game, and the Yankees tried not to be too down. Of course, nobody had ever come back to win a seven-game Series after being down two games to none. Could this be the one time?

Carl Erskine, his shoulder aching, drove home to his rented Brooklyn apartment near Fort Hamilton. Don Newcombe, also hurting, drove to his family home in New Jersey. Billy Loes was back in Queens by dark. Johnny Podres was back with his aunt and other family members as they enjoyed a dinner in Staten Island.

Jackie Robinson and Roy Campanella were with their families in St. Albans, Queens. Duke Snider, Pee Wee Reese, Don Zimmer, Rube Walker and George Shuba were home in the Bay Ridge section of Brooklyn. Sandy Koufax was with his parents in Bensonhurst.

Most of the Yankees were in their homes in northern New Jersey.

The sixth game of the 1955 Series, maybe the last baseball game of the year, was scheduled back in Yankee Stadium the next afternoon, October 3, 1955, at one o'clock.

Dodger fans were already lined up outside the bleacher entrance at 161st Street and River Avenue for the ticket sale starting that Monday morning.

If Brooklyn was to win that Monday game and win a World Series, all Brooklyn fans, it seemed, wanted to be there.

All the Dodgers had to do was beat Whitey Ford. Their pitcher would not be known until shortly before game time.

Next Year Is Here

We shoulda had Spooner sooner.

That was the cry around Brooklyn in 1954 when the left-hander from Oriskany, New York joined the Dodgers and broke into the big leagues with the remarkable debut of back-to-back shutouts. At the age of 23, he had a 2-0 big-league record, two shutouts and a 0.00 ERA. Not even Bob Gibson 14 years later could top that.

The Dodgers were too far back when Spooner joined the club in 1954 for that performance to make much of a difference.

In 1955, he was still impressive with an 8-6 mark in 29 games and a 3.65 ERA on a loaded staff. Walt Alston brought Spooner into the second Series game as a reliever and he shut out the Yankees over three innings with just one hit, a harmless Yogi Berra single in the fifth.

Now he was given the ball for the sixth game with Brooklyn up 3-2 in games and the teams returning to Yankee Stadium for what Dodger fans, the Flatbush faithful, certainly believed would be *the* day, their day, the day it all happened—a victory, a sixth-game triumph, a World Series win for the first time ever in the borough.

All the Dodgers had to do was beat Whitey Ford. All Billy Conn had to do was beat Joe Louis. All Purdue and Indiana had to do was beat Notre Dame. All Hitler had to do was beat the British.

"I remember that game like it was yesterday," said Bill (Moose) Skowron, on a July 10, 2004 visit to Yankee Stadium for Old Timers Day. "The Dodgers sent that lefty out there so I had to be ready."

When Skowron joined the Yankees out of Purdue University as a famous football player in 1954, he could hit a ball hard but he couldn't field.

"Casey [Stengel] saw me working out at first base in spring training and immediately said I was a lousy dancer. *A lousy dancer?* What did that have to do with playing first base? But Casey always knew what he was doing. He said my footwork wasn't good enough to play in the big leagues. In those days, with no DH, you had to be able to play a position. Casey sent me to an Arthur Murray Dancing School in St. Petersburg where we trained. When we went back north he kept me in that school, this time in the Bronx, and I really improved my footwork. Then he got me hitting straight away instead of pulling everything. That made my career."

Skowron hit .340 as a Yankee rookie in 1954 as the Yankees failed to win a Series for the first time in six seasons. He hit .319 in 108 games as a platoon first baseman with Joe Collins in the pennant-winning season of 1955.

Spooner, a hard-throwing lefty, was the sixth-game pitcher for Brooklyn, and Skowron was the Yankee first baseman.

"Our scouts told us he threw high and hard," said Skowron. "We had seen him for a couple of innings in relief, so I knew what to expect."

Back home in the Stadium, the Yankees retired the Dodgers in the first inning of the sixth game with Ford striking out Reese and Snider.

Rizzuto walked to start the Yankees first. Billy Martin struck out as Rizzuto stole second. McDougald drew a walk. Berra and Bauer both singled for a 2-0 Yankee lead. That brought Skowron up.

"The guy was down 2-0 with two on and only one out. I knew he would throw a strike. He threw a high pitch and I went after it," Skowron recalled.

The ball sliced off the end of Skowron's bat and curved in a strange way toward the low right-field wall. The baseball cleared the wall by a couple of feet as Furillo raced over to try for it.

"It was high and outside," said Spooner after the game. "I didn't think he could reach it. I was setting him up for the inside pitch so I could get a ground ball and get out of the inning."

"Nah, it was up in my eyes," said Skowron almost 50 years later. "And it was inside a little, too. I just leaned back and inside-outed it to the short porch, just the way Casey taught me."

The ball crashed into the eight or ninth row of seats and the Yankees had a five-run lead on Skowron's three-run homer. Spooner also had a waiting shower as Russ Meyer relieved for the Dodgers, gave up a single to Bob Cerv, playing in place of the leg-troubled Mickey Mantle and retired Elston Howard and Ford.

Meyer and reliever Ed Roebuck would shut the Yankees down the rest of the way in the 5-1 Brooklyn loss.

"It's too bad we couldn't make a comeback against Ford, with Meyer doing that kind of pitching," manager Walter Alston said later in the quiet Brooklyn clubhouse. "Whitey pitched a good game, much too good for us to spot him five runs right at the start."

It was a World Series game. Of course, Whitey Ford would pitch a good game. He collected 10 World Series wins in his 22 World Series starts.

"I just liked the fun of a World Series start," said Ford, half a century later. "If you didn't get turned on by a World Series start, you were in the wrong business."

Ford allowed only four hits in his nine-inning performance and put the Dodgers in a dour mood after the loss.

The Dodgers had a history in those days of second-guessing Alston, and a key loss like this created a perfect situation. It might have been Robinson who said it, or Campanella or Snider or maybe even Reese, but a still-unidentified member of the team suggested that Alston didn't even put the best Brooklyn lineup on the field for the sixth game.

One of the Dodgers told Roscoe McGowen of *The Times* that he would have liked to see Don Zimmer starting at second base and Jim Gilliam starting in left field instead of Gilliam at second and left-handed-hitting Sandy Amoros in left against lefty Ford.

Gilliam was slow in covering second base on Rizzuto's first-inning steal and off the mark in chasing after Berra's ground-ball hit. Writers tried to give Gilliam an excuse but the classy Dodger said, "I just didn't get the ball Berra hit. There was no bad hop."

Spooner didn't suggest Gilliam's play cost him the game. Skowron's homer did. He answered a question about Berra's ground-ball hit by saying, "I guess I should have struck him out."

Spooner, a handsome lad, was already dressed in street clothes by the time the press was allowed into the Dodger locker room after the loss, ready to return to his Brooklyn hotel room at the Bossert.

The Brooklyn players walked slowly out of the locker room, headed down the ramp to the outside gate, climbed a few steps and walked towards the team bus outside.

Police officers guarded their entry onto the Greyhound bus as they boarded for the ride back to Ebbets Field where their cars were parked.

"The guys were down," remembered Johnny Podres, who was named the Brooklyn starter for the seventh game by Alston as soon as the sixth game ended. "I kidded around as I got on the bus. I wanted everybody to have a laugh. I had already beaten the Yankees in the third game. I didn't see any reason why I couldn't beat them again in the seventh game."

"Hey, we'll be all right tomorrow if you guys get me a few runs," Podres said.

Nobody answered the young left-hander. Then Pee Wee Reese, the Brooklyn captain and the one man who dated his Yankee disappointments back to 1941, looked up at the left-hander and quietly asked, "Will one run do?"

⚾ ⚾ ⚾

On July 25, 2004, the Baseball Hall of Fame inducted its latest members, Paul Molitor and Dennis Eckersley, in touching ceremonies in Cooperstown, New York.

Fifty living members of the Hall of Fame attended the weekend event. A few of them played with or against the 1955 Brooklyn Dodgers at Ebbets Field. I asked for their reminiscences of that experience.

"I remember after we clinched the pennant and we were going from Milwaukee to Chicago. We had two buses," Duke Snider said.

"[Manager] Alston said the guys who wanted to drink a little champagne could get on one bus and the other guys could get on the second bus. Everybody moved to the first bus. Alston and the driver were the only guys on the second bus. When we got to Wrigley Field for the next day's game Alston said all the regulars would start so they could stay sharp for the Series. I was feeling no pain. Ernie Banks hit a line drive and I saw two balls. I put up my glove and one ball nicked my nose. I caught it off the nick. I could have been another Babe Herman, famous in Brooklyn for getting hit on the head with a fly ball."

Ernie Banks said the Brooklyn fans were very supportive of the team. He said the knothole kids of Happy Felton really added to the atmosphere.

"They would be screaming all game but they understood and appreciated baseball. I liked the way they cheered for us if we made an exceptional play," says Banks. "I liked playing in Brooklyn and then playing the next series in the Polo Grounds in Manhattan. That way you could stay in New York City for a week or more and go to those great restaurants, the theater and all the tourist attractions. The Polo Grounds, with Leo Durocher, was fun, too."

"The Polo Grounds would have been a great place to test an atomic bomb," said Snider.

Harmon Killebrew saw only one game in Ebbets Field.

"I was a rookie with the Washington Senators in 1955 and we were in town for a series against the Yankees. We had an off day and I went over to Brooklyn. We didn't see much big-league baseball where I grew up in Idaho. We did hear the games on the radio with Al Helfer doing the broadcasting. The Dodgers were my favorite team and Pee Wee Reese was my favorite player. I go to this game in Brooklyn and somebody hits a popup to shortstop. Pee Wee goes back and then he drops it. I didn't know if I was good enough to play in the big leagues then but when the great Pee Wee Reese dropped a fly ball I figured *anybody* could make an error, maybe even me. I thought maybe I could play in the big leagues."

"I played my first Series game in Brooklyn at Ebbets Field in 1953 against the Dodgers," said Whitey Ford. "I was from Queens and all my family came to the game. I had to buy 20 or 30 tickets. I pitched one inning and they knocked me out. That was embarrassing. I tried to keep it from my family that I was pitching the sixth game in 1955. I was able to win that one to tie the Series."

"It was always more fun to play against the Dodgers at the Polo Grounds or Ebbets Field," said Willie Mays. "We beat them in 1951, and then I was in the Army in 1952 and 1953. I probably lost about 80 homers those two years but winning was more important to me than individual numbers. I learned about that when I was a kid playing with the Birmingham Black Barons."

Mays said the neighborhood kids would watch him come home after a game in Brooklyn and go up to his apartment on 155th Street.

"A bunch of kids would come up with me and put me to bed. They would watch me fall asleep before they left. No kidding. I think they were betting on the games. If they saw me go to bed and knew I was getting my rest they would bet on me and the Giants. If I was out somewhere they would bet on the Dodgers."

Mays said the fans in Ebbets Field really took the game seriously.

"One day I hit a home run and had two or three other hits. We beat Brooklyn bad. Across the street from the park, where we parked our cars, in 1955, I had this green Cadillac. I came out after that game and they had slashed my tires. The only visiting guy they liked and left alone there was the Stan 'The Man' Musial. He could do anything against Brooklyn and get away with it."

Mays said that baseball fans always talk about his 1954 World Series catch off the bat of Vic Wertz of Cleveland as his best catch. Mays disagrees.

"My best catch was against Bobby Morgan in Ebbets Field in 1952 before I went off to the service. He was a pinch hitter for Brooklyn and hit a huge drive to right center. I raced over and caught the ball just as I was hitting the wall. It knocked me out. When I looked up Leo Durocher and Jackie Robinson were staring down at me. Leo wanted to see if I was still alive and Jackie wanted to make sure I held on to the ball."

Monte Irvin, a New York Giants teammate of Mays, recalled how he also ran out to the outfield to see how his pal was after the crash.

"Buck, Buck, are you all right?" Irvin asked in a frightened voice.

"Just resting," replied Mays.

Yogi Berra saw Ebbets Field for the first time in the World Series of 1947.

"I got on the subway with two teammates, Billy Johnson and Spec Shea, and we took the train over to the ball park. Nobody bothered us. I had just come up. Nobody knew us."

Berra said he liked playing in Ebbets Field, and by 1955 when he was a Yankee star, he began complaining a little.

"The clubhouse was too small and by then we came on the bus from the stadium. The wives could ride the bus, so Carmen got on with me and she pointed out all the sights in Brooklyn. I forgot what they were," he said.

Yogi played in two Series in Brooklyn, 1947 and 1949, with teammate Joe DiMaggio.

"I remember Joe talking about how much he loved the park," Berra said. "Even when we won in 1955 and Joe was long retired he said to me, 'Boy, if I had played here.' He knew he was a perfect Ebbets Field hitter."

Robin Roberts was the National League-leading winner with 23 victories in 1955. He always loved Ebbets Field, even that great Brooklyn year.

"We had beaten the Dodgers in the last game of the 1950 season when Cal Abrams was thrown out at home by Richie Ashburn. We went to the World Series against the Yankees and that was my favorite season. Even in '55 I won more games in Brooklyn than in Connie Mack Stadium in Philadelphia. The only way to pitch in Brooklyn was to get ahead of the hitters, don't walk anybody and stay away from the three-run homer. I think I gave up more homers than anybody in my time, but I didn't give up many three-run homers," Roberts said.

Monte Irvin remembers that shortly after Jackie Robinson's signing to break baseball's color line in 1945, he was almost signed by the Dodgers.

"I had been in the war and was still a little shaky over it," Irvin said. "The Dodgers wanted to sign me for the next season. The owner of our team, Effa Manley, said she had a $5,000 deal with Brooklyn. She wanted more but Branch Rickey wouldn't give her any more. Then the Giants came along and offered the same $5,000. This time she took it.

I asked her if I would get any of that sale money to go up to the Giants. She said, 'No, I'm buying a new fur stole with that money.' Sure enough, in 1973, when we had a reunion of Negro League players, there she was wearing the fur stole she got with my money."

Irvin said he loved the excitement of playing in Ebbets Field. He played in only 51 games with a .253 average in 1955 as age and injuries took their toll.

"It was always fun to have the Dodger Sym-phony play us back to our seats on the bench. I tried dozens of times to fake them out, start to sit and jump up, but I never could do it. In 1955 they got me every time without a fight. I was too old by then to fight back."

"Holy cow, Ebbets Field and the 1955 Dodgers," Phil Rizzuto said. "I had been turned down by the Dodgers. Casey Stengel was the manager, and he told me I was too small and I should get a shoebox and forget baseball. But I tried out with the Giants and then the Yankees and the Yankees signed me. They were smarter than the other teams, right? The '55 Series was disappointing because they beat us and I always wanted to beat Brooklyn. Podres won that last game for the title. Mickey was injured and didn't play. It night have been different if Mickey was in the lineup that last day."

ββββ

"Brooklyn's long-cherished dream finally has come true," John Drebinger wrote in *The Times* after the Brooklyn Dodgers won the 1955 World Series. *"The Dodgers have won their first World Series championship.*

"The end of the trail came at the Stadium yesterday. Smokey Alston's Brooks, with Johnny Podres tossing a brilliant shutout, turned back Casey Stengel's Yankees, 2-0, in the seventh and deciding game of the 1955 baseball classic."

"They won't make October 4 a red-letter day in Brooklyn," wrote Joe Trimble in the *Daily News. "They'll print it in letters of gold from now on because it is only the greatest day in the history of the batty borough—the day those darling Dodgers finally won the World Series. At exactly 3:45 yesterday afternoon at the Stadium, the Brooks got the third out of a 2-0 victory over the Yankees in the seventh and deciding game."*

Trimble pointed out in his article that on October 4, 1861, the Union forces massed to form the Army of the Potomac and the Erie Railroad opened (probably not on time). On that date in 1940, Hitler and Mussolini met at the Brenner Pass. On October 4, 1944, the U.S. Army broke through the German west wall. On October 4, 1944, beloved New York governor Al Smith died.

"As far as Brooklyn is concerned, nothing could match the events of yesterday when all the years of frustration and defeat were wiped out in one blazing afternoon," Trimble wrote.

The immortal tabloid front page of the New York *Daily News* for October 5, 1955 simply read, *WHO'S A BUM!* above Leo O'Mealla's howling cartoon of the classic Brooklyn bum.

"I guess I read every word of every newspaper story about the game in my hotel room at the Bossert the next day," Johnny Podres said in 2004 as he sat on his living room couch at home in Queensbury, New York. "I couldn't get enough of it."

Podres had driven over to Ebbets Field for the bus trip to Yankee Stadium that October 4 morning from his aunt's home in Staten Island. Gil Hodges parked his car across the street from Ebbets Field and climbed on the team bus. Pee Wee Reese, Don Zimmer, Carl Erskine and Rube Walker shared a ride as they always did. It was Reese's turn to drive.

Joan Hodges came with several family members and sat in the stands at the Stadium more than two hours before the game. Rachel Robinson, Dottie Reese and Bev Snider sat next to each other in the family section behind the third-base side visitor's dugout.

"I was so nervous before the game I could hardly catch my breath," Joan Hodges remembered as she sat in her Brooklyn living room in 2004. "I never thought about losing the game. I was sure we would win. I just thought of fainting from the excitement."

The Yankees were a pretty cocky bunch before the game started.

"We always won the World Series against Brooklyn," said Phil Rizzuto on a Stadium visit in 2004. "I didn't think that Series would be any different."

"I was all set for a golf date the next afternoon. I wouldn't have made it if I didn't think we would win," recalled Yogi Berra as he sat in the offices of his Museum at the Montclair State University.

Left-hander Tommy Byrne got the Dodgers out in order in the first inning with Gilliam grounding out, Reese flying out and Snider grounding out.

Dodger fans, among the 62,465 in the Stadium, gasped at the efficiency of the Yankees. Was this going to be another mortal blow for the Dodgers, overwhelmed by a left-hander when they were supposed to murder left-handers with all that right-handed power?

Podres was sharp in the first as he set the Yankees down in order.

"I didn't throw one changeup that inning. That was the pitch they were looking for after my first Series victory," Podres remembered. "I had used the changeup a lot, but I talked to Campy before the game and he said we should just go with the hard stuff early. They won't be expecting it."

The game stayed scoreless through three innings. Then Campanella doubled with one out, moved up on Furillo's grounder and scored on a line single to the left by Gil Hodges.

"All I could think of was the terror of Gil's 1952 Series when he didn't get a hit. Now he knocked in the first run. If that held up he would be the hero," said Joan Hodges. "I just started praying harder."

The sixth inning turned the game. Not so much for the run the Dodgers scored but because of the substitution Walter Alston made.

Reese started the Brooklyn sixth with a single. Snider bunted and was safe when Skowron dropped Byrne's low throw. Campanella bunted and both runners moved up.

Furillo was walked intentionally and Stengel decided to bring in righty Bob Grim to pitch to right-handed slugger Gil Hodges. Hodges hit Grim's second pitch for a long fly ball to center, and Reese scored easily on the sacrifice.

"Now I *really* thought it might happen. We really might win," said Joan Hodges, "and Gil had knocked in two of the runs."

Grim threw a wild pitch and Furillo moved to second as Snider held third. Don Hoak walked to load the bases.

Alston decided he could put the game away now with a base hit. He sent George Shuba up to hit for Don Zimmer. A base hit would give the Dodgers a four-run lead, and with Labine ready in the bullpen the Dodgers could lock it all up.

Shuba hit a hard ground ball right at Skowron. The big Moose collared it and threw over to Grim at first for the final out of the inning. The Dodgers would take a 2-0 lead into the bottom of the sixth.

First Alston had to replace Zimmer at second base. He brought Gilliam in from left and sent Sandy Amoros out to left field for the Yankee sixth.

"I liked that," said Podres. "I knew Sandy had great speed in left."

Billy Martin, the Yankees' famous overachiever, walked. McDougald laid down a surprise bunt and beat it out for a hit. Dangerous Yogi Berra, one of the game's most renowned clutch hitters, was up. He hit a half fly/half line drive to left field.

"I turned and saw it floating out there and I was sure it was an out," Podres recalled. "Then it began dying and curving away towards the rail. I saw Sandy chase it with his right hand outstretched for the ball. I wasn't sure if he would reach it. But thankfully he did."

He not only caught the ball, he fired a quick relay to Reese who fired to first as McDougald, who had advanced almost to second base, certain the ball would drop in. Hodges leaned into the infield, collected the throw from Pee Wee and recorded the second out for a double play. Bauer rolled out to Reese to end the mini-threat.

The Yankees sent the injured Mantle up as a pinch hitter for Grim in the seventh, and Mickey popped out to shortstop.

"Sure it might have been different if Mickey played the entire game," Podres said. "But maybe I would have struck him out a couple of times. Mickey struck out a lot, you know."

Rizzuto singled in the eighth, and McDougald singled after one out. With two on and one out, Labine was throwing hard in the bullpen. Berra hit a changeup (Podres started throwing a few in the late innings) to Furillo, and Bauer struck out.

Hodges fouled out to start the Brooklyn ninth, and Hoak singled to center. Amoros walked and the Dodgers had two on with one out. Podres was the hitter. Or was he?

"Some guys on the bench thought Alston was looking around for a hitter in the spot and he could finish with Labine. It never happened. I went up there, flew out and came back to the bench," Podres said.

Gilliam ended the inning with a fly ball.

Now it was the bottom of the ninth. Three outs to go. Three outs to Valhalla for long-suffering Brooklyn fans. Skowron grounded out. Cerv flew out. Rookie Howard, the first Negro on the Yankees eight years after Jackie Robinson broke in with Brooklyn, was at the plate.

He hit a Podres changeup to shortstop. Reese, who had played the position from Brooklyn for 15 years, fielded it cleanly. He threw to Hodges at first and the ball began to sink. Hodges, an artist around the bag, leaned to his left and caught the throw for the final out of the final game in the most joyous inning in Brooklyn history.

"I just burst into tears," Joan Hodges recalled.

"I squeezed Dottie Reese's hand so hard I thought I would hurt her," Rachel Robinson remembers.

"I leaped off the ground. I thought I could stay in the air forever," said Podres.

The borough of Brooklyn exploded with joy. People raced into the street to share the triumph with neighbors. Wall Street brokers opened windows and filled the air with confetti. School kids raced home to share the experience with neighbors. In Witherbee, New York, Johnny Podres' mom cried with the last out and cried and cried and cried as friends walked into her home to share her joy. Podres' father sat outside Yankee Stadium in his car for a long time, too emotional to connect with his son and congratulate him on the greatest Brooklyn victory of all time.

The Dodgers had raced into the clubhouse by now. There were the strange sensations of both tension and joy. There was not much cheering. Mostly it was silence as Pee Wee Reese stared at his locker.

The Dodgers knew they could win this one. They just didn't know quite how to handle it when it happened.

A Flag Flies in Brooklyn

The glow lasted all winter after the 1955 Brooklyn Dodgers World Series championship. For years, Yankee fans had tortured Brooklyn fans waiting for the early editions of the *News* and the *Mirror* at candy stores around the borough. Now Brooklyn kids stuck their fingers out at the hated Yankee fans. At the Bay Ridge bars, no one could ever get enough of Brooklyn baseball talk, especially about that handsome, cocky kid from upstate named Johnny Podres who *could* walk on water. The kids who ran the three batters/six hits betting pools all over Brooklyn junior high schools prepared their dimes for the next winning season. Women in babushkas on Bushwick Avenue bantered about the Dodgers, not so much about the title but more about how happy their kids were and how cute that pitcher was.

One ominous note filtered through the media. The Dodgers under owner Walter O'Malley were committed to a new stadium for the team. But where?

"Right now the matter is pretty much out of our hands," O'Malley told the press. "But I don't see how anyone would want to see the Dodgers leaving Brooklyn. Certainly we don't want to go anywhere else and I am now more confident than ever that something will work out which will enable us to build a new home befitting world champions."

O'Malley had this dream of a new Ebbets Field at Atlantic and Flatbush Avenues in Brooklyn, a site adjacent to the Long Island railroad station serving potential suburban fans.

"There were even plans drawn up for a domed stadium, an idea way ahead of its time," said Peter O'Malley, retired Dodger owner and son of the owner of the championship Brooklyn team.

Peter O'Malley, a native of Brooklyn, has been a strong force in keeping the connection between the Brooklyn and Los Angeles Dodgers as alive and viable as possible. He was a student at the University of Pennsylvania during that momentous 1955 season.

"Nobody in our family, nobody around the club in those days could possibly forget the joy that championship brought to all of us," O'Malley said from his Los Angeles office in 2004.

Peter O'Malley took over the team in 1979 after his father's death and sold it to News Corp in 1997. News Corp sold it quickly to Boston real estate magnate Frank McCourt in 2004.

⌐ ⌐ ⌐

All of the 1955 Dodgers were enjoying the most exciting off-season of their lives. Podres was the hero of a parade in his honor before his friends and family. In Witherbee and Mineville almost all of the 2,384 folks in those hamlets were out in the streets to greet him. Clem Labine got the same sort of greeting in Woonsocket, Rhode Island. Pee Wee Reese was feted in Louisville. Jackie Robinson and Roy Campanella were honored in St. Albans, Queens.

Bill DeLury, who was hired in the Dodger office in 1950, served as ticket manager and road secretary for the Dodgers before assuming his current part-time job as an assistant in the Dodgers broadcasting department.

"I was sitting in the Brooklyn office seats down the left-field line in 1955 when Podres won the seventh game. I still remember the catch Amoros made. If he doesn't make it we lose to the Yankees again," DeLury said.

In 2004 he returned to Brooklyn for a visit to the Bossert Hotel where the Dodgers partied after the win.

"It's not a hotel any more. It's a religious residence, but it is still standing. I walked around the area and it brought back a lot of memories. I have that '55 ring in a vault. When I die I want to be buried with it," DeLury said.

DeLury serves as an office assistant to Hall of Fame broadcaster Vin Scully.

In his 55th year with the Dodgers, Scully easily recalled the joys of the 1955 Brooklyn World Series triumph. It made up for the heartbreak of the 1951 playoff to the New York Giants.

"I started broadcasting in 1950 out of Fordham on a one-month option contract," Scully said. "I was standing behind Red Barber and Connie Desmond in the Polo Grounds booth at the 1951 game in case either of them couldn't go on. It was a gag line I have used for more than 50 years. I tell everybody I couldn't take that game lying down. Red made the quick call when Bobby [Thomson] hit it and then shut up. He let the crowd noise tell the story. I walked into the clubhouse later and saw Ralph [Branca] sprawled on the stairs. My heart was breaking for him. I had violated one of Red's commandments. 'Never get close to a player.' Ralph was my closest friend. Jackie Robinson and Pee Wee Reese were in the trainer's room. Pee Wee said, 'You know, Jack, the one thing about this game that keeps it from driving me crazy, there's always tomorrow.' Ralph was a tower of strength through all this."

Scully took over as the number-one Brooklyn broadcaster when Barber left after the 1953 season to join the Yankees. The Brooklyn Dodgers didn't win in 1954, but 1955 and Johnny Podres made up for everything.

The Dodgers could enjoy that winter of 1955 because their first Brooklyn World Series winning share amounted to a hefty $9,768 while the LOSING Yankees received $5,598. Would Alex Rodriguez have bothered to cash a check that small?

The Yankees soon took off on a six-week exhibition tour of the Far East while many of the Dodger players showed up for exhibition games near their own hometowns for a few extra dollars. The average Dodger salary on the 1955 team was $22,000.

As the 1956 season approached, the Dodgers needed some fine-tuning. The anchor players of the team, Reese, Robinson, Hodges, Snider, Campanella, Furillo, Newcombe were sliding the other way. Randy Jackson had become the third baseman. A kid named Don Drysdale was a hot prospect at 19 but not yet a big winner. Koufax was still in the dark, early stages of his future Hall of Fame career.

The Dodgers won 93 games and beat Milwaukee out for the National League pennant by one game. It was Brooklyn's sixth pennant in 10 seasons.

They faced the Yankees, of course, and lost another seven-game series. Don Larsen beat Sal (the Barber) Maglie with a perfect game in the fifth game, Jackie Robinson singled in the 10th inning to win the sixth game, and Johnny Kucks beat Brooklyn with a 9-0 shutout in the seventh game.

It almost didn't matter in Brooklyn. We'll always have 1955.

⚾ ⚾ ⚾

The Dodgers bought the Los Angeles club of the Pacific Coast League. They gained approval for a move west, after all negotiations failed in Brooklyn, due mostly to the tyranny of Parks Commissioner Robert Moses who wanted the Dodgers in Queens. How ridiculous was that? It all ended on September 24, 1957. The Dodgers were a third-place team.

Roger Craig, who helped save the 1955 Dodgers, pitched the last game for Brooklyn in Philadelphia.

Dodger executives took off for their new horizons, Chavez Ravine, Los Angeles, California.

The Dodgers started their California careers in the Los Angeles Coliseum and soon were playing in a jewel of a ballpark—Dodger Stadium, 1000 Elysian Park Avenue, Los Angeles.

They fell to seventh in 1958 and, incredibly, won again in their second year in Los Angeles. The Dodgers defeated the Chicago White Sox in the 1959 World Series for the first Los Angeles title, just four years after their 1955 triumph.

Press headquarters was at the downtown Biltmore Hotel in Los Angeles. Reporters gathered after each game in Los Angeles for drinks, food, chatter, gossip and a little exchange of information.

After work was done and stories were filed back to their home offices, sportswriters from around the country sat around press headquarters and compared notes on the games.

Don Drysdale won the first Los Angeles World Series game, reliever Larry Sherry won the next day and Bob Shaw outpitched Sandy Koufax 1-0 in the fifth game of the Series. The teams and the press would travel to Chicago for the last game of the Series the next day.

On Sunday night in Los Angeles, several hundred boisterous and enthusiastic media types, advertisers, baseball officials, friends, families and professional hotel hangers-on filled the Biltmore Hotel ballroom and ate Walter O'Malley's elegant spread.

By midnight with the food almost gone, drinks slowing down and the conversation running low, only a handful of sportswriters remained.

Four of them studied a huge banner on the left wall of the hotel ballroom. It was the championship banner of the 1955 Brooklyn Dodgers, 17 feet long, in block style, with large blue letters on a white background reading, WORLD CHAMPIONS 1955 DODGERS. For some strange reason, the word "BROOKLYN" did not appear on the flag. It flew on a pole in Ebbets Field in 1956 and 1957 and traveled with the Dodgers to Los Angeles. Before the demolition of Ebbets Field in 1960, the flagpole remained behind and was purchased in the Ebbets Field garage sale by a Brooklyn church for $24, the original price of Manhattan Island in the deal with the Indians.

One sportswriter, in particular, was irritated by the site of the Brooklyn championship flag in a Los Angeles hotel ballroom. That was Stan Isaacs, a witty and wonderful writer for *Newsday*, in Long Island, New York, a growing suburban newspaper. Isaacs had been born and raised in Brooklyn. He had a quirky sense of humor but had no loyalty to the Dodgers. Most of the kids in his Williamsburg neighborhood were Brooklyn fans and that caused conflict for Stan right from the start. In the 1930s, he had fallen in love with Mel Ott of the Giants, a high-kicking home-run hitter who sat on the New York bench next to managerial icon John McGraw while learning his trade.

Isaacs was so enamored with Ott that he visited his birthplace in the tiny town of Gretna, Louisiana, probably the only New York sportswriter ever to do that. There was nothing at Ott's gravesite to show what a great player he was. Unhappy with the fact that the city fathers were unappreciative of their local hero, Isaacs raised a rumpus. This was a funny can-do guy.

On this night in Los Angeles he sat with his boss, sports editor Jack Mann, a hard-drinking talented writer and complained as he stared at the banner, "What makes them think that flag belongs out here?"

Isaacs and Mann decided it did not. It belonged only one place. In Brooklyn. How to get it there and who, if anybody, should they ask about it?

They were joined by two other sportswriters, Chuck Sutton, a Brooklyn native now working in Long Beach, California, and Steve Weller, a Buffalo sportswriter understanding the right of recall of the banner.

"We weren't drunk," Isaacs later insisted in a *Daily News* interview with columnist Vic Ziegel. "This was an act of principle, not inebriation."

The press crowd had dwindled down to these four sportswriters. The Dodger officials were gone. Even the freeloaders were home now with their stolen press badges and hotel salt shakers. Petty thievery was a part of the milieu. Sportswriter Jack Lang of the *Long Island Press* once envisioned stealing a huge, handsome pepper mill from a fashionable San Francisco restaurant called The Blue Fox. When asked how this could be accomplished before such a huge restaurant crowd Lang replied, "I'll walk out holding hands with Tommy Holmes. This is San Francisco. Nobody will notice." Holmes, unrelated to the famed baseball player of the same name, was a one-armed sportswriter. The pepper mill was to be secreted up his sleeve.

On that eventful 1959 night in Los Angeles, all the two-armed sportswriters decided to just go for the banner. They walked to the sidewall, told the Mexican crew cleaning up the room they were from the *Herald-Tribune,* borrowed a pair of scissors from the workers and climbed up on a table.

Isaacs, Brooklyn curmudgeon and believer in right, climbed atop the two tables that had been placed one atop the other—high enough to reach the cords holding the banner and cut away.

"We gave it to Chuck Sutton to hold overnight," Isaacs said in 2004. "We figured if the Dodgers found it missing they would come after a New York sportswriter—not a California one."

There was a surreptitious banner exchange the next day at L.A. airport with Isaacs stuffing the 17-foot flag into his carry-on bag for the flight to Chicago.

Larry Sherry closed the White Sox down for the Series the next day, recording his second win to go with his two saves for the 4-2 Los Angeles Dodgers' first Series win.

Isaacs kept his bag next to him for a quick getaway.

"I got home to Roslyn Heights the next day after the game and my wife, Bobbie, wrapped it and put it in a plastic container. That's where it stayed for 10 years. We figured out how to get it out of L.A. but we didn't figure out what to do with it next."

Isaacs visited the Baseball Hall of Fame at Cooperstown and told his old pal, sportswriter Kenny Smith, now working for the Hall in Cooperstown, about the flag escapade. He explained that the flag was still in his Long Island basement. It was seen by nobody. He thought it deserved better.

"Kenny said he would take it and put it on display in Cooperstown," Isaacs said. "We also agreed that if, in the future, Brooklyn had a fitting place for the flag, it would be moved and displayed there."

The Hall of Fame was planning a display of old Stadium memorabilia. The flag would be a perfect centerpiece. It finally did get a distinguished spot at the Hall of Fame Museum in Cooperstown in the 1970s.

Enter Marty Adler. An assistant principal at the Jackie Robinson Junior High School, he had created by dint of his own energy and passion a Brooklyn Dodgers Hall of Fame. Players were named each year in impressive Brooklyn ceremonies. National Hall of Famers from Cooperstown were admitted automatically. The other players like Gil Hodges, Carl Furillo, Gene Hermanski, Ralph Branca and so many others who brought joy to Ebbets Field through the years were elected. Even sportswriters devoted to the Dodgers, such as myself and Isaacs, the Giants fan, gained the honor.

Adler thought the flag should go to the Brooklyn Hall of Fame. Isaacs agreed. The only problem was that the Brooklyn Hall of Fame existed in Adler's home and not in any public building.

When Isaacs asked the Cooperstown Hall of Fame's new curator, Bill Guilfoile, former Yankee PR director, for the Brooklyn flag to be shipped to Adler, Guilfoile demurred. He knew nothing of the Isaacs agreement with Smith about the banner coming home when Brooklyn had a home for it. There was no building, but Adler had an organization and dreamed of a future site, in the Brooklyn Historical Society.

Peter O'Malley, son of the championship owner, emerged as the hero of the epic. He persuaded authorities at Cooperstown to return the championship banner to its rightful site at the Brooklyn Historical Society.

The flag was finally delivered there but had not been seen much publicly. The Society had been undergoing renovations and no real proper site for display had been selected. All that was accomplished in 2005 after the 50th anniversary.

When Fred Wilpon, a Brooklyn native and former teammate of Sandy Koufax at Lafayette High, acquired the New York Mets, he vowed a return to Brooklyn. He lived up to the promise with the creation of a minor-league franchise in Coney Island, the Brooklyn Cyclones. The Brooklyn Dodgers Hall of Fame is located in a side wing of the charming KeySpan Park.

Isaacs said he once asked former Dodger general manager Buzzie Bavasi why he never came looking for the flag when it disappeared from the 1959 Dodgers hotel ballroom site.

"Why bother? We had another one made. It only cost $92," he told Isaacs.

So now the championship flags of the Dodgers, the 1955 flag, the 1959 flag, the 1963 flag, the 1965 flag, the 1981 flag and the 1988 flag fly proudly over Dodger Stadium.

The one flag that really counts to millions, the real 1955 championship banner, is on display at the Brooklyn Historical Society.

It also flew free from a pole held by several members of the 1955 Dodgers—Podres, Zimmer, Snider and Labine, in a 2005 Brooklyn 50th anniversary parade.

Brooklyn of the Mind

"Hey, Brooklyn," they used to yell at me when I was a soldier boy in Japan, sitting around the barracks in those desperate days of 1955, wondering if this might really be the year it happened.

The Dodgers were winning another easy pennant that year and I stayed up to date with the team's progress through *Armed Forces Radio* and *Pacific Stars and Stripes* newspaper.

Could the Dodgers beat the Yankees in the World Series?

Brooklyn is a borough, one of five in the great City of New York. I never heard anyone called Manhattan or Bronx or Queens or Staten Island in my Army days or any days since.

I never heard anyone called Detroit or Chicago or Pittsburgh or Los Angeles or Dubuque or Boston in those days or these days.

What *was* it about Brooklyn? Why did it gain that attention, that separation, that distinction, that recognition that no other hometown ever achieved? Mention Brooklyn as a hometown on a radio program and the audience howled. Cast a character from Brooklyn in a silly comedy or serious film drama and attention was paid.

Maybe it was the Dodgers, maybe it wasn't. Boston had two teams and so did Chicago. St. Louis won a lot.

The Yankees played in The Bronx. So what!

Brooklyn. It had a ring, uniqueness, a coda, a *je ne sais qua* that no other place had. You'd meet a guy from Brooklyn in a London pub and smile. Run across a Parisian charmer in a Paris café and everything got easier when the Brooklyn ID was revealed. Why, why, why?

No real answers. That's the way it was.

They are all from Brooklyn and share the link—New York City mayor Rudy Giuliani, senator Charles Schumer, ball players Sandy Koufax and Chuck Connors, entertainers and actors by the dozens, including Mel Brooks, maybe the funniest man ever. Alan King and broadcaster Larry King, Harvey Keitel and singer Robert Merrill, television icon Jerry Seinfeld, comedians Joan Rivers, Dom DeLuise and Woody Allen—all are from Brooklyn. Then there is writer Pete Hamill, novelist Irwin Shaw, actress Mary Tyler Moore, entertainer Mickey Rooney, Betty Comden, Pat Benatar, Vic Damone, Louis Gossett Jr. and Elliot Gould. There was Gould's former wife, Barbra Streisand, and the legendary Lena Horne, a star at 19 in segregated America, Paul Mazursky, Rhea Perlman, opera's Beverly Sills, Connie Stevens, Brenda Vaccaro and Eli Wallach. Even Michael Jordan, identified as a North Carolinian by his Chicago team, was born in Brooklyn.

Mae West and Rita Hayworth were from Brooklyn, and sports heroes Red Auerbach, Len Wilkens and Fuzzy Levane were born there. Big-league pitcher Harry Eisenstat, Olympian Marty Glickman, football Hall of Famer Sid Luckman and show business and sports impresario David A. (Sonny) Werblin were Brooklyn natives. Baseball player association executive Marvin Miller learned his negotiating in Brooklyn.

So actors, athletes, entertainers, movie stars and writers come from everywhere. Does anyone care? Are they linked? Never.

And so many of them recalled that October 4, 1955 afternoon when Johnny Podres walked on water, when Pee Wee Reese lifted from the ground, when Jackie Robinson, Duke Snider, Roy Campanella, Carl Furillo, Don Newcombe, Carl Erskine, Clem Labine, Don Zimmer, Gil Hodges, Sandy Amoros and the rest brought Valhalla to Brooklyn.

"I was thrilled," broadcaster Larry King said. "I could finally forget 1951 when I wanted to commit suicide by jumping off the Brooklyn Bridge but I figured the line would be too long."

"With the last out we ran into the streets at Sterling Place, just a long fly ball from Ebbets Field," said Marty Hanfling, a longtime business executive and musician. "It was madness. We had done it. We had finally won. It was now OK that I stayed up late for all those night games until I could see the lights go down at Ebbets Field. A cousin of mine even became part of a game because he was wearing a visor while watching the game from his roof. It was shining in Duke Snider's eyes across the street. The cops had to come to the roof to make him take the visor off."

"I was a senior at Brooklyn College," said retired teacher Phyllis Kusinitz Cash, "and the people ran into the streets yelling and smiling and pounding at each other. The streets of Brooklyn were like a mosaic of people."

Bob Rosen, a statistician for the famed record keeper Elias Sports, had seen his first Brooklyn game on June 11, 1944.

"We were scheduled to go, my dad and I, June 6, 1944. That was D-Day. They called all the games off and we were told to pray for the troops. We went five days later. I fell in love with the Dodgers. On October 4, 1955, I was a student at Brooklyn College. I got home from school for the last two innings . . . 'Howard hits a ground ball to shortstop . . . Pee Wee has it . . . The throw . . . in time . . . The Brooklyn Dodgers are the World Champions.' There has never been a moment like it. We were sad in my house that week. My grandmother, Anna Brauner, had died that week. Now we could smile again."

Alan Boroff was out of the Army and at Harvard Law School. He had grown up in Bensonhurst.

"I brought the radio to school and listened to the game. What a thrill! The only other times I ever brought the radio to school was when Sandy Koufax was pitching. I had to hear every inning of every game. I can still hear that final game," Boroff said.

Joel Martin, a Philadelphia native, was serving in the Coast Guard at the New York docks on that October day in 1955.

"I heard the boat horns go off and the fire whistles and all the engines clanging and the bells ringing in the river. I looked out from my office window across the water to the Brooklyn docks and it was packed with people all screaming and dancing and jumping around. It was a wild scene. I had never experienced anything like it. Then people in my office began yelling, 'The Dodgers won the series, the Dodgers won the series!' It was unbelievable. All these years later, half a century later I can still hear those boat horns and all that screaming," Martin said.

Dr. Alvin Ehrlich of 440 Lenox Road in Flatbush was six in 1941 when the Yankees beat the Dodgers in the first of a string of World Series setbacks for Brooklyn.

"We were all Dodger fans then, of course, but my uncle came over to the house after that last 1941 game and told us the Yankees beat the Dodgers in the Series," Ehrlich recalled. "I burst into tears."

He then announced to his family after the tears ceased that from that day on he would be a Yankee fan.

"I wanted to root for a winner," he said.

It happened to some.

He was home in Brooklyn from Lafayette College in 1955 when the Dodgers finally won.

"All the noise in the streets didn't bother me," he said. "I knew we would probably win again the next year."

James McDonald, director of security for HBO, was a student at Brooklyn Technical High School.

"We ran out of the school, down to the nearby barber shop. I heard it there. I can remember every pitch, every pitch. No game could possibly compare to that," McDonald said.

Artie Balomey, a Grumman Aircraft builder, went to the first night game at Ebbets Field in 1938. Cincinnati's Johnny Vander Meer pitched a no-hitter.

"After that I was hooked on the Dodgers. I heard every game. I was at the factory in Beth Page, Long Island that October day. We just listened and listened. When Howard came up the line stopped. When he hit the last ground ball out the world stopped. Nothing else was ever like that," he said.

Betty Carter, a nationally known family therapist, recalled her days as a Brooklyn Catholic schoolgirl more than half a century ago.

"We were all in the auditorium one day and the Mother Superior came on the stage. She told us the Brooklyn Dodgers had two runs on base and Pee Wee Reese was up. 'I want all of you to say 10 Hail Marys.' Then she left the stage. A few minutes later she returned. She had the largest smile on her face I had ever seen. 'Pee Wee doubled and both runners scored,' she informed us. She turned once again and left the stage. She was a happy woman."

And now it is time for me to remember. It was at Camp Drake, Tokyo, Japan. The date was actually October 5, 1955, because of the International Dateline I had crossed by ship on the way to Army duty. It was 4:45 a.m. The snores and heavy breathing by 48 guys from Fargo, North Dakota; Denver, Detroit, Los Angeles, Augusta, Maine, Plattsburgh, New York and Columbus, Ohio could easily be heard. The cleaning boys, the papa-sans, elderly men we paid to clean our Army barracks, quietly drank tea on the corner floor of the building. The charge of quarters would not blow reveille for another 45 minutes.

An Army footlocker sat in the center of the floor. It was covered with $200 in GI script, the $100 that was my full net worth and the $100 put up against it by the others.

"Ahh, Brooklyn, forget it," one soldier said before he pulled a GI blanket over his head. "The Dodgers never win."

I kept the radio low all through the night. All the guys slept. I listened. The Dodgers lead 2-0. It is the ninth inning. Skowron grounds out. I lick my lips. Cerv flies out. I crack my knuckles and hold my hands together. Howard is up. Howard swings. Howard hits a ground ball to shortstop. The sound of the radio is clear. I hear the words, *"Brooklyn Dodgers win . . ."*

There is a computer chip in my brain holding that game report. It never leaves me. It was with me on my wedding day, on the day my kids were born, on the day grandchildren entered my life. It is with me half a century later.

The Brooklyn Dodgers defeat the New York Yankees. The Brooklyn Dodgers are World Champions.

In less than two years they were on their way to Los Angeles. Who cares? October 4, 1955. It can never be taken away from us.

Maury Allen is the author of more than 30 books on baseball, including best sellers on Joe DiMaggio and Casey Stengel and rambunctious biographies of Billy Martin and playboy Bo Belinsky. He has been a working sportswriter for nearly half a century with time as a columnist for the *New York Post*, the *Gannett Journal News* and other newspapers. He has written hundreds of magazine articles and made frequent appearances on radio and television as a baseball expert.

Allen has won many prizes for his work through the years and is a member of many sports Hall of Fame, including the Brooklyn Dodgers Hall of Fame, an emotional landmark for this Brooklyn-born author.

Brooklyn Remembered: The 1955 Days of the Dodgers is his first book on his favorite team.

Also by Maury Allen

Yankees: Where Have You Gone?	*The Incredible Mets*
Our Mickey (with Bill Liederman)	*Joe Namath's Sportin' Life*
All Roads Lead to October	*Reprieve from Hell*
China Spy	*Ten Great Moments in Sports*
Jackie Robinson: A Life Remembered	*The Record Breakers*
Ron Guidry: Louisiana Lightning	*Memories of the Mick*
After the Miracle	*Jim Rice: Power Hitter*
Roger Maris: A Man for All Seasons	*Greatest Pro Quarterbacks*
Sweet Lou (with Lou Piniella)	*Baseball's 100*
Mr. October: The Reggie Jackson Story	*You Could Look It Up*
Damn Yankee: The Billy Martin Story	*Big-Time Baseball*
Where Have You Gone, Joe DiMaggio?	*Bo: Pitching and Wooing*
Baseball: The Lives Behind the Seams	*Voices of Sport*
Reggie Jackson: The Three Million Dollar Man	*Now Wait a Minute, Casey*